MAGIC, RHETORIC, AND LITERACY

An Eccentric History of the Composing Imagination

WILLIAM A. COVINO

State University
of New York
Press

The following publishers have generously given permission to reprint or adapt portions of the following copyrighted works: From "Magic and/as Rhetoric: Outlines of a History of Phantasy," by William A. Covino (*Journal of Advanced Composition* 12.2 [Fall 1992]: 349–358). Reprinted and adapted with the permission of the *Journal of Advanced Composition.* From "The Grammar of Advanced Writing," by William A. Covino. In *Teaching Advanced Composition,* ed. by Katherine H. Adams and John L. Adams (Boynton/Cook Publishers, Inc., Portsmouth, NH, 1991): 113–122. Reprinted and adapted with the permission of the publisher. From "Objections to Astrology: A Statement by 186 Leading Scientists," by Bart J. Bok, et al. (*The Humanist* 35.5 [Sept./Oct. 1975]: 4). Reprinted with the permission of *The Humanist.* From "Phantastic Palimpsests: Thomas De Quincey and the Magical Composing Imagination," by William A. Covino. In *Composition in Context,* ed. by W. Ross Winterowd and Vincent Gillespie (Southern Illinois University Press, Carbondale, IL, 1994: 169–179). Reprinted and adapted with the permission of the publisher. From "Alchemizing the History of Rhetoric," by William A. Covino. In *Writing Histories of Rhetoric,* ed. by Victor Vitanza (Southern Illinois University Press, Carbondale, IL, 1994: 49–58). Reprinted and adapted with the permission of the publisher. From "Magic, Literacy, and the *National Enquirer.*" In *Contending With Words,* ed. Patricia Harkin and John Schilb (MLA, New York, 1991: 23–37).

Published by
State University of New York Press, Albany

Production by Susan Geraghty
Marketing by Theresa Abad Swierzowski

Printed in the United States of America

For information, address State University of New York Press,
State University Plaza, Albany, N.Y., 12246

Library of Congress Cataloging-in-Publication Data

Covino, William A.
Magic, rhetoric, and literacy : an eccentric history of the composing imagination / William A. Covino.
p. cm. — (SUNY series, literacy, culture, and learning)
Includes bibliographical references and index.
ISBN 0-7914-2083-3 (hc). — ISBN 0-7914-2084-1 (pb)
1. Rhetoric. 2. Literacy. 3. Magic. I. Title. II. Series.
P301.C66 1994

93-41344
CIP

10 9 8 7 6 5 4 3 2 1

To Debbie, My First Love

CONTENTS

ACKNOWLEDGMENTS

My students have been my toughest and most generous audience; they deserve credit for all occasions of honesty and clarity in this book.

A number of colleagues have given me their support, encouragement, references, and advice, and others have offered bracing criticism and expressed friendly alarm, since I began in 1988 to put together magic, rhetoric, and literacy: James Berlin, Don Bialostosky, Gerald Bruns, Sharon Crowley, Theresa Enos, Marcia Farr, Susan Geraghty, Tom Hall, Patricia Harkin, John Huntington, Clark Hulse, Nan Johnson, George Kalamaras, Michael Lieb, Peter Manning, Don Marshall, Chris Messenger, Gary Olson, Alan Purves, Priscilla Ross and SUNY Press, Gene Ruoff, John Schilb, James Sosnoski, Victor Vitanza, W. Ross Winterowd, and Marjorie Woods.

I am also grateful to the University of Illinois Institute for the Humanities, for granting me the time and resources to complete this project.

INTRODUCTION: ARTICULATE AND INARTICULATE POWER

Hundreds of thousands of people in advanced Western societies practice various kinds of magic, from witchcraft to palmistry, and millions read newspaper horoscopes daily. But the official post-Enlightenment response to magic is disbelief and fear. In 1975, 186 leading scientists, including 18 Nobel Prize winners, publicly repudiated astrology, and magic in general, in their "Objections to Astrology" published in *The Humanist*:

> One would imagine, in this day of widespread enlightenment and education, that it would be unnecessary to debunk beliefs based on magic and superstition. Yet, acceptance of astrology pervades modern society. We are especially disturbed by the continued uncritical dissemination of astrological charts, forecasts, and horoscopes by the media and by otherwise reputable newspapers, magazines, and book publishers. This can only contribute to the growth of irrationalism and obscurantism. We believe that the time has come to challenge directly, and forcefully, the pretentious claims of astrological charlatans. (Bok 4; Grim 18)

Worried about what we are able and liable to read—the literature of popular astrology—these scientists declare war on an unofficial literacy. The literacy enfranchised by a magical epistemology and represented by astrological charts is encroaching upon the "reputable" world of print media and, we must presume, replacing the language of science with "irrationalism and obscurantism." The scientists characterize themselves as a collective under siege, facing a crisis, determining that "the time has come" to fight back.

Fear of magic has always been with us, in particular the fear of magic words—curses, incantations, spells, horoscopes—which claim to define or alter reality. As Peter Brown explains, the *emphatic* expression of such fear may signal a clash between two incommensurate literacies, which he distinguishes as *articulate* and *inarticulate* powers. Focussing on the fourth century C.E.,

Brown constructs a general theoretical framework to explain the sharp increase in both sorcery belief and public accusations against sorcerers:

> It is here that we find a situation which has been observed both to foster sorcery accusations and to offer scope for resort to sorcery. This is when *two systems of power* are sensed to clash within the one society. On the one hand, there is *articulate* power, power defined and agreed upon by everyone (and especially by its holders!): authority vested in precise persons; admiration and success gained by recognized channels. Running counter to this there may be other forms of influence less easy to pin down—*inarticulate* power: the disturbing intangibles of social life; the imponderable advantages of certain groups; personal skills that succeed in a way that is unacceptable or difficult to understand. (124, emphasis in original)

Brown conceives a clash between those empowered by the official explanatory lexicon—the literate establishment—and those who seek knowledge and success outside of this lexicon. The representative of magic—the sorcerer—speaks an occult (and thus illegitimate) language: "he has brought in the unseen to redress the balance of the seen" (124). Unlike the articulate voices in our own time, sorcerer accusations in the fourth century do not question the existence or efficacy of magic. Sorcery is to be condemned because it is incongruous with the developing stability of the Christian state; it is a menace of demons who disrupt the community in ascendency:

> If there are sorcerers, they are usually seen to work outside the Christian community (hence the pervasive identification of paganism and magic in Christian sources); if there is misfortune, it is divorced from a human reference and the blame is pinned firmly on the "spiritual powers of evil." Hence, perhaps, the snowball effect of the rapid rise of Christianity. Men joined the new community to be delivered from the demons; and the new community, in turn, resolved its tensions by projecting them in the form of an even greater demonic menace from outside. (Brown 138)

Concentrating on a period when religion and society were beset by unfixed epistemologies, Brown indicates that the conflict between articulate and inarticulate power, between an exclusive, vested literacy/rhetoric and an ambiguous, licentious alternative, between the nonmagical and the magical, arises at historical periods when articulate power "feels challenged, through conflict, to uphold an image of itself in which everything that happens, happens through *articulate* channels only . . . and where wisdom is the exclusive preserve of the traditional educational machine" (Brown 124).

While the *Humanist* scientists do condemn magic as a mode of illegitimate knowledge-making, and thus define it as a threat to official culture, what they stress are the dangers of mesmerized passivity: a magical world view leads to uncritical faith in "a destiny predetermined by astral forces beyond our control" (Bok 4). Magic is the product of evil rhetors—charlatans—who prey on our susceptibility to "comfort" in "uncertain times" (Bok 4). This construction of magic and its dangers joins a number of similar statements that appear in the 1970s and 1980s, statements issued by representatives of articulate power who want to release the inarticulate from the oppression of a magical world view. Advocates of nonmagical thinking would agree with those who repudiate astrology, urging active, critical intellectual engagement rather than passive superstition because, as the *Humanist* scientists conclude, "we must all face the world, and we must realize that our futures lie in ourselves, and not in the stars" (Bok 4). The most radical opponent of "magic consciousness" is Paulo Freire, whose work we will examine more extensively in chapter 4. Freire, no friend to the sort of exclusive meritocracy that the *Humanist* club of 186 embodies, nonetheless joins the scientists when he contrasts critical consciousness with magic consciousness, associating the latter with the illiteracy of oppressed classes. Magic consciousness "apprehends facts and attributes them to a superior power, [leading people to] fold their arms, resigned to the impossibility of resisting the power of facts" (*Education* 44). The victim of magic consciousness says, in effect, "That's the way it is," which is not an acceptance of truth examined, but of circumstance enforced.

Influential distinctions between "product" and "process" models of literacy instruction follow Freire's castigation of magic consciousness, and strengthen the negative connotations of magic that the *Humanist* scientists emphasize and that Peter Brown attempts to complicate. By counterposing "magical" and "nonmagical" formulations of composing in 1981, Janet Emig identified the process movement in rhetoric and composition studies as a reaction against writing-as-magic. In "Nonmagical Thinking: Presenting Writing Developmentally in Schools," Emig connects current-traditional rhetoric with magical thinking, and "reinvented" or "new" rhetoric with nonmagical thinking. In the magical classroom, writing is a silent, solitary product fully formed in the writer's consciousness, and it materializes on demand; in other words, the writer is the passive recipient of an astral gift. In the nonmagical classroom, writing is an active, erratic process of gradual, constant revision according to changing factors such as purpose and audience and the advice of collaborators. The year 1982 saw the appearance of Richard Young's "Concepts of Art and the Teaching of Writing," in which he cites Jacqueline de Romilly's *Magic and Rhetoric in Ancient Greece* in order to distinguish between pedagogies that feature, respectively, "the spell of the irrational and the desire to master it by means of reason" (Young 139, quoting de Romilly).[1] Dismissing the pedagogical emphasis on a magical imagination, which he calls the "new romanticism," as a position that renders writing so mysterious as to be unteachable, Young proposes that heuristic procedures such as tagmemic exploration may help to make imagination more teachable and accessible to writers. Like Young, W. Ross Winterowd associates the magical imagination with "Romantic solipsism," and rates magical-romantic composition as "idiosyncratic, mysterious, and inexplicable" and "powerless in the very centers that largely determine the fate of literacy: for example, the National Institute of Education, the foundations, and Congress" ("Philosophy" 346).[2] For Emig and Young, magical thinking denies students a teachable, practical skill; for Winterowd, it also places them outside the halls of articulate power.

The rejection of magical thinking corresponds with an appreciative emphasis on contributions to developmental literacy from science and social science (Emig 135–40; Young 137–38). Such emphasis is central to the "emerging paradigm" for writing instruction and developmental literacy generally (see North 318–36), which Maxine Hairston summarizes in her definitive 1982 article, "The Winds of Change." Hairston notes that "for the first time in the history of teaching writing we have specialists who are doing controlled and directed research on writers' composing processes," and proposes that "changes in [composition] theory probably started, in the middle 1950s, from intellectual inquiry and speculation about language and language learning that was going on in several fields, notably linguistics, anthropology, and clinical and cognitive psychology" (23, 18).

The recent conjunctions of magic, rhetoric, and literacy that I have reviewed may be read as related responses to contemporary conflicts between inarticulate and articulate powers. First published in 1970, Peter Brown's piece seems something of a prognostication: It presages a decade of "culture wars" (Shor) between the voices of a quasi-mystical, visionary, protest movement against establishment militarism, education, and social policy,[3] and the "conservative restoration" of school and society as an authoritarian "information delivery system" (Shor, *Culture Wars* 159); a decade marked both by an occult "publishing explosion" (O'Keefe 565–66) and by the 1975 alliance of 186 scientists for the defense of nonmagical "enlightenment and education." The English translation of Freire's *Education for Critical Consciousness* appears in 1973, and becomes another document that attempts to place magic within the conflict of literacies in that decade, associating the rejection of magic consciousness with the rise of a newly articulate, and newly empowered, peasantry. The advocacies of a nonmagical writing process that dominate the 1980s castigate the teacher-as-sorcerer, a creature of obscure pronouncements and occult skills who keeps students inarticulate by mystifying composition. Even in our nonmagical world, magic remains a conceptual construct for appraising the powers of language, and while magic is understood by some as a liberatory alternative to established rationalism, the prospect of a magical epistemology is a fearful one even for those who endorse literacy as a disruptive force.

Making language has long been regarded as, in some sense, magical; as a *spell* (spelling, even in its ostensibly nonmagical sense, denotes the visible materialization of invisible thought [e.g., Daly, *Wickedary* 23]). Modern discussions of magic and language in tandem continue centuries of commentary by sophistic, hermetic, gnostic, cabalistic, and patristic intellectuals, about the powers that supervise our ex nihilo creation of discourse for altering reality. The longstanding centrality of magic to this commentary is evident in the early meanings of *grammar*: in its various Medieval forms—*gramarye, gramaire*, and *grimoire*—grammar at once denoted general erudition, literacy, and sorcery (OED 1187, Daly 289, Kuhn 2594, de Romilly v). The master of such grammar might serve God and the Good: Jewish and Christian cabalists held that specific combinations of letters and words contain and convey spiritual energies, whose understanding brings spiritual enlightenment (Yates, *Giordano Bruno* 92–93). Or the master of such grammar might invoke demons and do evil, as the Faust legend attests. In 415 B.C.E., the sophist Gorgias had warned that speech can "bewitch the soul with a kind of evil persuasion" ("Encomium" 41), voicing the ancient worry that words could be vehicles for diabolical forces (De Romilly, *Magic* 25–43). Nearly two thousand years later, the most famous of the Renaissance magicians—Cornelius Agrippa—warns against the evil uses of "the occult virtue of words," while he admits that a magus can change others with his speech, "with so great a power, that often [words] change not only the hearers but also other bodies" (1.69, 211; *Opera* 1, 139).

The magical world is one in which language can bewitch the soul, and it is also unstable and dynamic, spirited and licentious. For the magus, words transform reality, and facility with language makes multiple realities possible. The magical affront to institutionalized stability is what provokes the articulate powers Peter Brown conceives. These powers are further represented in the rationalist campaign against magic that gathered force in the seventeenth century, waged in England by the Royal Society of London For the Improving of Natural Knowledge and its spokesman, Thomas Sprat. In 1667, Sprat's *History of the Royal Society* warns against the licentious imagination that invents an unverifiable reality, and against stylistic amplifications that ambiguate true knowledge:

> The Ornaments of speaking . . . are so much degenerated from their original usefulness. . . . they give the mind a motion too changeable, and bewitching, to consist with *right practice.* Who can behold, without indignation, how many mists and uncertainties, these specious *Tropes* and *Figures* have brought on our Knowledge? (112, emphasis in original)
>
> The *Poets* began of old to impose the deceit. They to make all things look more venerable than they were, devis'd a thousand false *Chimeras*; on every *Field, River, Grove,* and *Cave,* they bestow'd a *Fantasm* of their own making. . . . And in the modern *Ages* these *Fantastical Forms* were reviv'd. . . . But from the time in which the *Real Philosophy* has appear'd, there is scarce any whisper remaining of such *horrors.* . . . The course of things goes quietly along, in its own true channel of *Natural Causes* and *Effects.* (340, emphasis in original)

With the association of figurative language and witchery, and the counterposition of "real philosophy" to chimeras and phantasms in these passages, Sprat and the Society impugn rhetoric and magic together, and dictate acceptable parameters for the literate intellect. Within the seventeenth century establishment of official science and official religion, "the imagination is particularly dangerous when it allows an individual to create a phantasm and impose it on the world for reality" (Vickers, "Royal Society" 60).

The *Humanist* scientists continue the Society's reaction against magic words, at a distance of three hundred years, within a remarkably similar set of values and warnings. Together, the two statements begin to define the conceptions of magic, rhetoric, and literacy that are usually *at issue* in considerations of their interrelationship, and point us toward the definitions of these three terms that will inform this study. For both seventeenth- and twentieth-century scientists, good rhetoric is conventional, correct, and certain. Sprat values these characteristics explicitly, directly castigating figurative and poetic language as "horrors" that depart from "real philosophy," while today's scientists imply a wrong and a right rhetoric by counterposing the astrologer and his false certainties to the self-evident verity of science.

"Science" is a term that coincides here with the advocacy of certain conservative attitudes toward knowledge and language, but I recognize that—as Paul Feyerabend argues—the actual practice of science is usually not "scientific"; that is, the scientist at work recognizes that the world of her investigations is "a complex medium containing surprising and unforeseen developments [that] demands complex procedures and defies analysis on the basis of rules which have been set up in advance and without regard to the ever-changing conditions of history" (Feyerabend *Against Method* 11). What Sprat and the humanists represent is the public advertisement of science, advertisement that is not insincere (the writers seem to believe their own publicity), and which refuses the importance of a scientist's recourse to uncontrollable and arguably "magical" variables such as imagination, intuition, and instinct. Leaving out the vagaries of science would seem necessary for maintaining the public perception of its strength as a reliable knowledge-making system. Sprat himself was not a scientist, and the *History* was always intended as an apologia that would valorize the Society in the public mind (Cope xii–xiv). Likewise, "Objections to Astrology" is published for an educated nonacademic *Humanist* audience. In both cases, the advertisement of science entails vigorous claims for what Sprat calls "right practice," and maintains a dichotomy between phantasy and reason which—as we will see in the course of this study—influences the institution of rhetoric and literacy, and their enforcement in public discourse.[4] Part of my purpose is to dispell the opposition of magic and science; at the same time, because that opposition prevails as a utility for maintaining one or the other camp, acknowledging it here reflects the state of things.

Current composition and literacy theorists who seem *allied* with Sprat and the scientists in their explicit dismissal of magical thinking (Emig, Young, Winterowd, Hairston, Freire) are also decided advocates of the *transformative* powers of literacy and writing: one learns to write in order to create and explore alternatives to any monolithic "right practice."[5] In "Literacy and Freedom," Janet Emig asks

> What is it we must imagine? Alternative social, economic, and sexual structures and arrangements, since so many we have are obviously bankrupt. Can there be economically only capitalism, socialism, communism? Does only the nuclear family provide the magnet to which most human values and feelings can adhere? Are only schools and churches the arches under which communities can come together and find coherence? (177)

Emig, Freire, and their like-minded colleagues fear the magical thinking that *disallows alternatives to authorized knowledge*: Freire's South American peasants are under the spell of official facts, and their illiteracy is their inability to question. For Emig, this sort of illiteracy is also enforced in North American classrooms: "Most North American schools are temples to magical thinking, with the focus not only on explicit teaching but on a specific form of explicit teaching—adults performing before large groups of learners" ("Nonmagical Thinking" 21). The literate individual, then, is one able to question and resist the performative pronouncements of an institutionalized sorcerer, standing ready with a critical lexicon of counter-spells.

Magic is, in one sense, the imposition by the powerful few of binding constraints upon the unquestioning many: a program of spells for *arresting* discourse. This is the sorcery of autocratic teachers and governments; it operates in many forms of mass media, notably advertising, and is practiced in some measure by the ostensible detractors of magic, voices of science who attempt to constitute official knowledge. Magic is, in another sense, the practice of disrupting and recreating articulate power: a (re)sorcery of spells for *generating* multiple perspectives. As we will see, generative magic is a dialogical critique that seeks novelty, originating at a remove from the mass culture it would interrogate. However, insofar as generative magic seeks social and cultural change, it enters the world it questions. Thus generative magic is at once private and public, occult and common, an esoteric critical discourse of "specialist" communities that define themselves in opposition to the mainstream, and an amplification of possibilities for action.

By explicating the interrelatedness of rhetoric, magic, and literacy in key texts, from antiquity forward, this study will examine the ways in which a magic world view can define and affect conceptions of rhetoric and literacy. However, I will seek less to impart historical "information" or offer a comprehensive survey than to construct a suggestive framework for appreciating the magic of the composing imagination. In brief, my "spell" here means to cast out prohibitive distinctions between the magical and the nonmagical; to recognize that magical thinking can coincide with the enfranchisement of a wide and wild plurality of literacies; and to associate different *forms* of discourse with the *powers* that they invoke. Chapter 1 defines magic, rhetoric, and literacy as working concepts that each address the causal powers of language, and that may be either arresting or generative. Chapter 2 initiates a history of phantasy, the central but always suspect activity of the composing imagination, by tracing classical traditions that influenced a revival of philosophical magic in the Renaissance. Chapter 3 describes the replacement of magic by Enlightenment mechanism, and locates the reappearance of the writer-as-magus in the Romantic prose of Thomas De Quincey. Chapters 4 and 5 concentrate on the arresting magic that informs American mass culture in this century, and present radical social critiques—by philosophers and witches—that call for the return of the generative magical imagination.

CHAPTER 1

Magic, Rhetoric, and Literacy

MAGIC

Daniel Lawrence O'Keefe, in his compendious and uniquely comprehensive social theory of magic, defines magic as the "audacious individual use of existing powerful symbols" (73) in which "there is always a curious tension between the traditional and the surreptitious, and hence between syllogism, implications from accepted truth, and an enthymeme that bends consensus to private ends" (85). Such tensions define a social context in which magic "works because people agree it works"(96).[1] O'Keefe's theory complements the core propositions of this study: Magic is not the instant and arhetorical product of an otherworldly incantation; it is the *process* of inducing belief and creating community, with reference to the dynamics of a rhetorical situation. Magic is a social act whose medium is persuasive discourse, and so it must entail the complexities of social interaction, invention, communication, and composition. Thus magic becomes a term through which we can address the ways in which words make real things happen.

Initially, O'Keefe divides the universe into magic "in the strict sense" and magic "in the weak sense." The former includes medical magic (e.g., the curative spells of the "medicine man"); black magic (malevolent witchcraft and sorcery); ceremonial magic (rainmaking); religious magic (exorcism); occultism (fortune telling); and the paranormal (ESP, flying saucers). Such institutions constitute magic in the strict sense largely because they are explicitly "designated as magical in many societies" (14).

O'Keefe is much more interested, however, in "magic in the weak sense," a category that becomes a misnomer during the course of his book, finally designating a broad range of symbolic actions that are *really* magical, exerting *strong* effects on society; but whose magical transformative powers are not fully and publicly acknowledged as such, because to do so would deny our rational, mechanistic epistemology:

> Newer magics of pseudo-science, mental technology and mass manipulation are invented almost daily. Occasionally, an "occult revival" like the present one becomes so blatant that we notice this persistence of magic; but usually we dismiss it as an exception and go on believing magic belongs to the past. As a result, the difference between modern and primitive societies is not that they had magic and we do not. The difference is that they accepted the magic around them, whereas we deny it. (xv)

What is this "magic" that exists despite our disbeliefs?

> Magic is real action. Something really happens, often something violent, usually something of consequence. People are shaken, influenced, healed, destroyed, transformed. The social situation is altered. . . . In fact, magic is more often than not *collective* social action. Solitary-seeming magics such as yoga and mysticism and the study of occult arts also have social objectives: in practice they translate into . . . the pursuit of power, prestige and authority over others. (25–34)

Put another way, magic is and always has been symbolic action (that is to say, magic never occurs apart from language), in the service of individual or social transformation.

Magic takes place, for the exorcist and the orator, the witchdoctor and the psychiatrist, when the parties involved agree to agree, when they enact what E. Fuller Torrey calls "a shared worldview." Torrey compares witchdoctors and psychiatrists, and finds little difference:

> The psychiatrist looked thoughtfully at his client. "You look angry when you talk about him. I wonder if something happened to you once that made you very angry at him." At this point the client broke down sobbing, blurting out a forgotten history of neglect and deceit by a thoughtless father toward a little girl. Afterward the client felt better. After several more sessions in which she was able to explore her feelings of anger, she began to get better.
>
> The witchdoctor stared solemnly at the small shells. They had landed in a pattern resembling the shape of a large animal. He picked up one shell and examined it minutely. "You have broken a taboo of your family. It has offended the sacred bear that protects your ancestors. That is why you are sick." The

> client and her family breathed a sigh of relief. It was as they had suspected. Now that they knew for certain what was wrong, they could proceed with the necessary sacrifices. After these had been made, the client began to get better. (17–18)

For both the psychiatrist and the witchdoctor, therapeutic transformation occurs through "operations on traditional collective ideas" that become "synthetic a prioris" (O'Keefe 110). These operations are often, O'Keefe reminds us, syllogistic; the psychiatrist and patient above come to share a syllogism: Expressing anger makes people feel better; I am expressing anger; therefore, I am feeling better. For the witchdoctor and his clients, the operative syllogism—with the major premise that offending the sacred bear is a cause of sickness—is nearly explicit in the witchdoctor's explanation.

In a nonmagical society, our classification systems are presumed to be scientific and logical, so that their origins in social rituals within a magical epistemology are forgotten. Time and space are concepts that govern the laws of modern science and society, which we abbreviate unreflectively in the memorization of common schoolroom formulas such as d(istance) = r(ate) x t(ime). As tokens of mechanism, they are entirely removed from ancient origins in ritual consensus, where time and space were "played out" in drama that attempted to establish our place in a universe driven by a cosmology of deities (O'Keefe 70–75). Jacqueline de Romilly traces, for instance, the orphic tendency to "present time as a first principle, and, through an identification of names, [turn] it into a divine being" (*Time* 34–35); Chronos eventually becomes established as a character in Greek tragedy. Ernst Cassirer surveys the ancient association of mental concepts with the correct utterance of an appropriate deity's name, and he concludes that ritualized word magic is the ground of "theoretical, practical and aesthetic consciousness, the world of language and of morality, the basic forms of community and the state" (44).

The belief in magic necessarily entails a sympathetic universe, in which master ideas emerge from the interaction of analogous spiritual and physical forces. In the exchange between the witchdoctor and his clients, the small shells are both natural and supernatural signifiers, in cooperative transaction with like signifiers: the shells "speak of" the great bear, and the clients are charged with reentering the cosmology of sympathies by offering sacrifices.

Distinctions between the natural and the social, corporeal and incorporeal, signifiers and signified, subjects and objects, do not operate here. The magical universe comprises a plurality of forces and powers that are all related, both metaphorically and really. The powers in this universe abrogate rules of binary logic, of contradiction and negation. O'Keefe extends the observations in Lévi-Strauss's *Primitives and the Supernatural*—that unresolved contradiction is a main element in primitive epistemology—to propose that binary Western logic is unable to *elaborate the possible* because it rules out the apposition of unlike categories, because it is locked in an "either-or" framework (87–91).

The elaboration of sympathies is not exclusive to primitive societies; it is central to the magic worldview that continues through the Renaissance. Even in sixteenth-century Europe, resemblances denominate consciousness:

> The world was seen as a vast assemblage of correspondences. All things have relationships with all other things, and these relations are ones of sympathy and antipathy. Men attract women, lodestones attract iron, oil repels water, and dogs repel cats. Things mingle and touch in an endless chain, or rope, vibrated (wrote Della Porta in *Natural Magic*) by the first cause, God. Things are also analogous to man in the famous alchemical concept of the microcosm and the macrocosm: the rocks of the earth are its bones, the rivers its veins, the forests its hair and the cicadas its dandruff. The world duplicates and reflects itself in an endless network of similarity and dissimilarity. (Berman 74; see also Foucault 17–45)

In a fourth-century C.E. memory spell that directs us to actually drink our writing, elements of the natural, the human, the celestial, and the supernatural worlds must be set into precise cooperation:

> Take hieratic papyrus and write the prescribed names with Hermaic myrrh ink. And once you have written them as they are prescribed, wash them off into spring water from 7 springs and drink the water on an empty stomach for seven days while the moon is in the east. But drink a sufficient amount.
>
> This is the writing on the strip of papyrus: "KAMBRĒ CHAMBRE SIXIŌPHI HARPON CHNOUPHI BRINTATĒN-ŌPHRIBRISKYLMA ARAQUAZAR BAMESEN KRUPHI NIPTOUMI CHMOUMAŌPH AKTIŌPHI ARTŌSE BIBIOU BIBIOU SPHĒ SPHĒ NOUSI NOUSI SIEGŌ SIEGŌ NOUCHA NOUCHA LINOUCHA LINOUCHA CHYCHBA CHYCHBA

KAXIO CHYCHBA DĒTOPHOTH II AA OO YY ĒĒ EE ŌŌ."
After doing these things wash the writing off and drink as prescribed.

This is also the composition of the ink: myrrh troglitis, 4 drams, 3 karian figs, 7 pits of Nikolaus dates, 7 dried pinecones, 7 piths of the single-stemmed worm-wood, 7 wings of the Hermaic ibis, spring water. When you have burned the ingredients, prepare them and write. (Betz 9)

A typical indicator of sympathetic magic, this spell also enforces the identification of magical action with symbolic action that O'Keefe stresses in two of his postulates:

> Magical Social Action Consists of Symbolic Performances—And Linguistic Symbolism Is Central To Magic.
>
> Magical Symbolic Action Is Rigidly Scripted. (21)

O'Keefe's distinction between magic and rhetoric turns on these postulates; a look at that distinction will lead us to consider the definition of rhetoric that follows from the acknowledgment of magic as social action. For O'Keefe, magic in the strict sense "must be said just right" (65); he agrees with Hugh Duncan, who writes in *Communication and Social Order*, "Magic spells must be handed down, without change. The slightest alteration from the original pattern would be fatal" (318, quoted in O'Keefe 65). For O'Keefe, such rigidity includes "speeches [that] are not extemporaneous or composed, but entirely traditional," for which "audience response is preordained." Further, real magic "does not try to 'persuade' [as does rhetoric], but to compel." But O'Keefe does admit, with reference to Plato and Aristotle, that the function of rhetoric (as persuasion) may be "wrenching the consensus and foreclosing it," and that "there is some resemblance to magic in this operation—in the attempt to suspend communal dialogue, in the first person singular speaking as the first person plural ['we believe'], in the partialism of the viewpoint." However, "magic itself" is rigidly scripted, while rhetoric is "much freer and more plastic." Strictly speaking, rhetoric "reminds us of magic" (81–84)

It is true that magic formulas are, in an important sense, formulaic. But at the same time, every particular effect that the magus seeks requires a particular formula; that is, there would seem to be a lack of "all-purpose" formulas. For example, *The Greek Magical Papyri* (just over 500 spells surviving from antiquity) contains 65 different love spells. There is a love spell to be "performed with the help of heroes or gladiators or those who have died a violent death" (Betz 64), a love spell to be recited "over myrrh which is offered," a love spell to be uttered "in conversation, while kissing passionately" (137), and so forth. The importance of making one's magic agree with circumstances continues through Marsilio Ficino's *Three Books on Life (Liber De Vita in Tres Libros Divisus)*, one of the most influential and popular statements of Renaissance magic. Ficino warns that even the slightest change in heavenly constellations affects both human behavior and the powers that magical discourse can invoke:

> Observe the daily positions and aspects of the stars and discover to what principal speeches, songs, motions, dances, moral behavior, and actions most people are usually incited by these, so that you may imitate such things as far as possible in your song, which aims to please the particular part of heaven that resembles them and to catch an influence that resembles them. (3.21; 359)

Ficino is calling, in a way, for a "rigid script." However, such rigidity is defined not by the invariableness of the symbolic act, but by the precise match that must be made between language and context. While it is perhaps true that magic as such can be identified with unalterable utterances and preordained responses, mainly in ritual ceremonial contexts, magic that performs social action and presupposes a sympathetic universe is essentially plastic.

Stopping short of concluding that magic *is* rhetoric, O'Keefe defines magic with rhetorical terms, and concludes that a complex of social/rhetorical contingencies accounts for its effects. Understanding magic as a social and discursive process allows us to analyze and critique the powers at work in the "plain rhetoric" that mesmerizes audiences with its seeming clarity and simplicity. Further, such a conception of magic may lead us to prefer a "magic rhetoric," if this means preferring a fertile, dynamic and fluctuant imagination to its opposite.

RHETORIC

In his commentary on Plato's *Phaedrus*, the same Ficino who advises the magus to adjust his discourse to constant, myriad changes, defines the perfect orator with like emphasis on the multiplicity and changeableness of the auditor's soul:

> The perfect orator must know that any human soul is intrinsically and naturally multiple (for it has reason, imagination, sense, and the powers of wrath and desire); and, likewise, that various souls use their various powers as much as possible and differently among themselves and are differently affected; and, again, that some of their differences are derived from the differences of their bodies. Moreover, he ought to know what kind of mental disposition is moved by what kind of discourse and accommodate his discourse to each one, just as a musician must bring various harmonies to various things. (Allen 204)

The call for systematic alertness to changing circumstances defines rhetoric from Antiquity through the Renaissance. In the sections of the *Phaedrus* to which Ficino refers above, Plato's Socrates insists that any true art of rhetoric must appeal to the multiform nature of the soul, through a repertory of changing speeches whose exact expressions cannot be predetermined (270c–72b; 549–55). Aristotle's *Rhetoric* emphasizes the complexity and diversity of proofs that will affect different auditors in differing contexts, and issues his famous sweeping definition of rhetoric, as "an ability, in each [particular] case, to see the available means of persuasion" (1355b; 35). Cicero's Crassus associates rhetorical power with broad learning and alertness to change: "The real power of eloquence is such that it embraces the origin, the influence, the changes of all things in the world, all virtues, duties, and all nature, so far as it affects the manners, minds, and lives of mankind" (*De Oratore* 3.20; 213). In 1708, Giambattista Vico—professor of rhetoric at the University of Naples—reasserts the importance of the broad exploration central to classical rhetoric, as he attempts to counter Cartesian educational philosophy, with its insistence on an unambiguous language of clear and distinct ideas:

> For how can a clear and distinct idea in our mind be a criterion of the true unless we perceive everything in, or related to, the thing itself? And how can anyone be certain that he has perceived everything, unless he has pursued every question pertaining to the matter under consideration? First [he should raise] the question whether it exists, lest he should be talking about nothing. Then the question what it is, lest his efforts be expended

> upon a name. Then how great it is, under which heading come color, taste, softness, hardness and the other tactile sensations. Then he must ask when it was created, how long it lasts, and into what it changes as it decays. And proceeding thus through the remaining categories, he must connect it to all the things which are in any way related to it, whether they be its causes or effects, or those effects it has when combined with objects which are similar, dissimilar or contrary, or when combined with those which are bigger, smaller, or equal. . . . On the other hand, anyone who is confident of perceiving something in a clear and distinct idea of the mind is easily deceived, and he will often think that he knows a thing distinctly when he still has only a confused consciousness of it, for he has not learned all the elements which belong to the object and which distinguish it from everything else. ("On the Ancient Wisdom of the Italians" 72–73)

In this century, the classical scope and dynamism of rhetoric reemerges in Paolo Valesio's ambitious proposition, "Rhetoric is *all* of language, in its realization as discourse" (7). Broadly inclusive formulations of the elements of rhetoric are presented by a diversity of scholars, including Kenneth Burke, I.A. Richards, Roman Jakobson, Ernesto Grassi, James Kinneavy, Ann Berthoff, and Terry Eagleton; all acknowledge that the *meaning* of any utterance varies with its *context*, and reinforce Valesio's conclusion that "the house of human discourse cannot be built on solid rock, that (*pace* Descartes) its only possible foundation is ever-shifting sand" (83).[2] Very recently, George Kennedy has proposed a definitive metaphor that recognizes the art of rhetoric as both the "coming into being" of discourse that accounts for interactive variables (see Kennedy in Aristotle 36, n. 34), and as a quasi-corporeal phenomenon that resists definition in material scientific terms:

> Rhetoric in the most general sense may perhaps be identified with the *energy* inherent in communication: the emotional energy that impels the speaker to speak, the physical energy expended in the utterance, the energy level coded in the message, and the energy experienced by the recipient in decoding the message. ("Hoot" 2, emphasis added).

We need not go very far from defining rhetoric as the interaction of different kinds of energy, and suggesting as Kennedy does that rhetoric is the *natural* practice of both animals and humans acting under the aegis of a common communicative urgency, to calling rhetoric the invocation of invisible powers within a sympathetic universe of widely shared signifiers; that is, magic.

Indeed, the magician and the rhetor are similar figures, and often the same figure, throughout Western intellectual history. Mythic and literary origins of rhetoric and literacy occur at the juncture of magic and writing, in the person of the ibis-headed god or divine man who was variously named Thoth, or Theuth, or Hermes. He is the inventor of writing, and as Frances Yates has shown, this originary writer was also the originary magus:

> The Egyptian God, Thoth, the scribe of the gods and the divinity of wisdom, was identified by the Greeks with their Hermes and sometimes given the epithet of "Thrice Great." The Latins took over this identification of Hermes or Mercurius with Thoth, and Cicero in his *De natura deorum* explains that there were really five Mercuries, the fifth being he who killed Argus and consequently fled in exile to Egypt where he "gave the Egyptians their laws and letters" and took the Egyptian name of Theuth or Thoth. A large literature in Greek developed under the name of Hermes Trismegistus, concerned with astrology and the occult sciences, with the secret virtues of plants and stones and the sympathetic magic based on knowledge of such virtues, with the making of talismans for drawing down the powers of the stars, and so on. (*Giordano Bruno* 2)

One of the many identities of Theuth/Thoth/Mercury/Hermes is "the Egyptian Prometheus" (Burger 90). Like Prometheus, Theuth would bestow knowledge and skills on humankind that—as his superior Thamus warns—can only be employed truly by gods. Recounting the story of Theuth and Thamus in the *Phaedrus*, Plato's Socrates describes Thamus's worry that those who can read and write "will read many things without instruction, and will therefore seem to know many things," thus exercising "a power the opposite of that which they really possess" (274e–75a; 563). The preemption of godliness is forbidden.

The dialogue between Thamus and Theuth, between the supreme god and the emissary of occult knowledge to humankind, represents the central worry that trails both writing and magic through their histories, namely, that they will get into the wrong hands. Outside the control of an originary authority, writing and magic might be made to do the work of illusion, as rhetoric. Jacqueline de Romilly, in *Magic and Rhetoric in Ancient*

Greece, has emphasized their common goal as illusion, holding the Sophists responsible for illusions of truth achieved via the incantatory spell of language, and reminding us that Plato's Socrates often charged his opponents with bad magic, while also weaving his own spells (see especially 26–27, 36).[3]

Although reactions against the Sophists contributed to the establishment of rhetoric as *techne* without magic, associated with political and institutional control and stability, the link between magic and rhetoric persisted. In Greco-Roman antiquity, the magician "served as a power and communications expert, crisis manager, miracle healer and inflicter of damages, and all-purpose therapist and agent of worried, troubled, and troublesome souls" (Betz xlvii). Through the Middle Ages and into the Renaissance, many of the prominent humanists are also occultists (Thorndike's *History* presents repeated instances); teachers such as Isidore of Seville wrote textbooks on both rhetoric and magic, and a typical government advisor in the Middle Ages was a "practicioner of magic and rhetoric, a supplier of skills to ruler and crown—administrative, ideological, rhetorical, historical, liturgical, and architectural skills" (Ward 101).[4] While there is a continuing post-classical emphasis on technical rhetoric, there is also "a revival of the Greek sophistic notion of rhetoric as magic" (Ward 107–9).

The need for magic, which Susanne Langer (after Cassirer) posits as part of the "inventory of human needs" (38), seems to coincide with the need for technical rhetoric; as John Ward points out, "high points in the history of rhetoric are also high points in devotion to the occult" (87). The proliferation of new facts—which marks the beginning of each of the traditional epochs of progress in Western history—provokes doubt about what's "really" true, and drives those who would manage a newly more complex world to magic, and to magic rhetoric. Thus the overtly magical Sophistry of early Antiquity, the renewed reliance on both magic and technical rhetoric in the late Middle Ages and the Renaissance (Ward 107–9), the appropriation of magic to empirical methodology in the Enlightenment (see below, chapter 3), and the growth of both New Age occultism and data management systems in our own "information age," may all be instances of the appeal of both magic and rhetoric, or of magic as rhetoric, at times when the influx of new knowledge and patterns of life puts us in search of a spell to control the demons of change. Bestseller lists in recent years include both Shirley MacLaine's *Out On A*

Limb, which offers a reactionary mysticism that has us looking backward for selfhood, constructing our identity by invoking our past lives; and E.D. Hirsch's *Cultural Literacy: What Every American Needs To Know*, a reactionary pedagogy that has us looking backward for a common language of established facts, constructing our identity by means of a *Dictionary of Cultural Literacy*, a list of the terms that we must memorize and speak to transmigrate into the mainstream, a virtual lexicon of incantations.

Insofar as they provide schema for public discourse, programs such as Hirsch's constitute a technical rhetoric. The congeniality of magic and technical rhetoric results from the real power of the latter to design and alter reality: the mastery of institutional discourse makes one an insider who can, in turn, invoke and impose facts and formulae. As Kenneth Burke writes, this power exists because "the magical decree is implicit in all language; for the mere act of naming an object or situation decrees that it is to be singled out as such-and-such rather than as something-other." Magic is a "coercive command," the "establishment or management by decree," and insofar as it is intrinsic to language, is unavoidable. Further, all magic is a *strategy* calculated to address a *situation* "in the name of" a certain *power* (*Philosophy* 3–5).[5] Strategy, situation, and power are the elements of magic, and (I would add) the elements of rhetoric, when embodied in discourse.

I have proposed that magic can be generative or arresting, a mode of creating novel possibilities for action or a mode of constraint. Just so, rhetoric can be identified with a play of ambiguities, or with the absolute determination of meaning, by decree. The recognition that discourse is made of shifting sands, or energies, enfranchises rhetoric as *invention*, and encourages the generation of multiple solutions, perspectives, formulations, in behavior variously associated with imagination and creativity. But alertness to ambiguity also makes possible its restraint, in the interest of clarity, certainty, authority, and power. Manifest in slogans, maxims, and laws, the restraint of ambiguity is an arresting rhetoric.

Herbert Marcuse emphasizes the force of an arresting magic rhetoric operating on mass culture:

> At the nodal points of the universe of public discourse, self-validating, analytical propositions appear which function like magic-ritual formulas. Hammered and re-hammered into the recipient's mind, they produce the effect of enclosing it within

> the circle of the conditions prescribed by the formula. (*One Dimensional Man* 88)

For Marcuse, "the closing of the universe of discourse" is effected by "magical, authoritarian and ritual elements [that] permeate speech and language": "It is the word that orders and organizes, that induces people to do, to buy, and to accept" (84–86). Abbreviated thought and thoughtless behavior are the consequences of the tendency in media and government institutions to prefer the abridgment of information: "In its immediacy and directness, [media language] impedes conceptual thinking; thus, it impedes thinking" (95).

Typically, magic rhetoric *arrests* ambiguity. The "arresting" magician issues a "coercive command"; because such commands are intrinsic to language, and really do make and re-make reality, we "do magic" when we "do rhetoric," and vice-versa. Such magic/rhetoric transforms the *phenomenal* world through *noumenal* enchantment. For the Greek orator, the Renaissance magus, the Romantic poet, and the variety of present-day institutional authorities who invoke a cosmology of sanctioned forces in every act of official discourse, language alters the social situation. Consider, for instance, the especially potent force of the speech acts J. L. Austin has called *performatives*, and which Daniel O'Keefe renames "magical power prescriptives" (54). When George Bush issued a performative declaration of war against Iraq in 1991, we were reminded that all such declarations, from the cleric's "I pronounce you husband and wife" to the professor's "Your final grade is an A" to the boss's "You're fired," are instances in which saying makes it so. In such cases, the rhetor performs magic by effecting real action; in the event that any of us employ powerful words to change a situation, or are ourselves changed by what we read or hear, we participate in a magical transactive transformation.[6]

Pierre Bourdieu gives repeated attention to the magic of performative utterances in *Language And Symbolic Power*:

> The mystery of performative magic is . . . resolved in the mystery of ministry . . . , i.e., in the alchemy of *representation* (in the different senses of the term) through which the representative creates the group which creates him: the spokesperson endowed with the full power to speak and act on behalf of the group, and first of all to act on the group through the magic of

> his slogan, is the substitute for the group, which exists solely through this *procuration*. Group made man, he personifies a fictitious person, which he lifts out of the state of a simple aggregate of separate individuals, enabling them to act and speak, through him, "like a single person." Conversely, he receives the right to speak and act in the name of the group, to "take himself for" the group he incarnates, to identify with the function to which "he gives his body and soul," thus giving a biological body to a constituted body. *Status est magistratus*; "l'Etat, c'est moi." Or what amounts to the same thing, the world is my representation. (106)

While magic may be intrinsic to language, the power of an utterance resides in the social designation of a speaking symbol, enacting a phenomenon common to both magic and rhetoric: "the first person singular speaking as the first person plural" (O'Keefe 83). Thus, "Stop in the name of the law" is only effectual when uttered by the law incarnate, the police officer who represents the codification—by some consensus—of right behaviors.

What is at issue then is not *whether* rhetoric is magic, but what sorts of magi/rhetors, under what sorts of conditions, produce what kinds of effects. Still enclosed in the Enlightenment privileging of plain, unambiguous maxims, and often presuming their speakers' authority, we are too often the victims of a repressive magic that *limits* the possibilities for action. The most obvious examples of such magic come from advertising, which Raymond Williams has called "a highly organized and professional system of magical inducements and satisfactions, functionally very similar to magical systems in simpler societies, but rather strangely coexistent with a highly developed scientific technology" (*Problems* 185). In a popular Nike commercial, all of the reasons to avoid exercise (and the Nike apparel that goes with it) disappear with the injunction, "Just Do It." This is the magic of authoritarian, simplistic incantations passed from salesperson to consumer, from teacher to student, incantations that identify preferred public discourse as instantaneous, formulaic, and absolute. Arresting magic operates more subtly in "info-tainment," in popular combinations of information and entertainment represented by "prole weeklies" (Paul Fussell's term) such as the *National Enquirer*, by digests for the astute such as *Harper's* magazine, and in television talk shows; in these cases, as we will see in chapter 5, inculcation can masquerade as the interanimation of perspectives.

Ioan Couliano associates an arresting magic with the hypnosis induced in a "police State," in contrast to the flexible but inefficient "magician State":

> But the essential difference between the two, the one which works altogether in favor of the [magician State], is that magic is a science of metamorphoses with the capacity to change, to adapt to all circumstances, to improve, whereas the police always remains just what it is: in this case, the defender to the death of out-of-date values, of a political oligarchy useless and pernicious to the life of nations. The system of restraints is bound to perish, for what it defends is merely an accumulation of slogans without any vitality. The magician State, on the other hand, only expects to develop new possibilities and new tactics, and it is precisely excess of vitality which impedes its good running order. (105-6)

Within a paradigm that privileges machine virtues such as "good running order," and values stability and efficiency, the discourse of slogans and the authority of sloganizers are prevailing sorceries inimical to social vitality. The prospect of *generative* magic rhetoric begins with the recognition of this fact.

LITERACY

Arresting literacy upholds determinate correspondences between signs, meanings, and behaviors; this is the literacy celebrated in "liberal and right wing discourse . . . tied to narrowly conceived economic interests or to an ideology designed to initiate the poor, the underprivileged, and minorities into the logic of a unitary, dominant cultural tradition" (Giroux, "Literacy" 2–3). It is the literacy we need to be "functional," which Ira Shor summarizes as

> The ability to interact with political, legal, commercial, occupational and social demands in daily life, such as voting, filing tax returns, applying for work, signing leases and contracts, following printed instructions, passing a driver's written exam, balancing a checkbook, comprehending instructions in a phone book or in an employee benefit plan, etc. (*Culture Wars* 189)

This conception of functional literacy becomes, in Linda Brodkey's view, a trope that a nation or culture can use to justify social inequity (161). Brian Street adds that "what governments and companies want from literacy is primarily technological competence and improvement. The relationship between this and 'intellectual competence' is problematic. . . . literacy programmes will still be justified on the grounds of 'productivity.'" (185). Jonathan Kozol, with his insistence that literacy is more than the incorporation of "adult nonreaders into the accepted mainstream of noncritical America" (182), has identified "fundamental humane literacy" with capacities that disrupt routine functionalism:

1. Informed Irreverence
2. Tolerating Indecision
3. Political Sophistication
4. Respect for History
5. Counteraction of Violence
6. Wise Anger
7. Taste ("the willingness to state that some things count a lot, others much less, and some things not at all")
8. Global literacy (as against "geographical myopia")
9. Ability to Decode Doublespeak (174ff)[7]

Defining the literate individual as broadly informed, critical, participatory, and skeptical, Kozol realizes that this individual "portends some danger for the social system as a whole" (133), through the counteraction of public emphasis on literacy as unreflective and obedient behavior.

The elements of Kozol's fundamental literacy are associated by others with *critical* literacy, that is, the ability to interrogate, challenge, complicate, transform, redefine, and elaborate ostensibly neutral social and institutional facts.[8] This literacy requires the capacity for dialectical thinking, by positing knowledge-in-language as an ongoing critique, in which conclusions lead to further questions, oppositions, and relationships. The dialectician is interested in how meaning can change in light of new connections and contradictions. Her practice exhibits critical inquiry that is necessarily ideological, because it embodies a belief in the value of change. Herbert Marcuse reminds us that dialectical thought can be the weapon of revolution against a formalist establishment:

> Its function is to break down the self-assurance and self-contentment of common sense, to undermine the sinister confidence in the power and language of facts, to demonstrate that unfree-

> dom is so much at the core of things that the development of their internal contradictions leads necessarily to qualitative change: the explosion and catastrophe of the established state of affairs. (qtd. in Giroux, *Theory and Resistance* 19)

Stepping back from explosion and catastrophe, I want to associate *generative* literacy with a dialectical habit of mind: the mind in motion rather than the mind foreclosed. Michael Basseches, whose presuppositions about learning in the 1980s recall Vygotsky's emphasis on the dialectical interaction of mind and society, investigates what may be called the society of ideas in the mind, that is, the dialectical interaction of contradictory propositions and perspectives that he associates with adult development. Basseches would extend Piagetian cognitive theory to account for post-adolescent development. He concludes that "Piaget has never described particular methods of transcending the stability provided by the closed-system structure of formal operational thought so that continuing dialectical progress in the construction of knowledge can occur" (54). Basseches interviewed thirty-six students and faculty members (nine freshmen, nine seniors, nine professors) at Swarthmore College about "the nature of education." From transcriptions of these interviews, he abstracted "moves-in-thought . . . which seemed clearly related to dialectical outlooks and analyses" drawn from "the work of many writers within the dialectical tradition" (68, 72; e.g., Hegel, Marx, Engels, Ollman, Unger, Kosok, Gould, Von Bertalanffy, Piaget). These moves-in-thought, which occurred most frequently in the older students and the professors, are represented as twenty-four dialectical schemata:

1. Thesis-antithesis-synthesis movement in thought.
2. Affirmation of the primacy of motion.
3. Recognition and description of thesis-antithesis-synthesis movement.
4. Recognition of correlativity of a thing and its other.
5. Recognition of ongoing interaction as a source of movement.
6. Affirmation of the practical or active character of knowledge.
7. Avoidance or exposure of objectification, hypostatization, and reification.

8. Understanding events or situations as moments (of development) of a process.
9. Location of an element or phenomenon within the whole(s) of which it is a part.
10. Description of a whole (system, form) in structural, functional, or equilibrational terms.
11. Assumption of contextual relativism.
12. Assertion of the existence of relations, the limits of separation or the value of relatedness.
13. Criticism of multiplicity, subjectivism, and pluralism.
14. Description of a two-way reciprocal relationship.
15. Assertion of internal relations.
16. Location . . . of contradictions or sources of disequilibrium [within and among systems and structures].
17. Understanding the resolution of disequilibrium or contradiction in terms of . . . transformation. . . .
18. Relating value to [movement].
19. Evaluative comparison of forms (systems).
20. Attention to problems of coordinating systems (forms) in relation.
21. Description of open self-transforming systems.
22. Description of qualititative change as a result of quantitative change within a form.
23. Criticism of formalism based on the interdependence of form and content.
24. Multiplication of perspectives as a concreteness-preserving approach to inclusiveness. (74)

One of Basseches's interviewees serves to sum up the process of dialectical thinking: "I test my schema all the time because it tells me how to react to the world" (139). Such "metaformalist" thought, and dialectical thought in general, conceives the world, and the ideas and institutions that populate it, as transforming and transformative systems.

By arraying in lists the characteristics that Kozol and Basseches associate with mature intellection, I want to support a definition of generative literacy as the capacity to create and entertain a number of intellectual, social, and political positions with reference to any piece of "data." More pointedly, I call generative literacy *alertness to ambiguity in spoken or written discourse.* This literacy becomes a foundation for generative magic rhetoric: alertness to ambiguity is a "competence" that makes possible its own "performance," as transformative rhetoric.

Generative literacy can be understood as a "philosophical condition" that continues the sympathetic polytheism central to magic. We perform literate alchemy by presuming that a plurality of relationships and articulations may affect the transmutation of any "pure" substance, fact, idea, condition. David Miller, James Hillman, and Margot Adler value the polycentric/polytheistic "belief" in plural meanings and shifting definitions (Hillman 35, Adler 28–34):

> Socially understood, polytheism is eternally in unresolvable conflict with social monotheism, which in its worst form is fascism and in its less destructive forms is imperialism, capitalism, feudalism and monarchy. . . . Polytheism is not only a social reality; it is also a philosophical condition. It is that reality experienced by men and women when Truth with a capital "T" cannot be articulated reflectively according to a single grammar, a single logic, or a single symbol system" (Miller 4, qtd. in Adler 29).

James Hillman connects dialogic literacy with both polytheistic magic and psychic health when he proposes that

> Even should unity of personality be an aim, "only separated things can unite" [Jung], as we learn from the old alchemical psychologists. Separation comes first. It is a way of gaining distance. This *separatio* (in the language of alchemy) offers internal detachment, as if there were now more interior space for movement and for placing events, where before there was a conglomerate adhesion of parts or a monolithic identification with each and all, a sense of being stuck in one's problem. (31)

The *separatio* that informs generative magic, rhetoric, and literacy is essentially patho-logical, a term whose Greek roots denote "suffering discourse." Dialectical transformation, the rearrangement of parts into new but temporary wholes, aims at disorder and de-formation, at the dis-ease of the original conceptual or institutional "organism." Imagining and arraying alternatives to a presumably healthy body of official knowledge: these are the traditional practices of the *magus*, and are always potentially wicked.[9]

TRICK OR TREAT?

I must admit, preliminary to a more patient investigation of our title terms, that equating magic and the language of social action is something of a trick; one might argue that they merely have a "family resemblance," insofar as both "make things happen." In that case, what this study accomplishes by replacing "rhetoric" and "literacy" with "magic" is an extended lexical shift. This both is and is not so. Allying rhetoric and literacy with magic because all three entail generation, production, and transformation, in order to assert that they are common identities as well as conceptual analogies, is a sleight-of-definition. But perhaps it seems so only because we have forgotten their real commonality. Recalling that commonality affords us the new stressing of an essentially forgotten epistemological framework, and re-presents the powers that we enforce in every instance of theoretical and applied rhetoric, theoretical and applied literacy.

CHAPTER 2

The Interanimation of Phantasms

Literacy, the alertness to linguistic ambiguity, and rhetoric, the performance of literacy, are both possible because meaning is always plural, always susceptible to transformation. Roland Barthes characterizes that susceptibility in terms of magic:

> The text, in its mass, is comparable to a sky, at once flat and smooth, deep, without edges and without landmarks; like the soothsayer drawing on it with the tip of his staff an imaginary rectangle wherein to consult, according to certain principles, the flight of birds, the commentator traces through the text certain zones of reading, in order to observe therein the migration of meanings, the outcropping of codes, the passage of citations. (14)

Reading is generative magic: the prognostication of changeable meanings within an infinite cosmology of signifiers. Barthes's soothsayer, observing the "migration of meanings," is our rhetor, who sees in each changing circumstance differing means/meanings of persuasion.

Today electronic and print media generate a seeming infinity of virtually instant images and words, a magical Barthesian "galaxy of signifiers" (5) that continually expands by virtue of both plurality of meaning and sheer quantity.[1] Surrounded by the production of knowledge, we are invited to participate in it, at the same time that we are prompted to ask the dominant ethical question: Should a plastic, magical imagination—of the very sort that our prognosticator/rhetor must develop—be entrusted with knowledge making? Plato asks this question in *The Sophist*, and is followed by centuries of philosophers occupied with the ethics of phantasy. In the Renaissance, Christian philosophers of magic become intensely occupied with the invocatory and generative powers of words, and the nature of an ideal rhetoric; they attempt to reconcile the human potential for interaction within a universe of intelligences with an obligation to avoid dangerous and heretical contact with ungodly ideas—personified by demons—that lurk everywhere. Cornelius Agrippa, one of the last Renaissance magi, asks Plato's question in the sixteenth century, and answers by writing like Barthes's soothsayer. He stands at the turning point of a long tradition that had licensed—with reservations—a magical composing imagination, a tradition which, after Agrippa, had its license revoked.

THE HISTORY OF PHANTASY

Phantasy is central to theories of magic and rhetoric through the Renaissance. The term has magical connotations for us, suggesting the play of imagination within an unreal world; phantasms, likewise, are the apparitions in such a world. For the ancients, phantasy denotes cognition, and all prevailing models of mind presume that one cannot understand without phantasms (Yates 71; Kristeller 234–38; Couliano 6–13; Watson, throughout). As Aristotle emphasizes in *De Anima*, phantasy is our only basis for speculative reasoning: "whenever one is contemplating, it is some image (*phantasma*) one is contemplating; for the images (*phantasmata*) are like sense data but without matter" (432a; 210). Sense impressions from the exterior world are presented to the mind-soul as phantasms, which are—generally speaking—likenesses of things. However, phantasms are not simply images, nor are they direct replications of the exterior world. A phantasm is produced when a sense impression takes residence in the mind-soul, transformed into something like an imaged archetype. Each phantasm functions as (1) the trace of an original sensation; (2) an analog to other phantasms in residence; (3) a cue for memory; 4) an interpretive guide to the meaning of new sense data; (5) an organizing principle for expression; (6) a basis for human language. Words at all levels of abstraction (e.g., *boat, justice, white*) originate from phantasms. Phantasms in combination, what Ioan Couliano calls "phantasms in motion" in order to emphasize their constant interaction and generation, constitute all intellection. In sum, the grammar of thought and expression is phantasy.[2]

Couliano traces the geography of the phantastic mind that predates its most-cited exponent, Aristotle, and prevails—*mutatis mutandis*—in the works of Augustine, Albertus Magnus, Roger Bacon, Thomas Aquinas, and the medieval encyclopedist Bartholomaeus Anglicus:

> The messages of the five "external" senses are transported by the spirit to the brain, where the *inner* or *common* sense resides. The action of common sense . . . occupies the three cerebral ventricles: the anterior, seat of the imagination; the median, seat of reason; and the posterior, seat of memory. Imagination translates the language of the senses into fantastic language so that reason may grasp and understand phantasms. The data of imagination and of reason are deposited in the memory. (11).

This description of phantasy in terms of faculty psychology is not expressly magical. Yet, at the same time that phantasy is a philosophical and scientific subject, it is also a mystical and spiritual phenomenon. The "language" of phantasms is occult; human language is a secondary representation of an inexpressible phantastic language (Couliano 5). Further, phantasms reside in an incorporeal *pneuma*, or spirit, made in the heavens of the same material as the stars and accompanying the soul as it begins its descent into body (Watson 107). Thus, phantasms are members of both the spiritual and physical worlds, and phantasy can be the contemplation of what is nonexistent in the sensible world (Bundy 148–52).

As a process for determining and producing human language; for mystical contemplation and philosophical speculation; and for generating vivid speech (*enargeia*; see Watson 69 and Eden 88–90), phantasy is closely and explicitly connected with both magic and rhetoric. It is always under suspicion, from Plato forward, as a tool of rhetorical deception; phantasy can create illusions that "charm" audiences.[3] For Plato, phantasy in cooperation with thinking and opinion (*dianoia* and *doxa*) constitutes discourse, which may be either true or false:

> Then since speech, as we found, is true and false, and we saw that thought is conversation of the soul with itself, and opinion is the final result of thought, and what we mean when we say "it seems" is a mixture of sensation and opinion (*phantasia*), it is inevitable that, since these are all akin to speech, some of them must sometimes be false. (*Sophist* 264a; 443. See also Watson 2, Eden 65–66.)

In general, when we investigate magic or rhetoric, we are looking at the process of inducing belief and creating community, and asking how the mind creates impressions and controls their powers and effects. Such is Plato's investigation, particularly in *The Sophist*, which he concludes with condemnation of the title character as a rhetorician whose stock in trade is deceptive image-making (*phantasia*):

> The imitative kind of the dissembling part of the art of opinion which is part of the art of contradiction and belongs to the [ph]antastic class of the image-making art, and is not divine, but human, and has been defined in arguments as the juggling part of productive activity—he who says that the true sophist is of this descent and blood will, in my opinion, speak the exact truth. (268d; 459)

Plato's Sophist is a magician (235a–b) who is especially liable to enchant youth with speech full of false images (*eikones*), "so as to make it seem that they are true and that the speaker is the wisest of men in all things" (234c; 329). This purveyor of "apparent truths in arguments" (*phantasmata*: 234e; 321) is dangerous because sophistic phantasy is protean. As Jacqueline de Romilly points out with reference to the *Euthydemus* (288b–c), Plato's figure of the dangerous magician is Proteus, "the symbol of elusive transformation; for, instead of fighting in a direct and honest way, he used to change himself into a number of deceptive forms and shift from one to the other" (de Romilly, *Magic* 28).[4]

The protean capability that seems a vice when associated with deceiving an audience is nonetheless essential to intellectual speculation, and to the practice of rhetorical *invention*, as Plato, Aristotle, and Cicero attest (see above, chapter 1).[5] Cicero considers phantasy in particular in the *Academica* 1.11.40–42 (449–51), where he tells us that the Stoic Zeno of Citium defined phantasy as the "presentation" (*visum*) of external impressions to the mind for its assent (*sensibus adsensionem*). Using his hand to demonstrate the nature of such assent, Zeno called it "graspable" (*comprehendibile*), midway between the closed fist of absolute knowledge and the empty hand of phantasy unapprehended. For Cicero's Zeno, phantasy is the mental entertainment of the graspable. It can lead to first principles, but it is also and more emphatically an agency for speculation. Through phantasy, "certain broader roads to the discovery of reasoned truth were opened up" (*latiores quaedam ad rationem inveniendam viae aperirentur*).

The Zeno we meet in Sextus Empiricus's *Against the Professors*, in his chapter "Against the Rhetoricians" (ca. 200 C.E.), distinguishes rhetoric from dialectic in a way that recalls the Stoic's definition of phantasy in Cicero:

> Hence, Zeno of Citium, when asked what is the difference between dialectic and rhetoric, clenched his fist and then opened it out and said, "This,"—comparing the compact and short character of dialectic to the clenching, and suggesting the breadth of the rhetorical style by the opening and extension of his fingers. (2.7; 193)

Phantasy and rhetoric are both associated with open and animate discourse,[6] counterposed to the closed fist of the absolute. Rhetoric, as the invention and elaboration of the "graspable," is necessarily phantastic. Mary Carruthers reinforces this point, with particular attention to the role of phantasy in *memory*, and the application of the phantastic memory to reading and writing. As one of the five canons of rhetoric, memory is most commonly understood in its technical sense, as the skill of memorization. For the ancients, however, memorization is one use of memory but does not indicate its whole operation. A full assessment of the nature of classical memory reveals that it is an interpretive and inventive faculty governed by phantasy. In her discussion of the interior senses described by Aquinas in the *Summa Theologica*, Carruthers notes the interaction of the composing imagination with the retentive imagination:

> Four powers are described: common sense; the fantastic (imagination: "as it were a storehouse of forms received through the senses"); the estimative; and the memorative. . . . In his "De potentia animae," cap. 4, Thomas defines the powers more particularly, enumerating five this time: the *sensus communis; phantasia* (retentive imagination); *imaginativa* (the composing imagination); *aestimativa seu cogitativa* . . . ; and *memorativa*. But the composing imagination (*imaginativa*) is elsewhere combined with *imaginatio* (or *phantasia*) and called simply *phantasia seu imaginatio*. (51)

This complex and unsettled psychological scheme describes a dynamic interplay of powers and sensations, memory and imagination, reading and writing. Carruthers explains that reading was considered a visual act that also relied on phantasms: "whatever enters the mind changes into a 'see-able' form for storing in memory" (18). The phantasms that enter when we internalize the sensible world—through reading or otherwise—are typically understood in terms of contemporary writing technology, often described as imprints on a wax surface. With attention to Plato,

Aristotle, Cicero, Quintilian, Aquinas, and Augustine, Carruthers concludes that "the metaphor of memory as a written surface is so ancient and so persistent in all Western cultures that it must, I think, be seen as a governing model or 'cognitive archetype,' in Max Black's phrase" (16). Consequently, the activity of rhetorical invention is a replication, or redirection, of the phantastic imagination. For Aristotle, the *topoi* that inform rhetorical invention are regions in the mind where arguments are stored as *phantasmata* for ready application (Aristotle, *Topics* 163b; Carruthers 29). And for Quintilian, "the greatest part of rhetorical activity involves the [phantastic] functions of the sensory soul, forming, combining, reacting to, storing, and recollecting sense images" (Carruthers 206). Quintilian initially associates phantasy with the vivid evocation of emotion in one's audience:

> There are certain experiences which the Greeks call *phantasiai*, and the Romans *visions*, whereby things absent are presented to our imagination with such extreme vividness that they seem actually to be before our very eyes. . . . When the mind is unoccupied or is absorbed by fantastic hopes or daydreams, we are haunted by these visions of which I am speaking to such an extent that we imagine that we are travelling abroad, crossing the sea, fighting, addressing the people, or enjoying the use of wealth that we do not actually possess, and seem to ourselves not to be dreaming but acting. Surely, then, it may be possible to turn this form of hallucination to some profit. . . . From such [phantastic] impressions arises that *enargeia* which Cicero calls *illumination* and *actuality*. . . . (6.2.29–32; 435)

Having a ready storehouse of phantasms is, for Quintilian, essential to eloquence:

> Consequently those vivid conceptions (*rerum imagines*) of which I spoke and which, as I remarked, are called *phantasiai*, together with everything that we intend to say, the persons and questions involved, and the hopes and fears to which they give rise, must be kept clearly before our eyes and admitted to our hearts: for it is feeling and force of imagination that make us eloquent.[7] (10.7.15; 141)

Quintilian describes the generation of *rerum imagines* in terms analogous to Sextus's Zeno in his characterization of the speculative power of phantasy, as a broadening of the road to discovery:

> Further the attention of the mind must be directed not to some one thing, but simultaneously to a number of things in continuous sequence. The result will be the same as when we cast our eyes along some straight road and see at once all that is on or near it, obtaining a view not merely of its end, but of the whole way there. (10.7.15; 141)

We are told in 10.7.18 that the phantastic imagination so essential to eloquent improvisation is developed through intellectual reverie,[8] or premeditation (*cogitatione praecipimus*), which may be more useful than practice by either writing or speaking. Quintilian characterizes such reverie in 10.6.1–4:

> Having dealt with writing, the next point which claims our attention is premeditation, which itself derives force from the practice of writing and forms an intermediate stage between the labours of the pen and the more precarious fortunes of improvisation; indeed, I am not sure that it is not more frequently of use than either. For there are places and occasions where writing is impossible, while both are available in abundance for premeditation. For but a few hours' thought will suffice to cover all the points even of cases of importance; if we wake at night, the very darkness will assist us, while even in the midst of legal proceedings, our mind will find some vacant space for meditation, and will refuse to remain inactive. . . . At length, however, our powers will have developed so far that the man who is not hampered by lack of natural ability will by dint of persistent [practice] be enabled, when it comes to speaking, to rely no less on what he has thought out than what he has written out and learnt by heart. (127–31)

For the ancients, invention involves recourse to a phantastic inner sense. In preparation for speaking the words of *De Oratore* 3, Cicero's Crassus devotes nearly two hours at midday "in the most earnest and profound meditation," settled into the "thoughtful posture" of "perfect stillness" that typically signals his involvement in rhetorical invention (3.5, 197). He enacts the composing imagination that defines rhetoric through the Middle Ages, as an act of phantasy and a process of reverie. As Mary Carruthers concludes, rhetorical invention—and for the most practiced intellects, formal composition as well—was a process in which the writer searched the places of memory in an exercise that "corresponds to what Aristotle calls the 'deliberative imagination,' a combination of *phantasia* with *dianoia*, or the power of constructing with conscious judgment a single image out of a number of images":

> So the act of invention, carried out by cogitation, was thought to be one of combining or "laying together" in one "place" or compositive image or design the divided bits previously filed and cross-filed in other discrete *loci rerum* when preparing to speak, and its close kinship is apparent to the technique of memorizing texts according to their *res*, which one would then shape into words to suit a particular occasion.
>
> For composition is not an act of writing, it is rumination, cogitation, dictation, a listening and a dialogue, a 'gathering' (*collectio*) of voices from their several places in memory. (Carruthers 197–98)

The *productive* and *combinatory* power of phantasy, and the value of "unfettered phantasia" (Watson 71) was a growing concern through the Middle Ages, as the classical emphasis on the metaphysics of phantasy gave way to the development of an aesthetic of imagination (Bundy 275–78; Watson 94–95). Consequently, the nature of proper intellectual conduct was at issue. The speech that Crassus invents in *De Oratore* 3 is not the speech requested: he was asked to survey the conventional elements of style in rhetoric; instead, he continues to explicate the relationship of philosophical exploration to rhetoric, and irritates his auditors, who want to hear "the ordinary knowledge of common affairs" (3.36, 234). Phantastic reverie can lead the rhetor into disapproved regions, or as with Sulpicius's response to Crassus, "despised" regions of discourse. As a human creative faculty for materializing the possible but nonexistent (those "visions" Quintilian refers to above), the impossible (e.g., a centaur), and the diabolical (given the rise of Christian demonology), phantasy can be dangerous. It is the enemy of a stable reality, as M. W. Bundy explains:

> Those who insisted upon the immutable and eternal character of reality had no place in their thought for a concept of phantasy; but those who conceived of reality as that which was progressively coming into existence, 'becoming' rather than 'being,' as the Greek phrased it, had for the phantasy an important function. This, of course, immediately suggests the bearing of the conflict of idealism and materialism upon the concept of *phantasia*. . . . From uncompromising idealism, with its contempt for matter, and its unwillingness to recognize the reality of the experience whereby mind comes into contact with a physical universe, there came no constructive view of phantasy. One

> is doomed to disappointment who comes to philosophical idealism expecting a lofty conception of phantasy and forgetting that the word itself suggests the contingent, the material, the fleeting,—in a word, the unreal. (271)

The conflict between ideal and material conceptions of phantasy, in a time when phantasy remained identified with the mind and its products, gets a definitive summary in Gianfrancesco Pico della Mirandola's 1500 treatise *De Imaginatione (On the Imagination)*. An appreciation of Aristotle's view of imagination in *De Anima*, Pico's work also synthesizes Neoplatonic, Stoic, and Christian perspectives, and offers a general assessment of the psychology and ethics of phantasy as it had emerged from the Middle Ages. Pico rejects the proffered Medieval distinction between phantasy and imagination, in which phantasy was associated with the *production of the unreal*, and imagination with the *reproduction of objects of sense*:

> The proposition of greatest weight, nay, the foundation-stone of the discussion we have undertaken, the proposition which in the eyes of philosophers and theologians is a clear and admitted fact, is that there exists a power of the soul which conceives and fashions likenesses of things, and serves, and ministers to, both the discursive reason and the contemplative intellect; and to this power has been given the name *phantasy* or *imagination*. For the opinion of Avicenna, whereby he separated the phantastic from the imaginative power, has long since been exploded, and that notion of his which attributed to phantasy supernatural powers of strength and efficacy has also been condemned by reputable philosophers.[9] (37)

On the primacy of phantastic imagination in human thought and behavior, Pico is emphatic: Phantasy is the "one, single power of the sensitive soul," which infuses imagination, common sense and memory (35). Further, "the life and actions of all animate beings are in great part ruled by phantasies" (39). With this position, Gianfrancesco Pico allows for the preeminent conjunction of phantasy, rhetoric, and topical philosophy in the Italian Renaissance; a conjunction that—as it was maintained by Renaissance magi such as Giovanni Pico, Marsilio Ficino, and Cornelius Agrippa—further defined rhetorical invention in terms of magic.

Gianfrancesco Pico proposes that a disordered imagination, to which "those devoted to the contemplative life" are particularly susceptible (61), can be cured by the light of faith (*fidei lumine*). Phantasms purified by this light have more persuasive power than "the reasonings of philosophers"; the light of faith reveals

> on the one hand, the lakes of fire and brimstone, tortures, demons, and the like; on the other hand, the golden ramparts of the heavenly Jerusalem, girt with precious stones, celestial banquets, the marriage of the Lamb, the societies of the blessed, choruses of angels chanting harmonious tunes, and whatever scenes of this kind there are, scattered through Holy Writ. (89)

For Gianfrancesco Pico, as with his classical predecessors, the invoked universe of images and associations is a persuasive force; both young and old are more influenced by "enlightened" phantasy than by image-less reason (91). Pico maintains phantasy as the central human generative power, which constitutes our very capacity to desire and create—in speech and writing—a vast cosmology: "Imagination . . . conceives not only what now is no more, but as well what it suspects or believes is yet to be, and even what it presumes cannot be created by Mother Nature" (29). For Pico, the recognition of this power corresponds with its restriction. The licentious rhetoric that phantasy allows must be reduced to the territories illumined by the pure light of faith.[10] Paradoxically, such insight lights the way beyond rhetoric and phantasy: "the intellect purified of phantasms" leads us to "the spirit hid beneath the bark" of human language, to wordless contemplation (93).

RENAISSANCE MAGIC RHETORIC IN THE LIGHT OF FAITH

Gianfrancesco Pico reiterates Plato's worry that our capacity for phantasy is potentially wicked. Reverie among phantasms can lead to regions of belief and persuasion outside of God and the Good. Pico's excursus on the phantastic imagination corresponds with terrific attempts by Renaissance magicians to explicate the magical powers of human language without committing heresy, to validate an expansive composing imagination that is also pious.[11] Gianfrancesco Pico is the nephew of the more famous Giovanni Pico, whose *Oration on the Dignity of Man* remains for many a definitive presentation of Renaissance humanism, as well as a "great charter of Renaissance magic" (Yates, *Bruno* 86) in its affirmations of magus's power as a medium for celestial deities. For the older Pico, the magus speaks the universe, and the speech moves its audience with cosmological force. Focussing on Giovanni's *De Genere Dicendi Philosophorum*, Ernesto Grassi notes his claim that "rhetorical speech cannot be replaced by rational speech." While Giovanni's contemporary Hermolao Barbaro says that "it is *brilliant and elegant* speech, or at least *clear and pure* speech . . . which brings fame and eternal remembrance to the writer" (Grassi 56); Giovanni says that this is merely technical rhetoric, whose "magical" power inheres in the manipulation of syntax and syllogisms that affects the ignorant (Grassi 58). Pico proposes that the alternative to the strictly technical and rational speech is the philosophical speech, in which the spirits of the cosmos speak through the orator; a speech that is plainly magical in its transformative power:

> They move not, they convince not (*non movent, non persuadent*), but they *compel*, they *stir*, they *impose* on you a force (*sed cogunt, agitant, vim inferunt*), those words of the Law, rough, simple words, but alive, animated, glowing, sharp (*rudia verba et agrestia, sed viva, sed animata, flammea, aculeata*), penetrating into the depths of the soul, transforming man through a wondrous power. (Grassi 60)

Giovanni Pico's conception of the godlike rhetor-as-magician influences grand models of the composing imagination. Frances Yates notes that, for instance, one of the most famous Renaissance memory systems, Giulio Camillo's memory theater, "proposed to show how Man, the great Miracle, who could harness the powers of the cosmos with Magia and Cabala as described in Pico's Oration on the Dignity of Man, might develop magical powers as an orator by speaking from a memory organically affiliated to the proportions of the world harmony" (*Art* 169). Renaissance fascination with the human prospects for expanded consciousness and control lent a distinctly magical cast to the concerns of philosophy, concerns that included the powers of imagination and rhetoric. Dominic La Russo generalizes the conjunction of magic and rhetoric that we note here in Pico as a humanist tendency that punctuates a long tradition, with foundations in Plato and in Scripture: "Many [Italian humanists] realized that the rhetorical act was the magical matrix; meaning was extracted from oral symbols and converted into energy that initiated action and reaction and left a residual feeling of spiritual fusion" (*Renaissance Rhetoric* 53; see also Copenhaver 206).

As we saw in chapter 1, Marsilio Ficino—who was Giovanni Pico's teacher and the preeminent Neoplatonic philosopher of the Italian Renaissance—defined the orator and the magus as similar figures. Just as the perfect orator must accommodate his discourse to the multiplicity and changing dispositions of each human soul, the magus must accommodate any invocation to the daily shifting positions of the stars, and the changing human behaviors incited by the heavens. Ficino presents natural magic—which includes astrology, medicine, and alchemy—as a rhetorical practice: the magus aligns the elements, and the right words, and the paths of the stars, with a variation in any one of them affecting all the rest.

Brian Copenhaver has noted that for Ficino, "man's chief magical faculty is the imagination, which as the Peripatetic common sense or as fantasy links corporeal objects to the incorporeal subject, soul or mind" (285). In a sympathetic universe, physical, spiritual, and intellectual bodies interact and affect one another; for Ficino, the phantastic imagination can determine their conjunctions. Ficino affirms a central tenet in the history of magic: Mind exists *in* matter, and language *affects* matter: words and things are themselves volitional forces, and the magus attempts to invoke and participate with those forces, to enter his own mind into the constant flux of "minded" elements and signs. Brian Vickers explains: "The sign is the thing it represents, and as such it works in us, and we can use it to work on the world. . . . The lute strings affect each other, the star's image affects us; by wearing a magic amulet we can tap the health-giving forces in the invisible world" ("Analogy" 123; see also Berman 69–113, and Foucault below). Modern magicians still follow these principles. The 1939 *Encyclopedia of Occult Sciences*, a standard reference in the trade, includes a section on "The Language of Flowers," which proposes that flowers "have been given a language" that allows for "mute dialogues" among lovers: "A well-arranged nosegay takes the place of a letter, lacks its perils, and for the timid, its disadvantages" (Maffeo 347). Certain combinations of flowers determine several, usually complementary, messages:

> Thyme + rosemary + elder + white jasmine + convolvulus + mignonette + everlasting flower = The sight of you thrills me.

> Your presence scatters my trouble. You comfort me in every sorrow. You are amiable and charm me. You qualities surpass your charms. Always yours. My friendship is without end. (346)

After offering similarly functional grammars for stones, colors, and other terrestrial and celestial elements, the *Encyclopedia* repeats a longstanding epistemological tenet of magic: "For the Alchemist everything lives. For the Occultist everything can become symbolical" (353). It is a belief that echoes Ficino:

> The life of the world, innate in everything, is clearly propagated into plants and trees, like the body-hair and tresses of its body. Moreover, the world is pregnant with stones and metals, like its bones and teeth. It sprouts also in shells which live clinging to the earth and to stones. For these things live not so much by their own life as by the common life of the universal whole itself. (Ficino, *Three Books* 3.6; 289)

With this view, distinctions between literal and figurative identity are impossible to maintain, because everything is both actual and symbolic: a talisman or a word signifies a magic power *and* is that power.

Participation in the universal mind, the central activity of the magus, depends upon an explication of the cosmology of powers that constitute that universe. For those who seek spells and rituals with determinate functions, such explication may become formulary. But in an ever-changing universe, in which signification is always—as Barthes puts it—migratory, the consequences of resemblance, analogy, and identity are never permanent. This is Foucault's point in his chapter on "The Prose of the World" in *The Order of Things*. Treating intellectual history more broadly than does Vickers, Foucault also proposes that up until the end of the sixteenth century, *resemblance* was central to knowing and creating; it was the basis of hermeneutics and semiology. Things resemble other things; signs resemble—through analogy and sympathy—other things and other signs. While antipathies can be posited (dogs repel cats), absolute and exclusionary distinctions cannot. To *know* a thing means to know all of its resemblances:

> Resemblance never remains stable within itself; it can be fixed only if it refers back to another similitude, which then, in turn, refers to others; each resemblance, therefore, has value only from the accumulation of all the others, and *the whole world must be explored if even the slightest of analogies is to be justi-*

> *fied and finally take on the appearance of certainty.* It is therefore a knowledge that can, and must, proceed by infinite accumulation of confirmations all dependent on one another. And for this reason, from its very foundations, this knowledge will be a thing of sand. (30; emphasis added)

The principle of resemblance allows for an infinity of interpretive possibilities, and necessarily replaces conclusive knowledge with *writing*, that is, with an inventory of identities that is definitive but never exhaustive:

> And indeed, when one goes back to take a look at the *Historia serpentum et draconum*, one finds the chapter "On the serpent in general" arranged under the following headings: equivocation (which means the various meanings of the word *serpent*), synonyms and etymologies, differences, form and description, anatomy, nature and habits, temperaments, coitus and generation, voice, movements, places, diet, physiognomy, antipathy, sympathy, modes of capture, death and wounds caused by the serpent, modes and signs of poisoning, remedies, epithets, denominations, prodigies and presages, monsters, mythology, gods to which it is dedicated, fables, allegories and mysteries, hieroglyphics, emblems and symbols, proverbs, coinage, miracles, riddles, devices, heraldic signs, historical facts, dreams, simulacra and statues, use in human diet, use in medicine, miscellaneous uses. (39)

Foucault concludes that, in the sixteenth century, to know any thing "is to gather together the whole dense layer of signs with which it or they may have been covered" (40); this gathering of signs traverses natural and supernatural realms of representation. We have seen that such an expansive process of naming is made possible by the model of cognition that had persisted since antiquity, which licenses productive and combinatory phantasy. Phantasy becomes human discourse through intellectual reverie, and the capacity for such reverie is identified with the mastery of rhetorical invention. The magical nature of this process is reaffirmed by Renaissance magi such as Giovanni Pico and Marsilio Ficino, who accord humanity the power to affect the circumstances of their lives, by creating language that identifies the sympathetic forces that populate the cosmos.

The magical imagination traffics in an infinity of signs, in part because it aspires toward containing a universe of resemblances, in part because, as Foucault points out with reference to Montaigne, "language contains its own inner principle of proliferation" (40): words generate more words, commentaries upon commentaries, interpretations of interpretations. Thus, final knowledge is inexpressible, "a thing of sand." However, the imagination's generative impulse harbors a nostalgia, even an urgency, for Truth:

> There can be no commentary unless, below the language one is reading and deciphering, there runs the sovereignty of an original Text. And it is this text which, by providing a foundation for the commentary, offers its ultimate revelation as the promised reward of commentary. . . . The language of the sixteenth century—understood not as an episode in the history of any one tongue, but as a global cultural experience—found itself caught, no doubt, between these interacting elements, in the interstice occurring between the primal Text and the infinity of Interpretations. (Foucault 41)

Plato's concern in the *Sophist*, that the composing imagination—"the juggling part of productive activity"—can operate at variance with Truth, is an expression of this tension between an infinity of interpretations (the Sophist's stock in trade) and a primal Text (the ideal Mind-Soul). In the Christian Neoplatonism of the Renaissance, theories of imagination and philosophies of magic grapple with reconciling the newly celebrated human potential for a purely *generative* magic with the moral necessity for an *arresting* magic: if human discourse can indeed determine and transform the cosmos, it must do so in the service of holy principles, in the light of faith.

Accommodating intellectual license to sovereign authority is the charge of the magus who would both preserve his own faith and escape punishment for heresy. Such accommodation meant taking care not to invoke *demons*, who draw the imagination away from the light of faith. The Medieval and Renaissance universes are full of demons: supercelestial, planetary, and elemental. Unlike the corporeal matter of the universe—stars and planets, rocks and trees—demons are not *neutral* agencies of sympathetic influence. Demons have *personal* identities; they possess volitional intelligences that can interact with and transform human intelligence. Even if the magus attempts to invoke a "good demon" (i.e., an angel), there is always the chance that a "bad" one will answer. So all demonic magic is potentially heretical; the magus risks allowing diabolical voices into his mind and soul. To avoid this, he must appeal only to unintelligent forces: When Ficino tells how to accommodate our words and songs to the health-giving forces of the stars, he is careful to indicate that the stellar influence to which we appeal is not itself volitional: "And do not believe that we are dealing with gifts which the stars are going to give by their own election, but rather by a natural influence" (3.21; 357). "Safe" magic, then, disallows all interaction with other *voices*. It can be interactive and sympathetic; the magus may attempt to harmonize his life with the beneficial—but dumb and soul-less—astrological influences emanating from, for instance, Saturn. But *dialogic* magic is dangerous. Any magic that employs words issues a general appeal—intended or not—to some other intelligence, and because we can never be sure who might respond, all word magic is *vehementer suspectus* (Nauert 244). For those who understand that the universe is both analogical and dialogical, every uttered word is necessarily *generative*, immediately migrating among resemblances and demons, into territories outside the light of faith; outside any regulative Text that would arrest the principles of proliferation that language enacts. The Christian magus who would draw power from the cosmos faces a central question: Can one both celebrate the protean powers of the discoursing imagination, and remain faithful to an ideal origin: to God, to Truth, to Justice? Cornelius Agrippa is at pains to address this question; in the course of doing so, he illustrates contradictory impulses that indicate the restlessness of the magical imagination and the range of rhetorics it can contain.

AGRIPPA'S OCCULT PHILOSOPHY

The works of Cornelius Agrippa (1486–1535) represent most fully the scope of Renaissance magic, and his influence is evidenced by the literary characters he inspired (Christopher Marlowe's Dr. Faustus and Goethe's Faust, Thomas Nashe's Agrippa in *The Unfortunate Traveler*, Rabelais's Her Trippa in *Tiers Livre*, Mary Shelley's Victor Frankenstein); the works modeled in some measure on his skepticism (Montaigne's "Apology for Raymond Sebond," Sidney's *Defence of Poesy*) and his astrological doctrines (Dürer's *Melencolia I*); the intellectuals who criticized him (Erasmus, Bacon); and the magicians who reckoned with and adapted his *Occult Philosophy* (Paracelsus, Giordano Bruno,

Francis Barrett).[12] Born in Nettesheim, near Cologne, Agrippa learned astrology from his parents, and pursued a general course of study at the University of Cologne, where he joined a secret brotherhood of occultists. His claim to doctorates in law and medicine has never been proven; however, he practiced both subjects, working for a time as *orator-advocatus* (both lawyer and official speechmaker) for the German city of Metz, where he successfully defended a woman accused of witchcraft; and as a court physician in French Lyons. A miscellany of stints in political and military service and an occasional university lecture on magic filled Agrippa's life of travels through Italy, France, Germany, and Switzerland.

Mindful that magic, skepticism, and rhetoric were all objects of wholesale reform by the end of the seventeenth century, we can locate Agrippa in the post-Medieval, pre-Reformation moment when intellectual enthusiasm for the imaginative and expressive possibilities of figurative language, skeptical philosophy, and occult sciences was high.[13] His uneven and inconsistent body of writing, together with his variegated and restless career in a number of professions, allows us to consider how a belief in magic may—perhaps must—coincide with an exploratory and even incoherent rhetoric. Agrippa's occult, antirational, and fideistic epistemologies intersect and contradict each other during his career of temporary professions, shifting religious and political allegiances, and failed appeals for patronage, and comprise a rhetoric of unsettled propositions that reflects both the magic belief in the plasticity of language, and the willingness of the magus to create provisional intellectual realities.

Drawing heavily from Ficino and Giovanni Pico, and perhaps from Gianfrancesco Pico as well (see above, n. 11), Agrippa's 1510 *De Occulta Philosophia Libri Tres* (*Three Books of Occult Philosophy*) portrays a fluctuant world of physical and metaphysical sympathies:

> In the Soul of the World there [are] as many seminal forms of things as *Ideas* in the mind of God, by which forms she did in the heavens above the stars frame to herself shapes also, and stamped upon all these some properties . . . so that every species [has] its celestial shape, or figure that is suitable to it, from which also proceeds a wonderful power of *operating*, which proper gift it receives from its own *Idea*, through the seminal forms of the Soul of the World (1.11, 65–66; *Opera* 1, 23).[14]

The elaboration of this infinity of seminal forms—with their accompanying figures (numbers and letters)—fills Agrippa's three books of occult philosophy. Sharing in and directing the powers of the cosmology of forms is a matter of complex astrological and cabalistic arithmetic. Agrippa provides tables of correspondences among numbers, letters, and their celestial, terrestrial, and infernal counterparts. The number *8*, for instance, corresponds to the letter *H*; the practice of justice (because it divides "fairly" into even numbers equally, two times twice two); the eight rewards of the blessed (inheritance, incorruption, power, victory, the vision of God, grace, a kingdom, joy); the eight visible heavens (of the stars, Saturn, Jupiter, Mars, the sun, Venus, Mercury, the moon); the eight particular qualities (dryness of earth, coldness of water, moisture of air, heat of fire, heat of air, moisture of water, dryness of fire, coldness of earth); the eight kinds of blessed men (peace makers, those hungry for righteousness, the meek, those persecuted for righteousness, the pure in heart, merciful, poor in spirit, mourners); and the eight rewards of the damned (prison, death, judgment, wrath of God, darkness, indignation, tribulation, anguish) (2.11, 202–3; *Opera* 1, 188–89).

The larger the number, the more correspondences entailed (Agrippa discusses numbers as high as one million); the process of constructing a cosmology of powers/signifiers is largely a matter of multiplication (2.15, 222; *Opera* 1, 201). The scope and complexity of such arithmetical operations is compounded by the fact that all is in constant motion, and that every element is in sympathetic relationship with every other element. When the magician employs "ingenious speech" in order to attract virtues or compel action, he will fail without comprehensive alertness to the sympathetic and causal medley in play:

> So the universal soul moves the particular soul; and the rational acts upon the sensual, and that upon the vegetable; and every part of the world acts upon another, and every part is apt to be moved by another. (2.60, 338–39; *Opera* 1, 304)

Agrippa repeatedly emphasizes both the power of words and the complex of contingencies any utterance must address. Delivered rightly, words and sentences can convey "the virtue of the speaker," and powerfully change "not only the hearers but also other bodies and things that have no life" (1.69, 211; *Opera* 1, 139). The writer of verses and orations must be alert to the myriad associations that attend the appeal to any star or deity (here Agrippa echoes Ficino, *Three Books* 3.21; 355–56):

> You must diligently consider what virtue any star contains, as, also, what effects and operations, and to infer them in verses, by praising, extolling, amplifying and setting forth those things which such a kind of star is wont to cause by way of its influence, and by vilifying and dispraising those things which it is wont to destroy and hinder, and by supplicating and begging for that which we desire to get, and by condemning and detesting that which we would have destroyed and hindered; and after the same manner to make an elegant oration, and duly distinct . . . with competent numbers and proportions. (1.71, 214; *Opera* 142)

The "effects and operations" of any star cannot be arrested by discourse; they are too complex and mobile, interacting in Agrippa's cosmology with "intelligences" in innumerable associations:

> An Intelligence is an intelligible substance, free from all gross and putrifying mass of a body, immortal, insensible, assisting all, having influence over all, and the nature of all intelligences, spirits, and angels is the same. . . . But of these according to the tradition of the magicians, there are those kinds, the first of which they call supercelestial, and minds altogether separated from a body, and as it were intellectual spheres, worshipping the one only God, as it were their most firm and stable unity or center; wherefore they even call them gods, by reason of a certain participation of the divinity; for they are always full of God, and overwhelmed with divine nectar. . . . The celestial intelligences do next follow these in the second order . . . they are divided into so many orders as there are heavens in the world and as there are stars in the heavens. And they called those Saturnine who rule the heaven of Saturn and Saturn himself; others Jovial who rule the heaven of Jupiter and Jupiter himself, and in like manner [the magicians] name diverse angels . . . and because the old astrologers did maintain fifty five motions, therefore they invented so many intelligences or angels; they placed also in the starry heaven angels who might rule the signs, triplicities, decans, equinaries, degrees and stars;[15] for although the school of the peripatetics assigns only one intelligence to each of the orbs of the stars, yet seeing every star and small part of the heaven has its proper and different power and influence, it is necessary that it also have his ruling intelligence, which may

> confer power and operate. . . . Thirdly [the magicians] established angels as ministers for the disposing of those things which are below. . . . [W]hence as these angels are appointed for diverse stars, so also for diverse places and times, not that they are limited by time or place, neither by the bodies which they are appointed to govern. . . . Therefore of these spirits of the third kind, as the opinion of the Platonists is, they report that there are so many legions, as there are stars in the heaven, and so many spirits in every legion, as in heaven itself stars. . . . (3.16, 390–93; *Opera* 1, 353–55)

Philosophical magic, as typified by Agrippa, is occupied with the multiplication of contingencies. The countless forces that the magus would invoke and control are always in transit; they cannot be stabilized or codified. Further, the good and bad intelligences that populate the universe cannot be clearly distinguished; the numbers of the "angels that failed" (*defertores angelos*) corresponds to the numbers of good angels, and the evil spirits are also distributed among the "stars and elements and parts of the world" (3.16, 393–94; *Opera* 356–57). The complexity of the universe one would master precludes conceiving and prescribing a particular invocation with a particular effect. Thus, the relationship between discourse and action is real but uncertain.

Still, words *do* make things happen. Throughout the *Occult Philosophy*, Agrippa's own experience complements the testimony of poets and philosophers that "by verses many wonderful things may be done, as corn to be removed, lightnings to be commanded, diseases to be cured, and the like" (1.72, 217; *Opera* 1, 145). Agrippa insists upon the verity of such happenings, noting that if magic were not possible, we would not legislate against it: "If these things were not true, there would not be such strict penal statutes made against them that should enchant fruit" (1.72, 217; *Opera* 1, 144). Significantly, the transformative power of words is not restricted to spoken utterances. Just as speech reiterates what is in the mind, so does writing: "And whatsoever is in the mind, in voice, in words, in operation, and in speech, the whole and all of this is in writing also" (1.53, 218; *Opera* 1, 146). The magus who knows the complex geography of the soul of the world, who—in effect—holds that universe *in mind*, can express and impose the powers of this cosmology through writing, if he masters "the proportion, correspondency, and reduction of letters to the celestial signs and planets, according to various tongues":

> God gave to man a mind and speech, which (as said Mercurius Trismegistus) are thought to be a gift of the same virtue, power, and immortality. The omnipotent God has by his providence divided the speech of men into diverse languages, which languages have, according to their diversity, received diverse and proper characters of writing, consisting in their certain order, number, and figure, not so disposed and formed by hap or chance, nor by the weak judgment of man, but from above, whereby they agree with the celestial and divine bodies and virtues. (1.74, 219; *Opera* 1, 146)

Here Agrippa places himself among the magi—including Ficino and Giovanni Pico—who sought an "alphabet of nature," a written language coincident with the elements of all creation, which could be used to command them.[16] The search for such a language developed initially in Spain in the Middle Ages, through the Jewish mystical hermeneutic study called Kabbalah, or Cabala as it was often known by its Christian adaptors. The Cabala is constituted by a body of speculative philosophy holding that God created the universe through the manipulation of a set of basic letters, expressed in divine speech. A text of "hidden meaning" is available to the trained Cabalist who understands this originary alphabet: like God, and in concert with Divine creation, he is also able to invoke and control natural forces. Frances Yates offers a summary view of the tradition:

> The Cabala . . . had as its basis the doctrine of the ten Sephiroth and the twenty-two letters of the Hebrew alphabet. The doctrine of the Sephiroth is laid down in the Book of Creation, or *Sefer Yetzirah*, and it is constantly referred to throughout the *Zohar*, the mystical work written in Spain in the thirteenth century which embodies the traditions of Spanish Cabalism of that time. The Sephiroth are "the ten names most common to God and in their entirety they form his one great Name." They are "the creative Names which God called into the world," and the created universe is the external development of these forces alive in God. . . . [W]hen words were calculated into numbers and numbers into words the entire organization of the world could be read off in terms of word-numbers, or the number of heavenly hosts could be exactly calculated as amounting to 301,655,172. (Yates, *Bruno* 92–93)

In cabalistic speculation, the magus must presume that there is a discoverable originary language that discloses the mind of God, and contains, for instance, the grammar of "seminal forms" that populate the universal mind-soul. This language cannot be conventional and ambiguous, it must be pure and natural. And, as Agrippa indicates, although the power of writing an originary name is considerable, the possibility of such writing is slim, because an act of human language can never be pure:

> Now, those words are of greater efficacy than others which represent greater things—as intellectual, celestial, and supernatural; as more expressly, so more mysteriously. Also those that come from a more worthy tongue, or from any of a more holy order; for these (as it were certain signs and representations) receive a power of celestial and supercelestial things, as from the virtue of things explained, of which they are the vehicle, and from a power put into them by the virtue of the speaker. . . . For the natural power of things proceeds, first, from the objects to the senses, and then from these to the imagination, and from this to the mind, in which it is first conceived, and then is expressed by voices and words. The Platonists, therefore, say that in this very voice, or word, or name framed, with its articles, that the power of the thing, as it were some kind of life, lies under the form of the signification. . . . Every voice, therefore, that is significative, first of all signifies by the influence of the celestial harmony; secondly, by the imposition of man, although oftentimes otherwise by this than by that. But when both significations meet in any voice or name, which are put upon them by the said harmony, or men, then that name is with a double virtue, viz., natural and arbitrary, made most efficacious to act as often as it shall be uttered in due place and time, and seriously, with an intention exercised upon the matter rightly disposed, and that can naturally be acted upon by it. (1.69–70, 211–13; *Opera* 1, 139–40)

Express connections between celestial harmony and human language are mysterious and rare. Such a connection is made more likely when a celestial signifier is uttered or written in the right circumstances: by a worthy and serious spokesman, at the right place and time (in the astrological scheme of things), in a manner appropriate to the matter one would affect. Noting that the conditions necessary for effective magic correspond to the factors that traditionally contextualize effective rhetoric (e.g., under the Aristotelian categories of ethos, logos, and pathos), we may propose once again that transformative word magic operates within rhetorical contingencies.

Caught among such contingencies, the magus acts out the tension between what Foucault calls "the primal Text and the infinity of interpretations." Keeping God in mind, and aspiring to the mind of God (to gain a full command of *human life*), Agrippa would establish a determinate set of associations among speaker, text, and context, within a dynamic cosmology of resemblances that evades any conclusive explication. The magical imagination can achieve, at best, a reverie of possible associations—among stars, spirits, virtues, vices, words, numbers, talismans, images, times and places, intentions and attitudes—subtended by a nostalgia for pure linguistic power.

For the magus, the realization that we participate in a cosmology of uncertain sympathies, and that the originary Text cannot be conclusively written, can allow for intellectual license that becomes licentious. This is, apparently, Agrippa's problem. His uneven and inconsistent body of work has puzzled and disturbed scholars. Ioan Couliano becomes exasperated with Agrippa because "ambiguities pile up within him" (200). Charles Nauert, whose full-length study of Agrippa remains a standard reference, says that Agrippa is "really incapable of deciding what he is about" (261), charging further that Agrippa does not write "orderly expositions, but mere chains of alleged facts, all having some connection, however slight, with the topic announced in the chapter title" (261). Brian Copenhaver concludes that "[Agrippa] overwhelmed his blatantly derivative theory with a tonnage of recipes and anecdotes that leave the impression of chaotic wonder-mongering . . . " (289). Richard Popkin laments that Agrippa "may not have contributed much that was lasting, only false starts" (xx–xxi). But Nauert also devotes a full chapter and more to "the odyssey of Agrippa's mind" (194–221), as a defense against a critical tradition that has dismissed his importance, concluding that Agrippa "personified . . . his epoch": "He was the magician, the cabalist, the Faustian doubter, the living embodiment of many of the enthusiasms and most of the gnawing doubts and uncertainties and fears of his age" (330–31).

What is most disturbing, from these modern vantage points, is that Agrippa seems to be of more than one mind at the same time. He completes *The Occult Philosophy* by 1510, but does not publish it until 1533, seven years after writing an ostensible *refutation* of magic, and rhetoric, and "any kind of learning" in *De Incertitudine et Vanitate Scientiarum atque Artium* (*Of the Vanity and Uncertainty of Arts and Sciences*); completed in 1526, the *Vanity* reflects an absolute skepticism initiated in writings ten years earlier.[17] The *Vanity* presents an especially pointed denunciation of the cabalistic art so important to Agrippa's philosophy of magic:

> And so this Cabala of the Jews is nothing but a certain most pernicious superstition, by which according to their own will they gather, divide, and transfer words and names, and letters placed here and there in Scripture . . . constructing from this [practice] words, conclusions, and parables from their own imaginings; they want to fit the words of God to them, defaming the Scriptures and saying that their imaginings arise from them; they calumniate the law of God and by impudently twisted computations of words, syllables, letters, and numbers, try to infer violent and blasphemous proofs of their perfidy. (Nauert's trans., 210)

Through the two major works that develop in tandem during his career, Agrippa has been said to exhibit a "credulity-incredulity-charlatanry" pattern (Nauert 200): the magus believes in the powers of mind and language to articulate the order of the universe, however provisionally and tentatively; the skeptic is a fierce anti-intellectual who explicitly retracts his *Occult Philosophy*:

> I being also a young man wrote of magical matters three books in a sufficient large volume, which I have entitled Of Occult Philosophy, in which books whatsoever was then done amiss through curious youth, now being more advised I wish that it be recanted with this retraction, for I have in times past consumed very much time and substance in these vanities. (*Vanity*, Cap. 48, 141–42; *Opera* 2, 104).

It is difficult to regard this retraction as final, given Agrippa's subsequent revision and publication of the *Occult Philosophy*, and his continued public interest in magic. The magus and the skeptic appear to contradict each other, and that contradiction has accounted for the dismissal of Agrippa as a confused thinker. Nauert attempts to save Agrippa's reputation by arguing that his anti-intellectual stance against conventional learning is consistent with the anti-rationalist nature of magic:

> Yet the usual assumption, that skepticism is incompatible with an interest in magic, is really quite unfounded; and a few recent historians have shown that enthusiasm for magic undermined

> the medieval belief in an orderly universe amenable to the workings of human reason. Although Agrippa's magical studies would not expose him directly to arguments directed against the validity of human reason, the intellectual foundations of magic would suggest that the real world far exceeds the scope of the rational understanding. (141)

The Agrippas of the *Occult Philosophy* and the *Vanity*, taken together, exhibit what Nauert (following Garin) has called "belief in magic and corrosive doubt about the validity of human reason and about contemporary civilization," which are "two aspects of the same mentality" (200). This mentality is what we might expect of a magus, who believes that realities can be invented and transformed, and practices intellectual travel among them.[18] In the *Vanity*, Agrippa's protean capacity for phantasy within contingent realities, coupled with fideism that is emphatic in the *Vanity* and also present in the *Occult Philosophy*, compel him to construct a paradoxical discourse that represents the magical composing imagination at play with conventional wisdom.

In the *Vanity*, Agrippa fears "new words springing up and the old decaying . . . so that there is nothing stable" (Cap. 100, 376; *Opera* 2, 302), and cautions us to disregard the sciences and arts, which are "nothing else, than traditions of men . . . and that all these do consist of no other thing but of doubtful things and opinions . . . and that all are not so uncertain as deceitful" (Cap. 101, 379; *Opera* 2, 304–5). Repeatedly, he insists that because human language is susceptible to multiple interpretations, it becomes matter for strategic contentions instead of truth, even among the scholastic theologians who should be pursuing Divine truth:

> Hereupon Scholastical Divinity in the end by little and little was turned to sophisms . . . and hucksters of God's word, who are not divine except the title be bought . . . going from school to school, moving questions, forging opinions, and wronging the Scriptures with intricate words giving them a contrary sense, readier to craftily deceive, than plainly to try out the truth, they have also presumed to invent infinite seed plots of brawling. . . . Afterward they having recourse to interpreting, to expounding, to glossing, and to syllogizing, do rather give [the meaning of Scripture] some other sense, than the proper meaning of the letter. If you instantly require an answer, and be earnest upon them, they will give evil language and call you Ass, as one who understands not that which is hidden in the letter: but as a ser-

> pent feeds on the earth alone, so there is none among them accounted as divines, but such as can brawl apace, and dispute against every matter proposed, readily to invent, and find out new understandings, and to make so great a noise with monstrous words, that not for the hardness of the matter, but for the strangeness of words that are understood by no man. And then these are called subtle, angelic, seraphic, and the divine doctors, when they have handled the matter so that they cannot be perceived, then the multitude of auditors rush about them, who believe whatsoever they have spoken. . . . (Cap. 97, 354; *Opera* 2, 283)

This attack upon the sophistry of scholars illustrates Agrippa's typical volubility throughout the *Vanity*, a volubility curiously at odds with the repeated insistence that human language is a useless means to Truth. Condemning rhetoric, logic, and sophistry as like materials for the "fortress of heretics" (Cap. 8, 55; *Opera* 2, 39), Agrippa castigates the associational fluency that informs rhetorical and sophistical facilities for constructing multiple arguments (Cap. 6, 42 and Cap. 8, 52–53; *Opera* 2, 28 and 36–37). But he demonstrates such facility throughout, especially in the progression of topics through the ninety-nine varieties of "arts and sciences." A discernibly conventional associational progression does operate in several collections of chapters. Chapters 3–8, for instance, treat Grammar, Poetry, History, Rhetoric, Logic, and Sophistry; chapters 42–47 treat Natural Magic, Mathematical Magic, Witchcraft, Necromancy, Theurgy, and Cabala. However, in a striking idiosyncratic departure from such conventional trains of analysis, Agrippa follows chapter 62, on Monks, with a chapter on Prostitution. He has decided to feature monks as whoremasters:

> Wheresoever these sumptuous churches and colleges of priests and monks are, for the most part there are at hand brothels; and also very many houses of nuns and Beguines are as it were private stews of harlots, whom we know also that monks and religious persons (lest their chastity should be defamed) have oftentimes maintained in monasteries under a monk's hood and man's apparel. I think it not against order in this place to join a discourse on the whoorish art, which many passing wise men have thought not only profitable, but necessary also for the governance of a well framed commonwealth. (Cap. 63, 201; *Opera* 2, 161)

With similar effrontery, chapters on War and the Nobility, which characterize the former as inexcusably murderous and the latter as war's originators, lead to a series of chapters on Medicine, which is for Agrippa "also a certain art of manslaughter" (Cap. 82, 295; *Opera* 2, 234). Connections between monks and whores, murderous kings and murderous doctors, are opportunities for Agrippa to invent long prose excursions (the longest excursions devoted to the most scandalous subjects, e.g., astrology and prostitution) in order to survey enthusiastically the moral ambiguities attendant to the societal categories of knowledge, power, and behavior; ambiguities he at once vilifies and celebrates. Agrippa's ostensible castigation of sexual pandering (*lenonia*, translated in 1569 as bawdry) presents a range of licentious associations that includes all practitioners of all the arts and sciences—especially grammarians, poets, and orators—as bawds:

> For all sciences do as it were serve bawdry. For first of all Grammar, the discipline or science to write and speak feigned salutations of love, prayers, lamentations, and flattering words. . . . Next to this Poetry. . . . Wherefore the Poets have always been the chiefest bawds. . . . After these the Orators . . . the artificers of deceitful flatteries and persuasions, and she is the happiest bawdress, to whom the Goddess persuasion is favorable. (Cap. 64, 211; *Opera* 2, 162–63)

Next come the bawdries of history, logic, arithmetic, music, architecture (which teaches how to make a rope ladder to climb into a lady's window), painting, astrology, palmistry, religion, and on and on. In sum, all written knowledge is bawdry, and as a voluble writer demonstrating his critical knowledge of such, Agrippa insinuates himself into the prostitution of mind and spirit that is at once their exuberant demonstration. His own characterization of the *Vanity* as an *oration* (the final chapter is titled *Operis Peroratio*) further suggests his ambiguous sense of his own work as a tissue of contradictions, a presentation of idiosyncratic associations within a general castigation of this sophistic tendency; a speech against speech; volubility in the service of silence; play in the service of absolute truth; fascination with vice in the service of virtue.

Such contradictions inform the magician's truth, a truth located in the motion of the imagination, which at once yearns for power over the elements of meaning that populate a divinely ordered universe, proposes that knowledge making is fraudulent, and devotes obsessive and undisciplined attention to the life of the mind. Agrippa is one of the last of such truthtellers; pressing a mode of topical exploration past the borders of conventional reason and conventional society in the *Vanity*, he takes rhetorical invention to extremes, illustrating through generative "wondermongering" the activity of the unfettered phantasy. In Agrippa then, we see the possible results of the thorough interpenetration of magic and rhetoric.

The play of the intellect and the spirit that Agrippa represents—the phantasy that is sanctioned but suspect in a magical world—is repressed fully during the course of the Reformation and the Enlightenment, in attacks on both classical rhetoric and phantasy that informed Ramism, and in the fear of both mystical enthusiasm and figurative language instituted by the Royal Society of London. The magic and rhetoric that disappeared were protean ways of knowing, at once visionary, practical, and politically charged. They elaborated the instability of intellectual and social realities, and it is not surprising that the normative impulses governing institutionalization in the seventeenth and eighteenth centuries would regard such progressive forces as subversive. Dismissed by the educated gentry, magic survives as an epistemological mode in secret societies such as the Rosicrucians and Freemasons (Johannisson). Magic rhetoric reappears as a speculative instrument of Romanticism, in efforts to reinvent a phantastic composing imagination, and to defend it against society.

CHAPTER 3

Parcels and Palimpsests

C. S. Lewis calls rhetoric and magic together "the greatest barrier between us and our ancestors." The Renaissance doctrine of *copia*[1] that would strike us today as "fantastic artificiality" coincided with an epistemology in which the terrestrial and the celestial, the figurative and the concrete, were elaborated and co-mingled to the point of indistinction:

> High abstractions and rarified artifices jostled the earthiest particulars. They [in the Renaissance] would have found it very hard to understand the modern educated man who, though "interested in astronomy," knows neither who the Pleiades were nor where to look for them in the sky. They talked more readily than we about large universals such as death, change, fortune, friendship, or salvation; but also about pigs, loaves, boots, and boats. The mind darted more easily to and fro between that mental heaven and earth: the cloud of middle generalizations, hanging between the two, was then much smaller. (Lewis 62)

In this realm, "Bacon and the magicians have the closest possible affinity. Both seek knowledge for the sake of power . . . both move in a grandiose dream of days when Man shall have been raised to the performance of 'all things possible'" (14).

Bacon stands here for the emergent science of the seventeenth century. While it is true that magic and science have common ambitions, they do—as Lewis points out—inhabit different lexicons. The magical imagination traffics in an enspirited universe, in which every utterance contains cosmological influences, intelligences, and virtues. The magus who would both explicate and control this universe realizes that a particular utterance does not guarantee a particular effect; the dynamic complexity of celestial and terrestrial intelligences that attend any word render it a calculus of possibilities. Because every utterance is at once invocative, value-laden, interactive, and indeterminate, language is an exploratory act, a range of appeals to the mysterious, a tissue of hunches with which we trace the geography of the macrocosm that constitutes our own "giant self." And every utterance is always dangerous, liable to invoke evil forces with the power to affect human bodies and souls.

When words lose their souls, and spirits are no longer alive in the material world, a language of facts becomes realizable, and magic rhetoric becomes alien. In the mechanical universe that houses a determinate language, we no longer require the resources of ambiguity: there are no antinomies and analogs and demons to travel among in discourse. Plain rhetoric, as the agency for communicating clear empirical evidence and the indicator of conventional literacy, becomes particularly congenial to the establishment of *national* standards of expression that reject the value of *copia*. By the later seventeenth century, Bishop Aylmer's 1559 declaration that "God is English" (Jones 209) has become an epistemological tenet of the Royal Society:

> So that even the position of our climate, the air, the influence of the heaven, the composition of the English blood; as well as the embraces of the Ocean, seem to joyn with the labours of the *Royal Society*, to render our Country, a Land of *Experimental knowledge*. And it is a good sign, that Nature will reveal more of its secrets to the English than to others; because it has already furnish'd them with a Genius so well proportion'd, for the receiving, and retaining its mysteries. (Sprat 115)

In England, the magician's search for a universal and divine language that infused and animated all existence is displaced by a style fit for the land of experimental knowledge.

FROM MAGIC TO SCIENCE

The epistemological shift from magic to science may have occurred for a number of reasons. Keith Thomas connects the decline of magic with the growth of certain kinds of security; improvements in communications and standards of living, indicated by the emergence of services and technologies such as insurance and fire-fighting, made the seventeenth century environment seem less threatening and mysterious. But Thomas concludes that "the change that occurred in the seventeenth century was . . . not so much technological as mental" (661), an assessment that Morris Berman has continued by arguing that economic and technological advancements made the seventeenth century mind receptive to a mechanical philosophy, inclined to "think in mechanical terms" (58–59). For Berman, the movement from an age of magic to an age of science is a movement from "to be" to "to do" (29), or likewise, a movement from the question "why?" to the question "how?" Fascination with the ways in which sympathetic cosmological forces participate in the expansion of the individual, a central project of the Renaissance, gives way in the seventeenth century to the reduction of the individual in the service of institutional collectives.

This shift follows from the very openness of the magical world, which, as Foucault suggests, prepares for the appearance of a "grid" that contains its wandering (50–62). As John Mebane explains, Renaissance magic is the acting out of revolutionary ideals in its emphasis on individual power, and can lead to the extreme effrontery of an Agrippa, or worse, a Thomas Harriot, who charges that "heaven and hell were merely fictions designed to enforce obedience to the state" (Mebane 79). Agrippa's fierce condemnation of and excursion through the categories of knowledge in the *Vanity* is the magician's attempt to know God by enlarging himself beyond language and all of its institutions. When the human potential for exploding conventional categories is carried far enough, via an excursive magical imagination, it poses a dangerous challenge to the preeminence of domesticating political and religious doctrine. The rise of science and the reform of language are reactions to this challenge.[2]

More precisely, science is a reactionary *outgrowth* of magic. Francis Bacon's criticisms of magic contain his acknowledgments of its power (Briggs, Mebane, Rossi, Walker). In *The Advancement of Learning*, he commends the "ends or pretences" of astrology, natural magic, and alchemy as "noble," but warns that because these practices "have had better intelligence and confederacy with the imagination of man than with his reason," their "derivations and prosecutions . . . both in the theories and in the practices, are full of error and vanity" (1.3.11; 29). The mistrust of magical practices represents Bacon's fear of an imagination unchecked by reason, as well as the advocacy of a regulative and rigorous scientific method:

> But for mine own judgment, if it be admitted that imagination hath power, and that [magical] Ceremonies fortify imagination,

> and that they be used sincerely and intentionally for that purpose; yet I should hold them unlawful, as opposing to that first edict which God gave unto man, *In sudore vultus comedes panem tuum* [In the sweat of thy brow shalt thou eat thy bread]. For they propound those noble effects, which God hath set forth unto man to be bought at the price of labour, to be attained by a few easy and slothful observances. (*Advancement* 2.11.3; 120)

While the Renaissance magus confronts group authority with individual power, the scientist acknowledges the limitations of the individual by disallowing the eccentric pursuit of truth. The autonomous and mistaken thinker is identified with magical beliefs:

> For the mind of man is far from the nature of a clear and equal glass, wherein the beams of things should reflect according to their true incidence; nay, it is rather like an enchanted glass, full of superstition and imposture, if it be not delivered and reduced. (*Advancement* 2.14.9; 132)

As D. P. Walker concludes, "Bacon still believed in the traditional doctrine of the magical power of imagination fortified by credulity," but he concluded that magic is wrong "because it makes experiments unnecessary, and Bacon liked doing and planning experiments" (200–202).

The scientific age that Bacon introduces is not, of course, founded simply on a "liking" for experiments. Scientific experiments, practiced with some uniformity by a growing community of antimagicals in the seventeenth century, express both the scientist's wish to implement social improvements, and his assumption that such improvements require a cooperative effort rather than the singular vision of an inspired individual who might disrupt the canons of knowledge. The goal of knowing and controlling nature—common to the magus and the scientist—thus becomes a normative activity; the magus-turned-scientist is a disciplined observer who requires the corroboration of colleagues, and seeks alliances with political and religious collective interests.

The condemnation of the magical imagination as an antisocial, anti-intellectual force motivates the establishment of the Royal Society. Abraham Cowley, in the poem that prefaces Sprat's *History of the Royal Society*, identifies Bacon with the new and plain magic of reason, which drives out those "Pageants of the Brain" that have created false knowledge:

With the plain Magique of tru Reasons Light,
He chac'd out of our sight,
Nor suffer'd Living Men to be misled
By the vain shadows of the Dead. (stanza 3)[3]

The ambitions of the prescientific magus—who would expand rather than contract the imagination—are condemned as heretical pride; as Cowley declares, "For 'tis God only who can find/ All Nature in his mind." A reformed composing imagination stands beneath the refocussed light of faith, which no longer illuminates phantasms reproduced from the mind of God. Science shines its light on the productions that a silent God has left behind, and the explicit repudiation of phantasy and phantasms becomes a doctrine of the Royal Society:

> First then, the Phantasms, and Fairies, and venerable Images of Antiquity, did long haunt the World: Against these we have had our Champions; and without all question, they had the better of the cause: and now we have good ground to trust, that these Illusions being well over, the last finishing of this great Work, is nigh at hand, and is reserv'd for this undertaking. (Sprat 30)

The victory over magic, historically determined in Sprat's view here, activates the "compass of [the Royal Society's] design":

> I will here, in the first place, contract into few Words, the whole *summe* of their *Resolutions*; which I shall often have occasion, to touch upon in *parcels*. Their purpose is, in short, to make faithful *Records*, of all the Works of *Nature*, or *Art*, which can come within their reach: that so the present Age, and posterity, may be able to put a mark on the Errors, which have been strengthned by long prescription: to restore the Truths, that have lain neglected: to push on those, which are already known, to more various uses: and to make the way more passable, to what remains unreveal'd. This is the compass of their Design. And to accomplish this, they have indeaver'd, to separate the knowledge of *Nature*, from the colours of *Rhetorick*, the devices of *Fancy*, or the delightful deceit of *Fables*. They have labor'd to inlarge it, from being confin'd to the custody of a few; or from servitude to private interests. They have striven to preserve it from being over-pres'd by a confus'd heap of vain, and useless particulars; or from being straitned and bounded too much up by General Doctrines. They have try'd, to put it into a condition of perpetual increasing; by settling an inviolable correspondence between the hand, and the brain. They have

> studi'd, to make it, not onely an Enterprise of one reason, or of some lucky opportunity; but a business of time; a steddy, a lasting, a popular, an uninterrupted word. They have attempted, to free it from the Artifice, and Humors, and Passions of Sects; to render it an Instrument, whereby Mankind may obtain a Dominion over *Things*, and not onely over one anothers *Judgements*. And lastly, they have begun to establish these Reformations in Philosophy, not so much, by any solemnity of Laws, or ostentation of Ceremonies; as by solid Practice, and examples: not, by a glorious pomp of words; but by the silent, effectual, and unanswerable Arguments of real Productions. (61–62).

This is a remarkable indication of the importance of perspicuous and ostensibly value-neutral *writing* to knowledge making. Sprat begins by indicating that knowledge is reducible to "few words" and "parcels," and that the best writing is the production of descriptive "records" that are to be corrected for errors and brought into line with real Nature. Rhetoric, fancy, and fables stand together in opposition to Nature and its knowledge. Given that these three "enemies" are all located in the imagination, and the knowledge of nature is here the same as knowledge in general, Sprat is maintaining the strict counterposition of the magical composing imagination to knowledge. The writing of natural knowledge is a public enterprise, not to be entrusted to the singular fancy *or* reason of an individual, or to private interests; at the same time, each individual must discipline his own expression, "settling an inviolable correspondence between brain and hand," between thinking and writing. Cowley expresses these sentiments in his prefatory poem, when he follows praise of the "new magic" of Baconian reason with mistrust in the "ideas and the images" of the phantastic imagination:

> Who to the life an exact Piece would make,
> Must not from others work a Copy take;
> No, not from *Rubens* or *Vandike*;
> Much less content himself to make it like
> Th'Ideas and the Images which ly
> In his own Fancy, or his Memory.
> No, he before his sight must place
> The Natural and Living Face;
> The real Object must command
> Each Judgment of his Eye, and Motion of his Hand.
> (Stanza 4)[4]

The Society would establish knowledge in language resistant to disruption, "a steddy, a lasting, a popular, an uninterrupted word." Reliable writing maintains the separation of observer and observed, and the "dominion" of the observer, through its reliance on empirical verities, "solid practice and examples," whose finality as the "unanswerable arguments" of Nature makes all writing not directly referenced to observable phenomena into empty ornamentation, "the glorious pomp of words."

By the end of the seventeenth century, the spiritual universe is a figurative rather than a literal entity: as Keith Thomas notes, the saying that once denoted demonic possession—"to have a devil"—becomes by the later 1700s merely "a kind of phrase or form of speech" (572). While such changes influenced the decline of witch persecution, they also constricted the universe; its very geography ceased to include, for instance, Hell. Magical language loses power because the forces it would invoke and the regions it would traverse have lost reality: "Accusations of diabolical witchcraft were thus rejected not because they had been closely scrutinised and found defective in some particular respect, but because they implied a [nonmechanical] conception of nature which now appeared inherently absurd" (Thomas 577). Nature does not invite a participatory consciousness, because Nature itself does not contain respondent intelligences. Silent material existence "speaks for itself" as an unambiguous presence, whose revelation is constituted by the recording of facts. God has withdrawn from that dialogue within the magical imagination that the Renaissance sought to elaborate, and the generation of resemblances within an enspirited sympathetic universe has become obsolete. With conjuration no longer "a meaningful ambition" (Thomas 643), understanding means recording God's silent design, by developing *discriminations*, "parcels," clear divisions between form and content, sign and signified, observer and observed (Foucault 42–43).[5]

NATURAL LANGUAGE NATIONALIZED

As students of the Cabala, Renaissance magi search for an "alphabet of nature," an originary language with creative power. This pursuit includes Marsilio Ficino, Giovanni Pico, Ludovico Lazarelli, Johannes Reuchlin, Cornelius Agrippa, William Postel, Paracelsus, and Jacob Boehme in the fifteenth and sixteenth centuries, and fascinates seventeenth century adherents of the Royal Society such as John Amos Comenius and John Wilkins (Coudert). In 1509, Agrippa had contrasted the Hebrew names of Eve and Adam, the former traditionally associated with life ("Eve" means "life-giver"), the latter with earth ("Adam" means "formed from the earth") and concluded from this the intrinsic preeminence of women to men:

> Since *names* are the signs of *things* . . . we may observe, that *woman* was made at first so much more excellent than man, by how much she had given to her a name more worthy than his: the word *Adam*, signifying but *Earth*, whereas *Eve*, is interpreted *Life*. Therefore, woman is no less to be preferred before man, than life itself before sordid and contemptible earth. Nor let any weak heads fancy this argument lame or invalid, because from names it passes judgment on things, since it must be acknowledged, that the *All-wise Contriver* both of names and things, well knew the things before he imposed names on them; and therefore (it being impossible he should be deceived) did undoubtedly bestow on them such fit and apposite names, as might best express their *intrinsic* natures and dignity.

Agrippa argues further that a Cabalistic analysis of "Eve" establishes its close relationship with the "ineffable" name of God:

> However, if we shall not be allowed the privilege of contriving such advantageous etymologies for the honor of the female sex, yet let us at least affirm from the mysterious learning of the *Cabalists*, that the woman's name in the original language, has a much nearer affinity with the ineffable tetragrammaton, or sacred name of the Divine Essence, than the man's, which bears no resemblance thereto either in characters, figure, or number. (*Female Pre-Eminence* 4–6; *Opera* 2, 505–6).

The belief in an originary language that could express and invoke the nature of things met decisive skepticism from early members of the Royal Society.[6] Robert Boyle, one of the founders of the Society, ridicules the powers of naming attributed to Adam, and denies that Hebrew is more natural than any other language:

> I will not urge the received opinion of divines that before the fall . . . Adam's knowledge was such, that he was able at first sight of them, to give each of the beasts a name expressive of its nature; because that, in spight of some skill . . . in the holy tongue, I could never find, that the Hebrew names of animals,

> mentioned in the beginning of Genesis, argued a (much) clearer insight into their natures, than did the names of the same or some other animals in Greek, or other languages; wherefore, as I said, I will not urge Adam's knowledge in paradise for that of the saints in heaven, though the notice he took of Eve at his first seeing her, (if it were not conveyed to him by secret revelation) may be far more probably urged, than his naming of the beasts. (100)

Though nostalgia for a natural language persisted, statements of its impossibility—like Boyle's—began to define the prevailing view. The appreciation for a *stable* language, along with resignation to the impossibility of a *natural* language, informs John Wilkins's influential 1668 *Essay Towards a Real Character and a Philosophical Language*:

> It were exceedingly desirable that the Names of things might consist of such sounds, as should bear in them some Analogy of their natures; and the Figure or Character of These Names should bear some proper resemblance to those sounds, that men might easily guess at the sense of meaning of any name or word, upon the first hearing or sight of it. But how this can be done in all the particular species of things, I understand not; and therefore shall take it for granted, that this character must be by Institution. (104)

The exhaustion of attempts to discover a natural language corresponds to the disappearance of the magical universe necessary to its operation; at the same time, *national* language becomes a replacement for natural language. In England, "plain English" becomes associated with the "real character" of its citizens. Wilkins, who was particularly instrumental in the reform of prose style by the Royal Society (Christensen), concludes that an institutionalized language is our closest possible approach to a natural one, and feeds the Society's desire to make English the *universal* language of knowledge. Once it becomes dominant, the English national language can function as the "natural" language of the world. Sprat expresses such a goal when he invites scholars from all "civil Nations" into the Society, where their knowledge is "naturalized" into a "Philosophy of Mankind" for the glory of England:

> As for what belongs to the *Members* themselves, that are to constitute the *Society*: It is to be noted that they have freely admit-

> ted Men of different Religions, Countries, and Professions of Life. This they were obliged to do, or else they would come far short of the largeness of their own Declarations. For they openly profess, not to lay the Foundation of an *English, Scotch, Irish, Popish,* or *Protestant* Philosophy, but a Philosophy of *Mankind*. . . . By their *naturalizing* Men of all Countries, they have laid the beginnings of many great advantages for the future. For by this means, they will be able, to settle a *constant Intelligence*, throughout all civil Nations; and make the *Royal Society* the general *Banck*, and Free-port of the world. (65)[7]

Sprat is inviting the world to speak and write English, the new originary language. As an international center, the Society will rouse "all our neighbors to fix their eies upon *England*." The Society has adapted the powers of a universal alphabet of nature to national interests, and has placed England in the center of a newly literate world, as the central bank of knowledge. Writing with what Cope and Jones have called "this almost mystic sense of a national unity of spirit" (xix), Sprat associates the "Universal Temper" of his countrymen, who "love to deliver their minds with a sound simplicity," with the establishment of the "Land of *Experimental Knowledge*" (114).

Fixing the language of knowledge suggests benefits in addition to international dominance, such as greater social cohesion and the more efficient development of social technologies. Further, uniform literacy requires a new kind of individual, one with neither rhetorical nor magical pretensions, that is, one whose state of mind bespeaks the same lexicon and follows the same patterns of association as the mind of State. Associational thinking, which had been central to the magical composing imagination since antiquity, is not banished from the land of experimental knowledge. However, the ancient recognition that the power of any associative link is a situational variable, along with the ability to essay the range of associations that might engage and transform an addressed body, becomes irrelevant.

What the modern individual gives up, then, is the power of persuasion, which requires in its practice both associative dexterity and belief in the possibility of changing present reality. Sharon Crowley explains that as the eighteenth century dawns in England it is presupposed that certain mental associations are right and others are wrong, or put another way, that if one makes the right mental connections, persuasion is not necessary: appeals to reason are appeals to a distinct and distinguished mental faculty that recognizes a proper association when it sees one: "The uniformity of human nature, in essence, obviated the need for persuasive appeals" (Crowley 31). The composing individual is a copy of other individuals with the same reasoning equipment who can be counted on the reach similar conclusions, all united in their self-contained objectivity, and in their alienation from their objects of study.[8]

John Locke's 1690 *Essay Concerning Human Understanding* ratifies intellectual uniformity, while it continues the Royal Society's effort to fashion an English epistemological frame for the rejection of magic and the reduction of rhetoric.[9] "Whatever is, is," the demonstrative proposition repeated throughout the *Essay*, is Locke's primary antimagical statement. With it, he denies a universe of vitalities; the Lockean universe is *formed* rather than *transformational*. A phantasmic universe is replaced by a mechanical one, or in Lockean terms, corpuscular. Matter has powers (like magnetism), but they are not intelligent, and they do not vary according to cosmological changes: in other words, material is not rhetorical, not subject to variable contingencies—Whatever is, is.[10] Associative thought works to combine simple ideas into complex ideas, but becomes dangerously "fantastical" when it imagines matter that is not empirically verifiable:

> On the contrary, those are *fantastical* [ideas] which are made up of such Collections of simple *Ideas* as were really never united, never were found together in any Substance: v.g. a rational Creature, consisting of a Horse's Head, joined to a body of humane shape, or such as the *Centaurs* are described; or, a Body, yellow, very malleable, fusible, and fixed, but lighter than common Water: Or, an uniform, unorganized Body, consisting as to Sense, all of similar Parts, with Perception and voluntary Motion joined to it (2.30.5; 374).[11]

Locke insists that correct human language depends upon the self-contained, "determined" ideas of the noncontradictory mind, a mind without phantasms, which expresses itself unambiguously in words whose relationship to the "object of the mind" is arbitrary, conventional, and precise:

> Upon this Ground I have thought *determined* Ideas a way of speaking less liable to mistake . . . and where Men have got such *determined* Ideas of all, that they reason, enquire, or argue

> about, they will find a great part of their Doubts and Disputes at an end. The greatest part of the Questions and Controversies that perplex Mankind depending on the doubtful and uncertain use of Words, or (which is the same) *indetermined Ideas*, which they are made to stand for. I have made choice of these terms to signifie, 1. Some immediate object of the Mind, which it perceives and has before it distinct from the sound it uses as a sign of it. 2. That this Idea thus *determined*, i.e. which the Mind has in it self, and knows, and sees there be *determined* without any change to that name, and that name *determined* to that precise Idea. If men had such *determined* Ideas in their enquiries and discourses, they would both discern how far their enquiries and discourses went, and avoid the greatest part of the Disputes and Wranglings they have with others. (*Essay*, "The Epistle to the Reader," 13–14)

The intellect that connects "loose and independent" ideas is especially dangerous, so liable to "set us awry" that "there is not any one thing that deserves more to be looked after." It is especially important to see to the education of children in this respect, "to prevent the undue Connexion of *Ideas* in the Minds of young People." A tendency to false associative thinking begins with a childish belief in *magic*: "*Ideas* of *Goblines* and *Sprights*," referring as they do to an unreal and frightening world, must not be the stuff of bedtime stories, lest a spirit world becomes part of the child's imagination "so long as he lives" (2.33.8–10; 397–98). Such magical thinking is born of false associations, in this case, the association of darkness with demons; and false associations are, at bottom, symptoms of *madness*:

> I shall be pardoned for calling it by so harsh a name as *Madness*, when it is considered, that opposition to Reason deserves that name and is really madness. . . . And if this be a Weakness to which all Men are so liable, if this be a Taint which so universally infects Mankind, the greater care should be taken to lay it open under its due Name, thereby to excite the greater care in its Prevention and Cure. (2.33.4; 395)

Locke's madman denies the silent stability and integrity of mechanism. He activates intelligences in a universe that is really mute, and creates associations that are unconventional and—because they range apart from those "unanswerable arguments" of the objectified world—unnatural. With this behavior, the madman represents all humankind's potential for deviant intellection, and as such is not only an advertisement for the prevention of this disease, as Locke would have it; he is also an important sign of the culture that has been left behind, as Foucault explains:

> The madman, understood not as one who is sick but as an established and maintained deviant, [performs] an indispensable cultural function. . . . [H]e sees nothing but resemblances and signs of resemblance everywhere; for him all signs resemble one another, and all resemblances have the value of signs. At the other end of the cultural area, but brought close by symmetry, the poet is he who, beneath the named, constantly expected differences, rediscovers the buried kinships between things, their scattered resemblances. (49)

Foucault's mad poet here is the Renaissance magus, the premodern rhetor, and—beginning in the late eighteenth century—the Romantic writer.

MAGIC AND ROMANTICISM

A rhetoric with imaginative scope and a cosmology of phantasms reemerges in the poetry and poetics of Romanticism, in the language of magic.[12] Romantic fascination with the magical imagination is explicit in Blake's visionary poetry, Wordsworth's and Coleridge's conjunction of the natural and the supernatural in the *Lyrical Ballads*, Percy Shelley's faith in the power of language and mind over cultural and political "matter" in *Prometheus Unbound, The Witch of Atlas,* and *A Defense of Poetry*, and Mary Shelley's portrayal of a magical world ravaged by a monster of science in *Frankenstein*. English Romantics turn to magic in order to license the powers of the composing imagination, to find a discourse for intellectual and political revolution, and to define writing as a liberatory force that constructs realities. Their major critical theses—Wordsworth's Preface to *Lyrical Ballads*, Coleridge's *Biographia Literaria*, Shelley's *Defense of Poetry*—claim that the time has come to react against scientific reductionism with visionary scope; like alchemists forging new realities, they call up a sympathetic universe, "coercing all things into sympathy" (Wordsworth, *Prelude* 2.390; 65). With the supernatural as his vehicle, Coleridge declares in the *Biographia* that "I will cause the world of intelligences with the whole system of their representations to rise up before you" (13; 297). Shelley writes in the *Defense* that the "alchemy" of poetic imagination produces new lexicons of thought, new associations that eventually resonate in the political reorganization of society: "[Poetry] marks the before unapprehended relations of things and perpetuates their apprehension, until the words which represent them, become, through time, signs for portions or classes of thoughts" that effect "revolutions in opinion" (111–15).

Anya Taylor's *Magic and English Romanticism*, the only full-length study of this relationship, surveys the attention to magic in the writing of Coleridge, Wordsworth, Shelley, Byron, and Keats, and concludes that the magical imagination is a dangerous thing:

> From an examination of several matters of significance in the period between 1740 and 1840, five conclusions emerge. First, the living powers of language, in all their complexity of source and effect, point to the inscrutability of the mind, as the ancients had traditionally imagined in their imagery of incantations. Second, a discernible rediscovery of these complexities—some irrational in spite of the prevailing stress on scientific verification and some empirically observable in the effects of poetic devices—occurs in the second half of the eighteenth century. Third, the conjunction of these rediscoveries about language and poetic powers with the wider need to prove that human beings are not mere organisms but possess spirit and miraculous will is explored within a theological context in the prose of Coleridge—and as a theurgical possibility in his poetry. Fourth, the dangers of such assertions of separateness to the stability of the moral being are evident in the substitution of words for things and in an obliviousness to steadying external realities, most clearly exemplified in Coleridge's [debilitated physical and spiritual] condition as it is perceived by Wordsworth. Fifth, the lure of spiritual freedom inherent in the tradition that language is magical is imagined [by Shelley] to have practical possibilities in political oratory, but its perhaps more sinister result is the obliteration of the self when the vital will paradoxically becomes a morbid airlessness, which is finally shunned by both Keats and Byron. (251)

Taylor stresses that for Coleridge in particular, the act of writing is the act of animating the universe, a materialization of spirit in matter. One of Wordsworth's quarrels with Coleridge centers on the latter's fascination with the supernatural. In the Preface, the announced division of the *Lyrical Ballads* into those in which the natural is supernaturalized (e.g., "The Rhyme of the Ancient Mariner") and those of the sensible world, suggests this quarrel:

> I have wished to keep the Reader in the company of flesh and blood, persuaded that by so doing I shall interest him. Others [Coleridge] who pursue a different track will interest him likewise; I do not interfere with their claim, but wish to prefer a claim of my own. (390)

Wordsworth associates Coleridge's physical decay with his withdrawal from the sensible world into a miraculous and improbable one. With her emphasis on this charge, Taylor sets aside Wordsworth's own illustrations of an interanimating imagination at work in a sympathetic universe, which we see, for instance, throughout the *Prelude*.[13] Overall, she worries that the magical imagination is an agent of escapism. Byron, Keats, and Shelley "enter into an interior world made up of disembodied words, charms, songs, and wishes" (248) only to realize—according to Taylor—that the realities of life and death are inexorable.

My purpose here is not to counter Taylor's reading of these poets; her singular contribution to our recognition of the presence of magic in Romantic writing is, as such, important, and must be acknowledged. I will note that we have seen before the dangers of magical imagination that she targets: it discounts scientific verification, confuses words for things, upsets moral stability, and multiplies the identities of the self to the point of self-obliteration. From an Enlightenment perspective, these are acts of madness; for Shelley, a vital representative of Romantic magic energy, they are attendant to revolutionary idealism. In the *Defense*, Shelley imagines that magical language—embodied in the poet as legislator—can become a revolutionary rhetoric, realized in an oratory that we have seen exhorted by Ficino and Pico. The identity of the poet is collapsed into that of the rhetor and the magus: "Poets . . . were called, in the earlier epochs of the world, legislators, or prophets: a poet essentially comprises and unites both these characters" (112). Their prophecy comes from participation in the mindedness of the universe: "A poet participates in the eternal, the infinite, and the one; as far as relates to his conceptions, time and place and number [categories of scientific reason] are not." In order to do social good, one must be able to identify oneself with the "other" that is the object of moral good; to this end, "Poetry enlarges the circumference of the imagination" (118), and "redeems from decay the visitations of the divinity in Man" (137):

> It transmutes all that it touches, and every form moving within the radiance of its presence is changed by wondrous sympathy to an incarnation of the spirit which it breathes; its secret alchemy turns to potable gold the poisonous waters which flow from death through life; it strips the veil of familiarity from the world, and lays bare the naked and sleeping beauty, which is the spirit of its forms. (137)

The Romantic conjunction of poet, rhetor, and magus, which Shelley announces in the *Defense* and exemplifies through characters such as the Witch of Atlas and Prometheus, gets its most thoroughgoing prose explication in the essays of Thomas De Quincey. It is De Quincey who demonstrates most elaborately the tension between transcendental and dialogical impulses that defines the magical imagination. That tension is not apparent in the most absolute Romantic statements of aspiration; for instance, Shelley's emphasis on "the eternal, the infinite, and the one," points in the direction of pure transcendence. At the same time, his conjunction of poet, rhetor, and magus portrays writing in terms of multiple identities, and his attempts to realize a poetic program in dramatic dialogues such as *Prometheus Unbound* and *The Triumph of Life* suggests that a vast plurality of names and voices indicates the circumference of the imagination. But still, the tradition of the Romantic as a visionary idealist of the strong, singular voice, with an uppercase Imagination, can be located in pronouncements such as Shelley's in the *Defense*, and in Coleridge's godlike representation of himself in the *Biographia*.[14]

Continuing to regard the magical imagination as an open dialogue among phantasms, subtended by nostalgia for pure creative power, I will associate Thomas De Quincey with the project of a generative magic that is transcendental in its resistance to both mortality and convention, and dialogical in its demonstration of the tendencies inherent in the human mind.[15] De Quincey joins the Romantic magi who appeal to the "witchery" of language to reorder the imagination and reform the public mind. As a meditative visionary, he issues a political indictment of the mechanistic, reductive discourses that he would replace with intellectual play within a universe of free signifiers, and the "flux and reflux, swell and cadence" of an incantatory style. Magic and rhetoric come together in De Quincey's *Suspiria De Profundis* (Sighs from the Depths), which he calls a mode of "impassioned prose ranging under no precedents that I am aware of," and which exhibits the Romantic fascination with intercourse between the spiritual and physical, dream and reality, with the interplay of magic and rhetoric.

DE QUINCEY'S PALIMPSEST

As David Masson points out in his 1890 Introduction to Volume 13 of De Quincey's *Collected Writings*, titled "Tales and Prose Phantasies," De Quincey aligns both "rhetorical prose" and "prose phantasy" against "the ordinary jog-trot prose which suffices for business-documents, books of information, etc" (5). Masson correctly notes that for De Quincey, rhetoric is "the art of conscious playing with a subject intellectually and inventively," and he allies prose phantasy with rhetoric because it is also a product of "solitary self-musing" or "long nocturnal reverie" (*Collected* 13; 5–7).[16] As De Quincey says in 1828, to practice rhetoric is "to hang upon one's own thoughts as an object of conscious interest, to play with them, to watch and pursue them through a maze of inversions, evolutions, and harlequin changes" (*Selected Essays* 97). De Quincey's rhetoric is associated with a premodern age; like magic, rhetoric has been obliterated by science and "public business," activities that prefer a determined and perspicuous intellect to an excursive one: "Rhetoric prospered most at a time when science was unborn as a popular interest, and the commercial activities of aftertimes were yet sleeping in their rudiments" (*Selected Essays* 100).[17]

Blackwood's Edinburgh Magazine published De Quincey's self-proclaimed masterwork (*Collected* 13; 4), the *Suspiria De Profundis*, in four installments through the spring and summer of 1845. De Quincey wanted to produce what he called "the *ne plus ultra*, as regards the feeling and the power to express it, which I can ever hope to attain" (Lindop, *Opium Eater* 355). Grevel Lindop summarizes De Quincey's plan:

> This new work was to be a series of interrelated prose poems, exploring the worlds of dream and reverie, tracing the deliberate metamorphoses whereby experiences of the outer life became transformed into the matter of dream, interwoven by

association, emotion and premonition into complex motifs or "involutes" which embodied the hidden patterns of life and the soul. (*Opium Eater* 352–53)

This plan was never fully realized, probably because of De Quincey's frustration with *Blackwood's* for not allowing him as much space as he wanted. In the years following its initial publication, De Quincey carved up and redistributed the original *Suspiria* as he prepared collections of his works (Lindop, "Introduction" xxiii–xxiv). David Masson published one of the later, pillaged versions in his edition of the collected writings, for this reason:

> The original *Blackwood Suspiria*, when read now, annoy one as a kind of clotted confusion, in which duplicates of portions of the *Autobiographical Sketches* and the enlarged *Confessions* interrupt and disturb the succession of the pieces of phantasy that constitute the *Suspiria* properly and essentially; whereas in De Quincey's reduction of that heterogeneous original these pieces are rescued into impressive independence and stand on their own merits. (Masson in De Quincey, *Collected* 14; 333)

I am discussing here the original Blackwood's version of the *Suspiria*[18] for precisely the reason that makes it objectionable to Masson: because it represents the undisciplined writerly imagination that is De Quincey's. As Grevel Lindop explains, attempts such as Masson's to establish a version that reflects De Quincey's final intentions, are "probably misguided" ("Introduction" xxiii). No analysis of De Quincey's revisions yields a plan, or allows us to conclude that some more refined intentionality was at work during De Quincey's final years. So, I choose to read the fullest and most complex version, the version most immediate to De Quincey's frustration with the space constraints imposed by his publisher, and to the social and personal conditions that prompted the essay.

De Quincey begins his meditation on imagination, addiction, childhood, and death with appreciation for the art of phantastic reverie, which has disappeared amidst the "fierce condition of eternal hurry" in his own time:

> Among the powers in man which suffer by this too intense life of the social instincts, none suffers more than the power of dreaming. Let no man think this a trifle. The machinery for dreaming planted in the human brain was not planted for noth-

> ing. That faculty, in alliance with the mystery of darkness, is the one great tube through which man communicates with the shadowy. And the dreaming organ, in connexion with the heart, the eye, and the ear, compose the magnificent apparatus which forces the infinite into the chambers of a human brain, and throws dark reflections from eternities below all life upon the mirrors of the sleeping mind.[19]

The faculty of dreaming "suffers from the decay of solitude" that defines modern life. Solitude is a necessary condition of the dreaming imagination, which for De Quincey corresponds to the composing imagination. When he is "lying awake, unable to sleep," De Quincey's memory for long unread verses begins to "blossom anew":

> I become a distinguished compositor in the darkness, and, with my aerial composing stick [both a printer's tool and, in this context, a kind of magic wand], sometimes I 'set up' half a page of verses, that would be found tolerably correct if collated with the volume I never had in my hand but once. (116–17)

De Quincey attributes this capacity to a faculty higher than the retentive memory, which surveys topics through an associative magic, and exercises "an electric aptitude for seizing analogies, and by means of those aerial pontoons passing over like lightning from one topic to another" (117). This sort of phantastic topical invention, which I associated with Cicero and Quintilian above, requires for De Quincey a "constitutional determination to reverie," but such determination is forcibly distracted by "the continual development of vast physical agencies" (87), that is, nature-perverting, chaos-producing modern *machines* that represent, throughout De Quincey's work, "the stresses of external experience inimical to an introspective consciousness" (De Luca 89).

Society's "colossal pace of advance" promises our spiralling collapse into a merely physical and mechanical existence, as it blows up a "storm of life so perilously centripetal towards the vortex of the merely human." The introspective consciousness can resist this force, by producing centrifugal "counter-forces of corresponding magnitude, forces in the direction of religion or profound philosophy" (87). As an argument for the momentous import of dreaming, the *Suspiria* is a manifesto for superhumanity, an oration on the dignity of the human potential for reaching beyond its mundane propensities, employing the meditative and magical imagination as an act of cultural insolence that is realizable, for De Quincey, in writing.

De Quincey clears a space for imagination and writing with opium. The *Suspiria De Profundis* is his admission that the addiction is permanent (91), and that it helps him "to dream more splendidly than others." Finding himself in an age where mechanical progress has displaced visionary scope, De Quincey recognizes that there is no longer—as in the prescientific past—a societal appreciation for reverie as a common habit of mind. He praises opium (while mourning his addiction) as an antisocial technology for maintaining a composing imagination: of all that might "assist the faculty of dreaming," opium is "beyond all others" (88). While the drug can be counted among the centrifugal counterforces that De Quincey musters, his emphasis on its powers in his writing may be more a literary device than a clinical assessment (Lindop, *Opium Eater* 390–91; Hayter 101–31, 226–54; see also n. 20 to this chapter). The human power for creating a network of associations among the present and the past, among supernatural and natural spirits and powers, relies less directly on opium than on De Quincey's conception of the mind as a magical surface, as a palimpsest.

A palimpsest is a writing surface, usually wax or parchment, which can be reused, on which erased manuscripts are still visible beneath the newest writing. Before paper was introduced to the West in the late Middle Ages, palimpsests were commonly used for composing in writing (Gaur 46–47). De Quincey recounts the discovery by medieval chemists of a way "to discharge the writing from the [parchment] roll and thus to make it available for a new succession of thoughts" without completely erasing what had been previously written, so that "the more refined chemistry" of De Quincey's age can "restor[e] all below which they had effaced" (141). This is modern chemical magic that surpasses the thaumaturgical claims of a Paracelsus; "by our modern conjurations of science, secrets of ages remote from each other have been exorcised [summoned] from the accumulated shadows of centuries" (143). The restored palimpsest that De Quincey imagines reveals a history of the literary imagination:

> In the illustration imagined by myself, from the case of some individual palimpsest, the Grecian tragedy had seemed to be displaced, but was *not* displaced, by the monkish legend; and the

> monkish legend had seemed to be displaced, but was *not* displaced, by the knightly romance. In some potent convulsion of the system, all wheels back into its earliest elementary stage. (145–46)

A succession of texts is transformed, by the "witch" of chemistry (143) into a simultaneity of texts. This magical process is an analog to human intellection:

> What else than a natural and mighty palimpsest is the human brain? Such a palimpsest is my brain; such a palimpsest, O reader! is yours. Everlasting layers of ideas, images, feelings, have fallen upon your brain softly as light. Each succession has seemed to bury all that went before. And yet in reality not one has been extinguished. (144)[20]

Locating the individual within the "everlasting" suggests, as V. A. De Luca notes, that the dreamer/writer "houses the infinite in his own finite corporeality, and it raises the substance of his experience" so that "the history of the individual imagination is thus a microcosm of the history of imagination in general."[21] Writing is thus *participation* in a "giant composite form" (De Luca 74) constituted by natural and supernatural objects and powers, and infinitely larger than the individual himself. In reverie, which is for De Quincey the product of an isolated, drugged, defiant, and haunted sensibility, one composes the giant self.

The 1845 *Suspiria* is divided into seven sections, six of which comprise "Part 1": (1) In the "Introductory Notice" De Quincey advocates the antisocial powers of the meditative imagination, discloses that his addiction to opium—along with an attendant vivid imagination—is now permanent, and proposes to write in particular of the childhood experience of his sister Elizabeth's death, which colored all his future thought. (2) "The Affliction of Childhood," though primarily autobiographical, typifies the *Suspiria* as it ranges through "a gamut that is infinite, of temperaments and characters, ascending from the very dust below our feet to highest heaven" (126), resonating from the memory of Elizabeth's death. She died from hydrocephalus, what we would now call cerebro-spinal meningitis (Lindop, *Opium Eater* 9), a disease that De Quincey terms "premature expansion of the intellect," and links with his own mental propensities. (3) "The Palimpsest" serves as an apology for the excursive license of the preceding section, while it describes the magical imagination in the act of writing. (4) "Levana and Our Ladies of Sorrow" portrays the dark goddesses who attend the magus/writer from birth, speaking occult languages that he must learn to read. 5) "The Apparition of the Brocken" reveals that a spectre appearing before one who ascends the Brocken (a peak in the Hartz Mountains) is really the shadow of the human spectator. 6) "Savannah La Mar" takes its title from a Jamaican port destroyed in a 1780 hurricane. De Quincey tours its wreckage with the Dark Interpreter, who speaks to the writer of time everlasting. With all the preceding constituting "Part 1" of the *Suspiria*, "Part 2" (only about 1/5 of the total essay) is De Quincey's return to childhood memories as the foundations for his future life.

De Quincey understands that his own tendency to pile up "everlasting layers of ideas, images, feelings" in the *Suspiria* will meet resistance from readers who want a perspicuous presentation of facts. The "kind" reader who does not cynically dismiss the narration of experience *in extenso* "will perceive that it is not for the mere facts that the case is reported, but because these facts move through a wilderness of natural thoughts or feelings; some in the child who suffers; some in the man who reports; but all so far interesting as they related to solemn objects" (93). A characteristic Romantic autobiographer, De Quincey refuses the validity of neutral observation, conflating narrative objectivity with a complexity of insights into personal and human history (see, e.g., Cafarelli 126).

Thus, De Quincey stands on a precedent established by medieval magicians, who, as William Eamon points out, "made no distinction between *experimentum* (experiment) and *experientia* (experience)." This is a precedent followed by sixteenth-century magi such as Agrippa, for whom "knowledge is a kind of [experimental/experiential] *making*, and that making itself is a form of cognition that generates true knowledge. This attitude . . . is echoed in almost every sixteenth century treatise on natural magic" (Eamon 126, 134). Though not autobiographical, Agrippa's *Occult Philosophy* argues from evidence that is by modern scientific standards entirely anecdotal, comprising a history of reported experiences:

> But some virtues are in things according to some parts of it, viz., only in the tongue, or eyes, or some other members and parts; so in the eyes of a basilisk is a most violent power to kill men as

> soon as they see them. . . . So also there were some certain women in Scythia, and amongst the Illyrians and Triballians, who as often as they looked angrily upon any man, were said to slay him. Also we read of a certain people of Rhodes, called Telchines, who corrupted all things with their sight, wherefore Jupiter drowned them. Therefore witches, when they would after this manner work by witchcraft, use the eyes of such kind of animals in their waters for the eyes, for the like effects. In like manner do ants fly from the heart of a lapwing and not from the head, foot or eyes. So the gall of lizards, being bruised in water, is said to gather weasels together; not the tail or the head of it. The gall of goats, put into the earth in a brazen vessel, gathers frogs together; and a goat's liver is an enemy to butterflies and all maggots. Dogs shun them that have the heart of a dog about them; and foxes will not touch those poultry that have eaten the liver of a fox. So diverse things have diverse virtues dispersed variously through several parts, as they are from above infused into them according to the diversity of things to be received; as in a man's body the bones receive nothing but life, the eyes sight, and the ears hearing. (1.20, 86–87; *Opera* 39–40)

By piling up dozens of such "facts" in the service of each general assertion, interpersing the observations of ancient metaphysical and medical authorities with hearsay, Agrippa constructs the kind of persuasion that is possible when authoritative evidence is not inconsistent with a medley of reportage; and creates a rhetoric that is plainly associative, moving through analogs that comprise a world of proofs.

Such a movement of mind, while part of the tradition of magic, also constitutes *rhetorical* persuasion for De Quincey, who gives this advice in his essay on "Rhetoric": "Like boys who are throwing the sun's rays into the eyes of a mob by means of a mirror, you must shift your lights and vibrate your reflections at every possible angle, if you would agitate the popular mind excessively" (*Selected* 139). He understands that the rhetor's restless and exhaustive approaches from multiple angles may alienate the readers they agitate: "You feel symptoms of doubt and restiveness . . . unless we explain what it is that we are in quest of" ("Style," *Selected* 190), and forewarns readers of the *Suspiria*: "I tell my critic that the whole course of this narrative resembles, and was meant to resemble, a *caduceus* wreathed about with meandering ornaments" (*Suspiria* 93). Here associations with magic, rhetoric, and venture into dangerous territory all coincide. A staff wreathed by serpents, the caduceus is the wand of Hermes/Mercury, the god who invents both magic and writing. The "meandering ornaments" are at once figures of thought realized in meandering language—those phantasms of rhetoric that Sprat and the Royal Society want to abolish—and poisonous snakes. The writer/wizard/god resists modern society with venomous imaginative energies, through a dialogue with voices at once interior and cosmological.[22] He is an especially sensitive medium in a forceful universe of live signifiers:

> Said but once, said but softly, not marked at all, words revive before me in darkness and solitude; and they arrange themselves gradually into sentences, but through an effort sometimes of a distressing kind, to which I am in a manner forced to become a party. (117)

In a tale that closes "The Affliction of Childhood," De Quincey recalls a childhood terror that reinforces his entrapment within the discourse of his own imagination. Having ordered a history of navigation from a local bookseller, the child De Quincey is anxious and uncertain as to how many volumes he has actually promised to purchase. Putting the question to a clerk, and getting the jocular reply, "maybe a matter of 15,000, more or less," the child dreads that the bookseller's company will track him down and deliver an impossibly unaffordable cargo of volumes:

> There would be a ring at the front door. A waggoner in the front, with a bland voice, would ask for "a young gentleman who had given an order to *their* house." Looking out, I should perceive a procession of carts and waggons, all advancing in measured movements; each in turn would present its rear, deliver its cargo of volumes, by shooting them, like a load of coals, on the lawn, and wheel off to the rear, by way of clearing the road for its successors. (134)

This imagined episode sticks in De Quincey's imagination because of its connection with a tale of magic, "one of the Arabian nights which had particularly interested myself and my sister":

> It was that tale, where a young porter, having his ropes about his person, had stumbled into the special "preserve" of some old magician. He finds a beautiful lady imprisoned, to whom (and not without prospects of success) he recommends himself as a suitor, more in harmony with her own years than a withered magician. At this crisis the magician returns. The young man bolts, and for that day successfully; but unluckily he leaves

> his ropes behind. Next morning he hears the magician, too honest by half, enquiring at the front door, with much expression of condolence, for the unfortunate young man who had lost his ropes in his own zenana [harem]. (135)

The young man denies that the ropes are his: "If you please, Mr. Magician, I never had money enough to buy so beautiful a set of ropes." But to no avail: this young "intruder upon the privacy of magicians" becomes the magician's captive porter for life. De Quincey concludes by pulling together the tale of the books and the tale of the ropes: "For what did it matter whether a magician dunned one with old ropes for his engines of torture, or Stationers' Hall with 15,000 volumes (in the rear of which there might also be ropes?)" (135).

In these tales, De Quincey demonstrates the caduceus of his thought while he conjoins the forces of magic and the forces of writing. Booksellers become magicians; books become magic ropes; the porter and the beautiful lady are transfigurations of De Quincey and his sister, whose death has prompted this entire reminiscence. De Quincey is in the grip of writing, magic, drugs, dreams, and death, all operating as analogs in his traversing of literary and human history; even as he creates with the caduceus of his writing, he is already written: "It appeared, then, that I had been reading a legend concerning myself in the *Arabian Nights*. I had been contemplated in types a thousand years before on the banks of the Tigris" (135). He is alert to the palimpsest of human history within which he is both inscriber and inscribed, realizing himself as a participant in a universe of signifiers. But this is not a happy consciousness; rather, the giant self is attended by "horror and grief" (135). Like Medieval and Renaissance magi, De Quincey's conversance with a cosmology of discourses makes him the vulnerable medium of dark and demonic voices. The trembling voice of the young porter, which De Quincey "ventriloquizes" in performance for his sister, is an early and childish instance of the ability to commune with "dark phantoms," whom he describes in "Levana and Our Ladies of Sorrow."

Levana first appears to De Quincey in 1806 or 1807, when he is about twenty-two and studying at Oxford; she "appeared first in his daydreams, where fantasy was partly under conscious guidance, but soon, by a process that was to become very familiar to him, [Levana and her sisters] made their way into dreams that came to him in sleep" (Lindop, *Opium Eater* 138). Levana was known in De Quincey's day as the Roman goddess of education, and probably came to his attention in Jean Paul Richter's 1806 *Levana, or the Doctrine of Education.* Richter's educational theory affirms "an education of experiences, as opposed to an education of rules . . . which enables the child to see through the falsities of his immediate society and to view truth and purpose in the magic crystal of time" (Burwick 20). De Quincey's Levana follows Richter's; she is the dark goddess who governs the revelation of the sympathetic universe to each newborn child; a parent acts for Levana when he lifts a child to the stars and says, "Behold what is greater than yourselves." She is also "the tutelary power that controls the education of the nursery"; however, the education she inculcates does not rest on spelling books and grammars:

> By the education of Levana, therefore, is meant—not the poor machinery that moves by spelling-books and grammars, but that mighty system of central forces hidden in the deep bosom of human life, which by passion, by strife, by temptation, by the energies of resistance, works for ever upon children—resting not day or night, any more than the mighty wheel of day and night themselves, whose moments, like restless spokes, are glimmering for ever as they revolve. (*Suspiria* 147)

Levana is both the product and the tutor of an expansive imagination that is propelled by the energies of resistance against the centripetal forces of the "merely human." Education into the "mighty system of central forces" portends the endurance of sorrow, pain, and death, "the agencies of human grief."

As the professor of those agencies, Levana is attended by "the powers that shake man's heart" (148): Our Lady of Tears oversees the deaths of children; Our Lady of Sighs is the goddess of the outcast; Our Lady of Darkness, the most furious, is "the mother of lunacies, the suggestress of suicides." The Sorrows speak an occult language, which the writer translates:

> Mighty phantoms like these disdain the infirmities of language. They may utter voices through the organs of man when they dwell in human hearts . . . *They* wheeled in mazes; *I* spelled the steps. *They* telegraphed from afar; *I* read the signals. *They* conspired together; and on the mirrors of darkness *my* eye traced the plots. *Theirs* were the symbols,—*mine* are the words. (149)

De Quincey the "aerial compositor" enacts the translation of phantastic language into human language. His translating imagination here recapitulates the ancient primacy of phantastic language, describes the nature of literate intercourse with dark powers, and exemplifies the worst fears of Sprat and the Royal Society, the rule of phantasms. A visionary cosmology becomes De Quincey's grammar, and it is a grammar that bespeaks both the darkest passions of human life and the pain of its disenfranchised: children, the outcast, the mad, whose pain De Quincey shares and represents. There is nothing idyllic here about the generative magic De Quincey works; Our Lady of Darkness describes the forging of his imagination:

> So shall he be accomplished in the furnace—so shall he see the things that ought not to be seen—sights that are abominable, and secrets that are unutterable. So shall he read elder truths, sad truths, grand truths, fearful truths. So shall he rise again *before* he dies. And so shall our commission be accomplished which from God we had—to plague his heart until we had unfolded the capacities of his spirit. (153)

The intelligences that speak through this writer-as-magus are not demonic, but they are ominous. For De Quincey, to fully realize one's intellectual and spiritual capacities is to wheel about in the darkness and read the unutterable.

"The Apparition of the Brocken" brings us to a site of natural magic, as De Quincey explains in a note that I must quote at length:

> "*Spectre of the Brocken*" This very striking phenomenon has been continually described by writers, both German and English, for the last fifty years. Many readers, however, will not have met with these descriptions: and on *their* account I add a few words in explanation; referring them for the best scientific comment on the case to Sir David Brewster's "Natural Magic." The spectre takes the shape of a human figure, or, if the visitors are more than one, then the spectres multiply; they arrange themselves on the blue ground of the sky, or perhaps they are strongly relieved against a curtain of rock, at a distance of some miles, and always exhibiting gigantic proportions. At first, from the distance and the colossal size, every spectator supposes the appearance to be quite independent of himself. But very soon he is surprised to observe his own motions and gestures mimicked; and wakens to the conviction that the phantom is but a dilated

> reflection of himself. . . . One reason why he is seen so seldom must be ascribed to the concurrence of conditions under which only the phenomenon can be manifested: the sun must be near to the horizon, . . . the spectator must have his back to the sun; and the air must contain some vapour—but *partially* distributed. (133–34n)

One who ascends the Brocken and sees the spectre is really looking at his own shadow. This phantasm is both an other and a double, a representation of the self and the agent of the god *Phantasus*. As an inscription of the motions and gestures of the observer, the spectre is both magical and written, both a spirit and a sign. De Quincey posits magic as an interdependency of observer and observed, dreamer and dream, writer and text, appearance and reality, belief and volition:

> You are now satisfied that the apparition is but a reflex of yourself; and, in uttering your secret feelings to *him*, you make this phantom the dark symbolic mirror for reflecting to the daylight what else must be hidden for ever.

Like the Dark Interpreter who attends De Quincey for part of the *Suspiria*, like the Greek chorus that narrates dramatic tragedy, the function of the spectre is "not to tell you any thing absolutely new . . . but to recall to you your own lurking thoughts . . . in immediate connexion with groups vanishing too quickly for any effort of meditation on your own part, such commentaries, prophetic or looking back, pointing the moral or deciphering the mystery, justifying Providence, or mitigating the fierceness of anguish as would or might have occurred to your own meditative heart—had only time been allowed for its motions" (157). Phantasms are agents for bringing into synthesized relief the palimpsest of one's whole selfhood—they are the writers of the cosmology that escapes our normal, time-constrained powers of meditation. The magus, like Coleridge's woodman in "Constancy of an Ideal Object," "*makes* (not knowing) that which he pursues" (qtd. by De Quincey, 154n). A sympathetic Nature must cooperate: the right atmospheric conditions help to materialize the apparition. But essentially, the magus/writer inscribes his own "lurking thoughts."

With his palimpsestic conception of memory, his invocation of a dialogue of phantasms, and his interpenetration of magic and writing, De Quincey resurrects a version of the medieval composing imagination, which we have described as "a listening and a dialogue, a 'gathering' (*collectio*) of voices from their several places in [a cosmological] memory" (Carruthers 198). In the nineteenth century, phantasy, like rhetoric, has "silently faded away before the stern tendencies of the age" (*Selected Essays* 97), so that practicing it requires determination and drugs. But while excursive and visionary writing allows De Quincey to resist mechanistic virtues that dissipate novelty and freedom of thought, it also places him at the dark edges of life. The magus-writer must contend with *all* of the intelligences populating a vast universe, and those at the outer reaches speak of madness and pain and doom.

CHAPTER 4

Magic Consciousness

> I believe in three doctrines . . . : (1) That the borders of our mind are ever shifting . . . and create or reveal a single mind, a single energy. (2) That . . . our memories are a part of one great memory, the memory of Nature herself. . . . (3) That this great mind and great memory can be evoked by symbols.
>
> —William Butler Yeats, "Magic" 28 (1901)

> The tendency to occultism is a symptom of regression in consciousness. This has lost the power to think the unconditional and to endure the conditional. . . . Occultism is the metaphysics of dunces.
>
> —Theodor W. Adorno, "Theses Against Occultism" in *Minima Moralia* 238–41 (1951)

William Butler Yeats recalls the magi who precede him, as he reinforces the coincidence of magic, memory, and imagination that informed premodern conceptions of phantasy, as well as the poetics and rhetoric of Romanticism. Magic power requires a dialogical memory that ranges among the intelligences of the universe. Elaborating multiple constructions of reality, in the enactment of a palimpsestic intellect, Yeats's magus would become a part of the super-intellect of the universal mind-soul. Seeing himself as one of the last Romantics, Yeats associates the reformation of society with the poetic regeneration of an imagination in harmony with the Great Mind and Great Memory; enacting such imagination in a world of unbelievers entails some risk, and requires the courage to "cry out" about one's beliefs, especially in one's art ("Magic" 52).[1]

For Yeats, redemptive magic power is located in a gifted few. Modern culture has lost its Memory; restoring that Memory is the work of poets, musicians, and artists, who are the magi of our time (48), because they are uniquely capable of communing with the ideal and eternal. Those who are not gifted with sensitive imagination—ordinary citizens—become associated with evil, to the extent that they are removed from a mystical sensibility set in a supernatural cosmology. Everyday life exudes evil and ugliness, which result from the general disappearance of the "quality of mind" that appreciates the validity of magical practices and aspires to unity with a superordinate cosmos (28). In modern society, the cosmological imagination that was once "common over the world" has withdrawn from mass culture. The rescue of society and culture, if it is possible at all, requires great, gifted, powerful, and autonomous individuals who are types of "the supreme Enchanter" whose vision traverses and transcends time and space, and who sings of the return of a golden age ("Magic" 52).

As Paul Stanfield explains, Yeats's belief in the value and power of an imagination that is "wholly free, wholly self-moving" leads to the position that "the best government comes from the 'antithetical' aristocrat who requires and heeds only self-imposed obligations" (184; see also Flannery 53). The Great Mind and Great Memory, repositories of the alphabet of Nature, can be invoked to restore truth, beauty, and justice to humankind, and also to ordain a master race. However, I am not featuring Yeats as a Fascist;[2] rather, I want to note that this most ardent practitioner of magic opens the twentieth century with a traditional, metaphysical construction of magic power that we may regard as a backdrop for the play of later social criticism of authoritarian magic. The magus has always been identified in some measure as an occult figure with power and knowledge that put him in an "antithetical" relationship to society, as Yeats proposes in "Magic" and *A Vision* (73). But the assignment of the antithetical individual to a ruling aristocracy (*A Vision* 104) raises the spectre of the tyrant who—in the name of social redemption—invokes a Great Memory. As Kenneth Burke reminds us with his analysis of the "crude Nazi magic" of *Mein Kampf*, the supreme enchanter of this century is Hitler, who attempts to redeem society by instituting an Aryan cultural memory (*Philosophy* 191–220).

The neo-Marxist Frankfurt School that develops through the middle of this century in response to modern authoritarianism also seeks to reform the "mind" of mass culture, and sees the direction of such reform as the democratic *expansion* of cultural memory. Focussing on American mass culture, Frankfurt School members Theodor Adorno and Herbert Marcuse see the imagination as a *counter-magic* for resisting the dehumanizing magic of autocratic social forces and their agents, who suspend generative literacy and rhetoric. Adorno and Marcuse present memory—understood as the range of the critical intellect—as the seat of magical power, but unlike Yeats, they understand redemptive memory as an ideological construct rather than a metaphysical force. With Kenneth Burke, who associates "correct" magic with the critical elaboration of competing perspectives, Marcuse and Adorno call for a "return" to phantasy, which can counteract enforced automatism by opening the universe of discourse.

BURKE'S MAGIC

Language creates, and so every utterance is always a magical decree.[3] Burke elaborates this position in all of his full-length works, stating it most definitively in *The Philosophy of Literary Form*:

> Magic, verbal coercion, establishment or management by decree, says, in effect: "'Let there be'—and there was." And men share in the magical resources of some power by speaking "in the name of" that power. . . . Today [1941], for instance, we are facing problems that arise from an attempt to fit private enterprise with the requirements of the citizenry as a whole. Think of the difference in magic if you confront this situation *in the strategic name of* "planned economy" or, employing a different strategy, *in the name of* "regimentation."
>
> The magical decree is implicit in all language; for the mere act of naming an object or situation decrees that it is to be singled out as such and such rather than as something other. Hence, I think that an attempt to *eliminate* magic, in this sense, would involve us in the elimination of vocabulary itself as a way of sizing up reality. Rather, what we may need is *correct* magic, magic whose decrees about the naming of real situations is the closest approximation to the situation named (with the greater accuracy of approximation being supplied by the "collective revelation" of testing and discussion). (4)

Burke's "correct magic" here coincides with the "true magic" he defines in *A Grammar of Motives*. While "false magic" is merely formulaic incantation that attempts to suspend or control "the laws of motion," true magic is action that creates action, words that create words. It is consequential, "making everything out of nothing," generative. Writers are assistants to the play of language, "where the act of the writing brings up problems and discoveries intrinsic to the act, leading to developments that derive not from the scene, or agent, or agency, or extrinsic purposes, but purely from the foregoing aspects of the act itself. . . . Our act itself alters the conditions of action, as 'one thing leads to another' in an order that would not have occurred had we not acted" (67). The power that generates true magic is *novelty*.

Like true magic, "correct magic" also entails revelation and change, but instead of the "pure" magic of words causing words, correct magic is social, a decree that is least coercive and most inclusive, approachable through the "collective revelation of testing and discussion," that is, dialectically and dialogically. Thus, correct magic entails what Burke calls "scope" (*Grammar* 59); it will account more fully for "the facts" by subjecting them to the broadest inquiry.

The *ideal* practice of correct magic is "possible only to an infinite, omniscient mind" (*Philosophy* 7). Here Burke alludes to the metaphysical nostalgia for an alphabet of nature, noting that the "goal of philosophy, uniting free will and determinism," has been the creation of a "chart" that perfectly matches the name(s) of a thing with its essence(s). He cautions, however, that the creation of such a chart would mean the end of magic; that is, the end of the linguistic process of "sizing up reality," the dialogue of competing "decrees" that make social action and social change possible. In other words, totalizing magic is self-destructive, while the correct magic of social wrangling "contains enough elements of self-cancellation to keep things from coming to a perfect fulfillment in a perfect Apocalyptic holocaust" (*Language* 21). Against the advisability of an alphabet of nature, and by analogy all universalizing uses of language that represent the human impulse toward perfection, Burke posits "a comprehensive undefinable *definiendum*, here called the infinite wordless universe," which we can only desire through our persistent narrative approximations: "the countless universes of discourse that story can make of it" ("Logology" 32).

Magic diverges from rhetoric whenever it occurs outside the realm of human *action*, as the "use of addressed language to *induce motion in things* (things by nature alien to purely linguistic orders of motivation)" (*Rhetoric* 42). To see modern rhetoric as some anthropologists have, as the "survival of primitive magic," is to forget that rhetoric is "*the use of language as a symbolic means of inducing cooperation in beings that by nature respond to symbols*," and to eliminate the *realistic* and *social* nature of magic. Magic implies rhetoric, and rhetoric functions as magic, when magic is understood as a social act, "involving ways of identification [of "sizing up reality"] that contribute variously to social cohesion" (44). The distinction here between arhetorical magic and magic rhetoric corresponds to the distinction between false magic and true magic in *A Grammar of Motives*; Burke aligns the former with sheer physical motion and the latter with human action.

In sum, the principles of magic that Burke instigates are these:

1. Magic is intrinsic to language.
2. Because it constitutes reality by decree, magic-language is a coercive force.
3. True-correct magic is *generative*, practiced as *constitutive inquiry*, or the *coercive expansion of the possibilities for human action*.
4. False-incorrect magic—distinct from both the pure novelty of true magic and the shared creativity of correct magic—is *arresting*, practiced as *enforced doctrine*, or the *coercive reduction of the possibilities for human action*.

This last principle extends the realm of Burkean "motion" to situations in which people are treated as things, in which the magus orders automatistic behavior.[4]

The modern epistemological shift from the spiritual to the material has affected the grounds of magic, by changing the name of the power that we decree "in the name of." This is the age of "Money as Substitute for God": confronting the great diversity of the twentieth century, Burke concludes that "Monetary symbolism is the 'simple,' the 'god-term,' in terms of which all this great complexity attains a unity transcending distinctions of climate, class, nation, cultural traditions, etc." (*Grammar* 110).[5] It is the overall public motive for discourse, the motive of motives: "Money is *not a mere agency*, in our civilization, but is a *rational-*

izing ground of action" (113).[6] In the realm of the "almighty dollar," the attendant subdeities become virtues and techniques that satisfy "material requirements" (*Grammar* 109); we issue our decrees in the name of, for instance, "planned economy."

Taking Burke's position, we see that economic productivity and stability fall under the new, secularized *fidei lumine* of this age, as institutionalized determinants of the scope of lawful magic. In an age of faith, the light of faith restricted phantasy, and cast heresy into the shadows (see above, chapter 2). The monetary motive acts similarly, but illuminates a different lexicon. To reach God, we improve our souls; this means, in sociocultural terms, thinking and speaking and writing ideas and images whose "goodness" is established by religious authority. To make money, we improve our material efficiency; this means thinking and speaking and writing mechanistically. As Burke concludes, once our "materiality" becomes our "ideality," we identify ourselves with its production, so that "in adapting ourselves to machinery [which represents and effects the quantification of material resources], we are adapting ourselves to an aspect of ourselves" (*Grammar* 109). In this realm, automatizing and automatistic rhetorics that uphold the deification of material conditions are enactments of both arresting magic and *piety*: "When you discern the symptoms of great devotion to any kind of endeavor, you are in the realm of piety" (*Permanence and Change* 83). Arresting magi issue instrumental decrees "in the name of" good running order.[7] As Adorno and Marcuse will insist, arresting magic vies for the consciousness of our time. Generative magic that seeks novelty and the elaboration of competing "decrees," desecrating the material conditions in place by reconstituting them dialogically, continues to be the rhetoric of *heresy*, but heresy against a cult(ure) of secular deities that is replacing the cult(ure) of God(s).

ADORNO AGAINST OCCULTISM

Adorno and Marcuse are early advocates of what we now call "critical thinking" (Giroux, *Theory* 7–41), and identify its repression with the automatizing magic of the "culture industry." Adorno's "Theses Against Occultism" (1951) and "The Stars Down To Earth: The Los Angeles Times Astrology Column" (1957) posit relationships between magical beliefs, a domesticated mass culture, and reduced literacy; these essays point toward Marcuse's 1964 analysis of the abbreviation of public discourse into "magic ritual formulas," *One Dimensional Man*. The magic that has closed the universe of discourse does not originate in the authoritarian regimes or dehumanizing industrialization of this century; these political and economic movements are themselves developments of the Enlightenment project represented by the Royal Society. This is the position of *Dialectic of Enlightenment*, the trenchant critique of Enlightenment thought written during World War II by Adorno and Max Horkheimer, and published in 1947; Adorno's and Marcuse's later work can be read as an elaboration of and response to *Dialectic* (Jay 256). In "The Concept of Enlightenment," which opens the volume, Horkheimer and Adorno mourn the loss of magical imagination:

> The program of the Enlightenment was the disenchantment of the world; the dissolution of myths and the substitution of knowledge for fancy. . . . The world of magic retained distinctions whose traces have disappeared even in linguistic form. The multitudinous affinities between existents are suppressed by the single relation between the subject who bestows meaning and the meaningless object. . . . On the magical plane, dream and image were not mere signs for the thing in question, but were bound up with it by similarity or names. The relation is not one of intention but of relatedness. Like science, magic pursues aims, but seeks to achieve them by mimesis—not by progressively distancing itself from the object. . . . The "unshakeable confidence in the possibility of world domination," which Freud anachronistically ascribes to magic, corresponds to realistic world domination only in terms of a more skilled science. (3–11)

In this construction of the Enlightenment, ***knowledge*** (***Wissen***) is the ***naming*** of nature, as an act of both separating the knower from the known, and of determining a single relationship—or identity—for the object of knowledge. *Fancy* (*Einbildung*)—here understood in connection with the pre-Enlightenment process of phantastic imagination—explores "multitudinous affinities between existents," on a magical plane where a name invokes a system of relationships and resemblances. The authoritarian temperament that Freud calls magical is really the product of an "all-inclusive industrial technology" (*Dialectic* 11) made possible by the separation of the naming subject and the determined object.[8] The objectification of the world, which Burke has called false magic, informs the occult beliefs popular in mass culture, which maintain a mechanistic rather than a sympathetic universe, constructed of "facts" that dominate everyday life. A by-product of the Enlightenment, such beliefs constitute what Adorno calls "the metaphysics of dunces."

Adorno's "Theses Against Occultism" occurs toward the end of his *Minima Moralia: Reflections from Damaged Life*, and serves as a link between his reflections on culture in *Dialectic of Enlightenment* and his study of astrology ("Introduction" 5). The *Minima* is a collection of fragments; this form is itself a reaction against the "totalitarian unity" instituted by the Enlightenment (Jay 277). With his inversion of Hegel's "the whole is the true" into "the whole is the false" (*Minima* 50), Adorno announces his advocacy of a radical cultural critique, or *negation*, realized in writing that resists monolithic thought.

For Adorno, popular occultism affirms and reproduces positivist rationality, instead of providing a mode of negation. Occult "information" is no longer the grammar of an animistic universe, no longer a panoply of phantasms that serves the animated intellect in its resistance to what De Quincey called the "merely human." The "extirpation of animism" (*Dialectic* 5) has turned nature into "mere objectivity" realized in "a linguistically expressed totality" (9–11). With no connection to the vitalities whose interaction once determined the range of conceptual thought, the occult has been co-opted by the language of commodities, and thus "menacingly objectified," offers the believer "non-existent experience":

> Because objects have frozen in the cold light of reason, lost their illusory animation, the social quality that now animates them is given an independent existence both natural and supernatural, a thing among things. (*Minima* 239)

The commodification of the larger society is represented in small by petty astrologers: "The bent little fortune-tellers terrorizing their clients with crystal balls are toy models of the great ones who hold the fate of mankind in their hands" (240), and "have blunt, drastic answers to every question" (242). Practical information is the stock-in-trade of the merchandisers of the occult, for whom "from the stars to [business] transactions is but a nimble step" (243). "Spirit," which suggests a cosmology of moving forces evasive of totalization, has been replaced by its lowercase equivalent, "the guardian angel of the established, despiritualized order," the oracle of the status quo.

"The Stars Down To Earth" is Adorno's "content study" of his "Theses Against Occultism." In "Scientific Experiences of a European Scholar in America," Adorno describes his approach:

> The method I adopted was that of putting myself in the position of the popular astrologer, who by what he writes must supply his readers with a kind of personal satisfaction and finds himself continually confronted with the difficulty of giving to people whom he knows nothing about apparently specific advice adapted to each individual. The result is a strengthening of conformist views. (366)

Emphasizing the astrologer as a *writer*, who is in this case a rhetor engaging a "semi-erudite" audience with practical advice, Adorno continues his interest in the merchants of abbreviated discourse, and in the nature of the *appeal* of arresting magic. Noting that the writer of the *Times* column is a particular individual—Carroll Righter—Adorno proposes that no individual can really exert an authorial identity in this medium. The astrology writer is largely controlled by "the objective requirements of his product more than his own urges of expression"; that is, the "rules of thumb, set patterns and mechanisms" (19) that are associated with the faceless social, economic, industrial, and technical "controls" that the writer must obey.

The writer's limited range of self-expression corresponds with the readers' appreciation for "conventional, conformist and contented attitudes" (41) that provide "a short-cut by bringing the complex to a handy formula" (23). Although astrology columns do not really contain authority about the subjects they treat, that is, human nature and human behavior, they are regarded as authoritative by people who "are thoroughly convinced that others (or some unknown agency) ought to know more about themselves and what they should do than they can decide for themselves" (17). Adorno resists making the manipulated responsible for their own manipulation, saying that if the appeal of formulaic advice answers a reader's need, that need has been "molded" by the publication itself; readers have been conditioned by this stimulus, which is "consciously calculated and institutionalized" by a totalitarian social system (18). Without castigating the readers of horoscopes, Adorno does assign them motives: the "semi-erudite" (in other words, the semiliterate) is not adept at complex, critical thinking, but desires status and understanding greater than that of "plain people" (41), understanding that the astrology column seems to promise. However, without either advanced analytical skills or requisite detachment from culturally conditioned desires, these readers can only apprehend the horoscope as a species of mystification, a presentation of results whose formulation occurs in some unapproachable realm of expertise (15).

As the materialization of authoritarian elements that are "entirely abstract, unapproachable and anonymous" (20), the "set patterns" of the astrology column reveal powers that govern both the writer's activity and the audience's susceptibility. Adorno identifies these patterns, based upon his reading of three months of *Times* columns, along with comparable material in astrology magazines. Here, I illustrate his general observations with typical examples from current nationally syndicated astrology columns by Sydney Omarr, the astrologer who has replaced the late Carroll Righter in the *Los Angeles Times*; Joyce Jillson, whose column faces Omarr's in the *Chicago Sun-Times*; and Linda Black, the astrologer for the *Chicago Tribune*. The columns I studied were printed from January through March, 1993. Taken together, they represent the newspaper horoscopes read in big-city middle America and throughout the country. Illustrating Adorno's analytical points with these sources, I wish to suggest the persistence of the set patterns he noted over thirty-five years ago. I will give further attention in chapter 5 to the explosion of arresting magic we are experiencing in today's "New Age," as a continuation of the patterns presented here.

Astrological advice is restricted to the small world of the individual, who seems "severed" from the "fate of mankind at large" ("Stars" 26). Exhibiting a telegraphic style, Sydney Omarr tends to couch such advice in lists:

> Attention revolves around home security, possible change of residence, income potential, marital status. (28 February 1993; 71)

> Attention revolves around property, sales, real estate, reputation, marital status. . . . Attend to basics, including mending, correcting mistakes, sharpening tools, testing recipes. . . . Change of residence or appearance of home dominates scenario. (11 March 1993; 71)

The terms home, personal property, security, family, marital status, and appearance cycle through each week of columns, defining the markedly small range of activity that is generally featured in popular astrology. Joyce Jillson maintains a similar range, with a less imperative approach than Omarr's: "Shoe shopping and housecleaning are favored, but wait until next week to dry-clean delicate items" (24 February 1993; 71). Jillson's weekend columns (Friday–Sunday) emphasize home projects and family outings, therebye maintaining not only the "small world" that Adorno perceived, but also the "bi-phasic" division of work from play that we will consider below. Linda Black often celebrates stellar constellations fortuitous for solitary recreation, thus maintaining the individual's dissociation from global concerns: "This is a perfect day to take back everything you received that doesn't fit. . . . It's also a good evening to spend reading a book" (13 January 1993; 5.2).

The language suggests "individualized" attention to the reader, through second-person address, when in fact such attention is impossible; this is "the makeshift of pseudo-individualization" (Adorno, "Stars" 29). Omarr, Jillson, and Black all offer "900" phone numbers for "personal" horoscopes. Phoning Linda Black on January 30, 1993, I am initially met by a strong male voice who identifies Linda Black as a corporate entity "brought to you by Tribune Media Services," and warns that "billing will begin in three seconds" (seventy-five cents a minute). Then a friendly female voice, which I presume belongs to Linda Black, invites me to punch in my birth date (or that of a "friend or loved one"), or to select some other option from the "main menu," such as a birthday greeting, an "information on astrology" message, or a reference to a local astrologer.[9] I am also welcome, says the recorded Linda, to leave a message for the live Linda, who "loves" my comments, but must admit she cannot answer all of them personally.

Punching in my birthdate, I hear "Hi Virgo" from the same nice voice who just arrayed my options. It is nearing February 1 and "the moon has gone into Gemini," so I should expect to be pushed to do something challenging and possibly "nerve-wracking" at work; but I'll "learn from it." My advisor speaks casually, tending to repeat herself, in relatively unrehearsed syntax that both suggests spontaneity and takes up time (and money) with its verbosity: "It can be, you know, that might be a little bit difficult for you right now . . . to get some stuff out, to start thinkin' about it." When this message is over, the male voice invites me to try the "Live one-on-

one psychic line," for $2.95 a minute. Feeling vaguely involved in a version of phone sex, I hang up recalling that Adorno associates "indulgence" in astrology with "passive sexual pleasure" ("Stars" 21).

By seeming to give personal advice, astrology columns appeal to narcissism and vanity (Adorno, "Stars" 30). Often in current columns, such an appeal is overt. Sydney Omarr's excited declarations consistently touch upon physical attraction and personal appeal, and exhort self-confidence: "You'll look better, feel better, more people will be drawn to you, will comment on your talent, potential. You get money, too!" (7 March 1993; 75). And apart from frequent explicit compliments (such as Jillson's "Others observe you and like what they see" [20 February 1993, 49] and Black's "A lot of what you get simply comes to you, attracted by your good looks and good luck" [20 January 1993; 5.5]), the columns define their readers as beneficiaries of personal success, according them positions of wealth and authority. In Adorno's view, horoscope readers are encouraged to imagine themselves as winning players in a challenging but rewarding socioeconomic system; "big shot[s] with some worries" ("Stars" 40). Omarr creates this image with his repeated calls for attention to financial speculation, property values, and spectacular business achievements:

> Emphasis on security, home, family, sale or purchase of property. . . . Financial picture bright, you locate missing link, ingredients. . . . You get almost everything you want if diplomatic. Long-range project dominates, ambition fulfilled, you gain added recognition, could be flirting with "fame and fortune." (8 March 1993; 55)

Likewise, Jillson and Black give repeated attention to investments and large purchases, forecasting the best days for readers to make the most of their money, with the coincident implication that readers actually are in the position to "make a deal on the golf course or the tennis courts" (Black, 27 February 1993; 1.25).

At the same time that the horoscopes praise individuality, the behaviors prescribed imply compulsive obedience and conformity, not social or intellectual autonomy. Thus the columns are "appeal[s] to agencies of psychological control rather than an attempt to unfetter the unconscious" ("Stars" 36). Readers must attend to efficient organization, constraints and deadlines imposed by superiors, and the completion of tasks; as Omarr insists unequivocally, personal and professional fortitude is all-important: "Complete assignment, project—you'll be tempted to 'wait'" (11 February 1993; 79). Jillson regularly stresses the importance of punctuality, completeness, accurate record-keeping, efficiency, organization, and decisiveness, warning in a variety of ways that we must "see a project through to the end" (19 February 1993; 58). With a similar emphasis on industrial virtues, Black adds the importance of avoiding distracting or dissatisfied coworkers, who are "dragging their feet" (19 January 1993; 5.3) or engaging in "crazy talk" (22 January 1993; 5.3) or "internal squabbling" (11 February 1993; 5.3); those who take issue with professional responsibilities and assignments are simply immature:

> Don't have a temper tantrum today, unless you want to be treated like a child. This time it will mean your decision-making privileges will be taken away. Appreciate what you have. (3 March 1993; 5.5)

In sum, the horoscopes' emphasis on individualism seems a token acknowledgment of a desired self-image; more often, advice leads readers in the direction of cooperation and dependence on authority figures (Adorno, "Stars" 66–69). Omarr never lets readers forget that some other astrological sign—embodied as a personal or business associate—is exerting influence on their lives: "Scorpio plays paramount role. . . . Libra involved. . . . Pisces is in picture. . . . Cancer native involved. . . . Leo plays key role. . . . Capricorn involved. . . . Virgo in picture" (4 March 1993; 77); and Black is especially intent on acquiescence to bosses: "If the boss insists on trying to teach you something, do your best to learn" (15 February 1993; 5.4).

"Friends" often serve the function of authorities, an ostensibly benevolent but oppressive collective that defines the reader's identity in their image, but because of its detachment from the reader's worries, knows better. As projections of the reader, the friends in the column say, "If you do what we tell you, if you only will be good, we will give you anything you want to have" (Adorno, "Stars" 76). The advice to readers to "talk over" issues or problems with another [usually a higher up] acts in the interest of closure and conformity" ("Stars" 81). Our three astrologers identify a "friend" as—variously—a source of the secrets of professional success, a motivator for high achievement, a voice of wisdom and experience, a valuable though disagreeable critic, a model of right thinking and behavior, and a stimulant for the imagination. In the presence of all of these friends, the reader would be wise to subordinate herself gratefully, realizing that listening to "strong" others often beats listening to one's "weak" self: "Exceptional efforts of a strong-minded family member or co-worker are just the help you needed; remember to express your gratitude" (Jillson, 5 March 1993; 63).

Continuing the themes of cooperation and subordination, astrology columns discuss the family as an ideally harmonious group, and warn that rifts in family relationships should be met with appeasement (Adorno, "Stars" 69–71). Omarr carries this message with his persistent incantation of "home" in his lists of significant factors for attention, and with particularly buoyant appreciations of family happiness: "Where there was bitterness in family relationships, there now can be joy, humor, plans involving future journey. You no longer will be 'locked in' to one course of action. Wake up with a happy shout!!" (4 March 1993; 77). Joyce Jillson's typical praise of family get-togethers and activities is unusually evident in her February 25, 1993 repetition of family value imperatives: "Spend time with family. . . . Mate's strength sustains you. . . . Daily family routine is your rock. . . . Time with the Family is well spent in March; their support brings goals within reach" (73). Linda Black likes to advise contact with siblings, who are sources of good times and heart to heart talks, and like Jillson she discourages stubbornness and arguments among family members, noting that "If you appreciate [the family] you have, you'll be able to build toward a secure future" (5 February 1993; 5.3).

Family time is, however, distinguished clearly from "work" time. These "contradictory" activities of life are to be managed by their distribution over different time periods. Work and leisure are given their respective times of day, and such apportionment comes to represent a "bi-phasic" reality (Adorno, "Stars" 41–51), in which work is dissociated from pleasure, pleasure must be "earned," and the characterization of work as the price for pleasure disallows a more incisive critique of its value. During the work week, all mentions of recreation place it after hours, and characterize it as an escape from nine-to-five life; in general, "some sort of drudgery has to be finished before you get to go out and play" (Black, 30 January 1993; 1.23). Weekend columns from all three astrologers abound with references to household repairs and chores; the presence of relatives; "music, art, beautification of surroundings" (Omarr, 7 March 1993; 75); shopping trips; exercise; churchgoing; romance. As Joyce Jillson says on Friday, February 26, 1993, "Try your best at work, and then go home and forget it for the weekend" (59). Such injunctions conceive pleasure as a kind of amnesia, with no understanding of the mutual exclusion of work and pleasure as a problem.

Yet life can be pleasant enough, if the horoscope reader follows the astrologer's advice. Not doing so is associated with some sort of usually mild threat; thus "threat and relief are somehow intertwined" (Adorno, "Stars" 30). But following the advice promises that everything will be fine; there is "this general pattern of the happy ending" (33). The same forces that threaten our safety and contentment can assure them, if we align our behavior properly. Typically, difficult and even painful experiences are featured as opportunities or stages on the road to success: "You'll be saying, 'At first I was leery of the challenge but now I've met it and I'm happy!'" (Omarr, 7 March 1993; 75). Losses, setbacks, arguments, sacrifices, and confusion are consistently characterized as obstacles from which a reader will "emerge victorious" through endurance and a positive attitude. However, if things go wrong, the reader is to blame:

> If you can move quickly when the situation changes, this day could turn out to be fun instead of a disaster. (Black, 29 January 1993; 5.5)
>
> Be willing to revise, to tear down for ultimate purpose of rebuilding on solid base. (Omarr, 7 February, 1993; 83)
>
> Refuse to give up. Reversals and changes are signs you are close to a bonanza. (Jillson, 7 February, 1993; 83)

Despite the professed importance of following through, there is more emphasis in astrology columns on avoiding than on doing (Adorno, "Stars" 35). This is implicit in the constant references to cooperation, which typically requires the avoidance of personal desires and compulsions. "Watch out," "Be careful," and "Don't get involved" are common commands from both Black and Jillson. For Omarr, it is most important that one avoid a negative attitude; the lexicon of terms that comprise his daily lists of salient behavioral elements exudes optimism and disparages gloom. Here is a catalogue, from February 15–March 15, 1993, of the aspects that Omarr wants his readers to emphasize: responsibility, wider horizons, communication, promotion, production, recognition, partnership, power, authority, achievement, universality, independence, freedom, prestige, spiritual awareness, reunion, cooperation, originality, courage, panache, leadership, innovation, talent, security, income potential, motivation, credibility, discovery, magnetism, sex appeal, romance, sophistication, adventure, sensuality, fun, confidence, showmanship, dedication, sensuality, health, creativity, variety, harmony, reputation, determination. In general, personal or professional failure results from a captious attitude: we are warned to avoid those people and behaviors that problematize life, and to proceed cheerfully with our responsibilities:

> Nothing's impossible if you're willing to work hard for as long as it takes. And you probably are! (Black, 26 February 1993; 2.5)

> Keep that positive energy flowing; you have every reason to assume that you'll benefit from changes transpiring now. (Jillson, 13 March 1993; 49)

The consistently euphemistic language of the columns, which never names the reader's weaknesses directly, or suggests any offensive behavior on the reader's part, is tied to "the fear of summoning some demon by mentioning his name" (Adorno, "Stars" 79). The language of negation is a kind of heresy against the social hierarchy that the column keeps in place; it would place the reader outside the secular "light of faith" that subtends the harmonies and hierarchies of modern social life. Omarr's, Jillson's, and Black's insistent positive attitude is regularly evident in the "birthday message" that characterizes the year ahead:

> Current cycle highlights possible change of residence, chance to increase income, participation in art, music, drama. . . . Aries, Libra persons play interesting roles in your life. September and November will be your most memorable, profitable months of 1993. (Omarr, 18 February, 1993; 76)

Adorno concludes that astrology is an "ideology for dependence," an "attempt to strengthen and somehow justify painful conditions which seem to be more tolerable if an affirmative attitude is taken toward them" (83).[10] With his emphasis on authoritarian set patterns that correspond to this ideology, Adorno features the involvement of formulaic writing and reading in the uncritical affirmation of popular occultism. In "The Essay As Form," which Adorno is completing at the same time that "Stars" first appears, he proposes the corrective to dunce metaphysics, positing excursive writing as a countermagic to cultural orthodoxy.

Adorno holds that one's conception of the essay determines one's attitude toward both reading and writing, one's literacy. The literate "technician" believes in the recoverability of authorial intention, the separability of style and content, and the importance of objectivity and conviction to writing. The "dreamer" practices the "spontaneity of subjective fantasy that is chastised in the name of objective discipline" (4). The dreamer's essay rejects the traditional distinctions between the eternal and the transitory, the historical and the personal. Its method is to proceed unmethodically. It is discontinuous, exploratory, and inconclusive, the ideal mode for a philosophy in defiance of Descartes' "clear and distinct idea."

Taking as its proper theme the relationship of nature to culture, the Adornian essay blurs that distinction, and maintains a mobile cultural critique rather than some metaphysical or theological "standpoint." To insist that writing maintain such a standpoint, that is, to abandon intellectual play for the maintenance of established truth, is a merely pedagogical necessity that "acts as though it were a metaphysical virtue" (20). With its play among a panoply of standpoints, the excursive essay recalls premodern rhetoric, before it decayed into a science of communication that prizes "undifferentiated unity":

> [A]bandoned by play, truth would be nothing but tautology. For historically the essay too is related to rhetoric, which the scientific mentality has wanted to get rid of since Bacon and Descartes—until, appropriately, in a scientific age it degenerated to a science *sui generis*, that of communications. . . . The essay retains, precisely in the autonomy of its presentation, which distinguishes it from scientific and scholarly information, traces of the communicative element such information dispenses with. (20)

Characteristics of rhetoric that might be suspected as tools for manipulation—"association, ambiguity of words, neglect of logical synthesis"—are in the essay the elements of truth content. They allow for expansive intellection that is prohibited by scientistic logical criteria that serve the "established system of values." As it proceeds, the Adornian essay reads itself, it is self-critical; it is more intensely responsible than writing that proceeds automatically, and more likely to reveal the hidden: "Hence the essay's innermost formal law is heresy. Through violations of the orthodoxy of thought, something in the object becomes visible which it is orthodoxy's secret and objective aim to keep invisible" (171). In sum, the essay illuminates regions of thought that the secular *fidei lumine* keeps in the dark. An artifact of un-Enlightened rhetoric, it enacts the magical composing imagination long associated with heresy, the imagination disallowed by the terse directives of the astrology column and the powers they represent.

MARCUSE'S UNIVERSE OF DISCOURSE

Herbert Marcuse repeatedly characterizes in magical terms "the powers that be and the powers of fact," which define and administer abbreviated discourse:

> Magic, witchcraft, and ecstatic surrender are practiced in the daily routine of the home, the shop, and the office, and the rational accomplishments conceal the irrationality of the whole. For example, the scientific approach to the vexing problem of mutual annihilation—the mathematics and calculations of kill and over-kill, the measurement of spreading or not-quite-so-spreading fallout, the experiments of endurance in abnormal situations—is mystifying to the extent to which it promotes (and even demands) behavior which accepts the insanity. It thus counteracts a truly rational behavior—namely, the refusal to go along, and the effort to do away with the conditions which produce the insanity. (*One Dimensional Man* 190)

The transformation of complex concepts into calculable and measurable "facts" creates "magic-ritual formulas" that are "hammered and re-hammered into the recipient's mind" (88). Creating a society that questions arresting magic, in which "recognition of facts is critique of facts" (118) requires phantasy, understood in connection with *memory* as the agency of both recognition and critique (99). Phantasy creates alternatives to the established order, alternatives that memory makes imaginable: "And in the personal events which reappear in the individual memory, the fears and aspirations of mankind assert themselves—the universal in the particular" (98–99). Because memory preserves history, with its complex of defining events, memory is a subversive force. Referring to Adorno's "spectre of man without memory" (*One* 99n), Marcuse presents a ghastly phantasm who cannot entertain alternatives to his fate or understand its causes: a phantasm without phantasy.

One Dimensional Man pits one kind of magic against another: the generative magic of a historical consciousness expressed in "contradictory predicates" contests the arresting magic of an ahistorical consciousness expressed in "hypnotic nouns" (100). In a discourse of contradictory predicates, judgment requires the elaboration of contradictions, and that elaboration follows from the assumption that multiple definitions are in play in any instance. This is the discourse of phantasy, as Marcuse has indicated in *Eros and Civilization* and *Negations*. Although he has not altogether delivered phantasy from the Freudian connotations that associate the imagination with regressive infantilism (Kellner 194), Marcuse does recognize its centrality to classical epistemology, and appreciates its power for generating ways of knowing that may constitute critical thinking and eventuate in the "Great Refusal" necessary to liberation from arresting magic (*Negations* 154–55):

> In its refusal to accept as final the limitations imposed upon freedom and happiness by the reality principle, in its refusal to forget what *can be*, lies the critical function of phantasy[11]. . . . Phantasy is cognitive in so far as it preserves the truth of the Great Refusal, or positively, in so far as it protects, against all reason, the aspirations for the integral fulfillment of man and nature that are repressed by reason. In the realm of phantasy, the unreasonable images of freedom become rational, and the 'lower depth' of instinctual gratification assumes a new dignity. (*Eros and Civilization* 149, 160)

In terms that recall De Quincey's characterization of introspection as a counterforce to "merely physical and mechanical existence" (Burke's *motion*), Marcuse devotes *One Dimensional Man* to the possibility for a dimension of mind that resists the individual's coordination (for De Quincey, "collapse") into society.[12] Allied to phantasy, this dimension of mind becomes the preferred realm of Reason. Marcuse would define Reason (to which he gives this uppercase prominence) as a dialectical process that enacts the "nature of thought" by revealing rather than censoring contradictions.[13] This idea of Reason seems inoperative now:

> Conversely, all *established* reality militates against the logic of contradictions—it favors the modes of thought which sustain the established forms of life and the modes of behavior which reproduce and improve them. . . . [This logic belongs] to modes of thought which are non-operational in their very structure; they are alien to scientific as well as common-sense operationalism; their historical concreteness [that is, their recourse to an expansive memory] militates against quantification and mathematization on the one hand, and against positivism and empiricism on the other. Thus these modes of thought appear to be a relic of the past, like all non-scientific and non-empirical philosophy. They recede before a more effective theory and practice of Reason. (*One* 142–43)

What has receded is the subversive intellection of the premodern magus. Speculating on "The Chance of the Alternatives" in *One-Dimensional Man*, Marcuse proposes the return to a transcendent, metaphysical world, the world that preceded the scientific one; perhaps, he says, further "progress" means a break with established doctrines of "quantity" and a return to "quality." Deciding that this cannot really happen, because our dependence on the existing system would make its disintegration an "unbearable nightmare," Marcuse returns to the importance of art, which—he reminds us—can still name "the otherwise unnameable" (247). However, the prevailing belief that "the real is rational and the system delivers the goods" (84) has contributed to the accommodation of art to the harmony of mass communications, and the impossibility of qualitative change: "If mass communications blend together harmoniously, and often unnoticeably, art, politics, religion and philosophy with commercials, they bring these realms of culture to their common denominator—the commodity form" (57). Critical theory is not able to remedy this situation (254): phantasy is not able to disturb cultural reality. What human imagination can maintain, perhaps, is an appreciation for "absolute refusal" that is our only hope. Adorno complements this view when he says that "The only philosophy which can be responsibly practised in face of despair is the attempt to contemplate all things as they would present themselves from the standpoint of redemption . . . all else is reconstruction, mere technique":

> Perspectives must be fashioned that displace and estrange the world, reveal it to be, with its rifts and crevices, as indigent and distorted as it will appear one day in the messianic light. (*Minima* 247)[14]

Methodologically, absolute refusal is the rejection of abbreviated thought, with the discourse of a "multi-dimensional universe" where meaning is the product of "interrelated, overlapping, and antagonistic 'systems'" (*One* 196). Such discourse is the true-correct magic that Burke encourages, counterposed to the "mere technique" that he calls false magic, and Marcuse calls "false consciousness" (145). False consciousness is closely connected to technological progress: as "operationalism" becomes our ethical as well as epistemological center, we are ourselves "operationalized" (156–59),[15] becoming instruments of an operationalism that is advertised in connection with happiness and freedom. A current example, "GE, we bring good things to life," illustrates Marcuse's association of false consciousness with "one-dimensional" language that abbreviates concepts in order to arrest their contradictions. The formula GE = Good Things suppresses the involvement of General Electric in building military weaponry which, we may say, brings good people to death. Language that presents concepts as formulas evades full meaning by taking a short cut from naming to judgment, impeding conceptual thinking that is inclusive of the contradictions and ambiguities that attend any name (*One* 95).

Once an abbreviation or slogan is used repeatedly in public discourse, it becomes an "official vocable" with the status of an "unquestionable fact" whose conceptual content remains hidden. Marcuse surveys the characteristics of this one-dimensional language with examples that emphasize the cold war climate of the 1960s: "abridgment of the concept in fixed images" (Edward Teller as the "father" of the H-bomb); "arrested development in self-validating, hypnotic formulas" (the Western bloc is the Free World); "immunity against contradiction" through reconciling the irreconcilable (clean bomb); "identification of the thing (and of the person) with its function" ("nuclear-powered, ballistic-missile-firing submarine"); "suppression of history" ("AFL-CIO" hyphenates and "entombs" the radical historical differences between the two organizations). In the one-dimensional universe, history is regularly *invoked*, but with terms that are presented ahistorically: the regular intonation of "freedom" in a political speech sets aside the variegations and complexity of that term (*One* 90–100). The following current terms, to the extent that they operate as hypnotic formulas that maintain a "fixated structure of institutions, attitudes, aspirations" (*One* 91) for the uncritical reader, and serve to arrest reflection, are part of the one-dimensional language of the 1990s:

> fast food, CIA, PLO, abortion rights, economic recovery, fat-free, AIDS, OPEC, global warming, SCUD, family values, free trade, ROM, RAM, DOS, megabyte, software, Iraq-gate, "give us twenty-two minutes, we'll give you the world," global competitiveness, growth industry, environmental management, crisis management, data management, poverty line, job development, "you deserve a break today," information age, virtual reality, HDTV, word processor

Some of these terms are perhaps "two-dimensional," provoking *contrary* definitions from *competing* groups; as in the case, for instance, of the pro-choice and pro-life forces (whose own group names are each one-dimensional) on abortion rights. However, when neither side will transgress the "closed analytical structure" that protects its interests, each side is—in Marcuse's view—refusing to think (*One* 88).

Bringing Marcuse's argument to a present realization, we can cite recent directives by the U.S. Department of Labor Secretary's Commission on Achieving Necessary Skills (SCANS). In its 1992 *Skills and Tasks for Jobs: A SCANS Report for America 2000*, the Commission catalogs the skills it judges essential for fifty different jobs.[16] Particularized job skills are grounded in a set of all-purpose "Foundation Skills":

> Basic Skills: Reads, writes, performs arithmetic and mathematical operations, listens, and speaks
>
> A. Reading—locates, understands, and interprets written information in prose and in documents such as manuals, graphs, and schedules
>
> B. Writing—communicates thoughts, ideas, information, and messages in writing; and creates documents such as letters, directions, manuals, reports, graphs, and flow charts
>
> C. Arithmetic/Mathematics—performs basic computations and approaches practical problems by choosing appropriately from a variety of mathematical techniques

D. Listening—receives, attends to, interprets, and responds to verbal messages and other cues

E. Speaking—organizes ideas and communicates orally

Thinking Skills: Thinks creatively, makes decisions, solves problems, visualizes, knows how to learn, and reasons

A. Creative Thinking—generates new ideas

B. Decision Making—specifies goals and constraints, generates alternatives, considers risks, and evaluates and chooses best alternative

C. Problem Solving—recognizes problems and devises and implements plan of action

D. Seeing Things in the Mind's Eye—organizes, and processes symbols, pictures, graphs, objects, and other information

E. Knowing How To Learn—uses efficient learning techniques to acquire and apply new knowledge and skills

F. Reasoning—discovers a rule or principle underlying the relationship between two or more objects and applies it when solving a problem

Personal Qualities: Displays responsibility, self-esteem, sociability, self-management, and integrity and honesty

A. Responsibility—exerts a high level of effort and perseveres towards goal attainment

B. Self-Esteem—believes in own self-worth and maintains a positive view of self

C. Sociability—demonstrates understanding, friendliness, adaptability, empathy, and politeness in group settings

D. Self-Management—assesses self accurately, sets personal goals, monitors progress, and exhibits self-control

E. Integrity/Honesty—chooses ethical courses of action (Rosenheim, "SCANS," taken from United States *Skills* 2.8–2.9).

The skills that SCANS recommends are intended to drive most government-supported programs for job training and literacy development (Rosenheim, "What Works"). Specific applications of these skills vary from job to job. For instance, the Beauty Shop Owner needs writing to

Establish a network of customers by writing personal notes. To perform the task, the beauty shop owner obtains personal infor-

> mation from clients who enter the salon. Following appointments, the owner writes notes of appreciation to clients, expressing pleasure in meeting them and a desire to see them again. Further, the owner indexes a client's name, services, and products for future reference. Task ID#: 7021361. (United States *Skills* 3.176)

The SCANS material is remarkable for its encouragement of conformity and cooperation, identification of the individual with automatistic functions, abbreviation of complex processes into simple directives, and inattention to critical thinking. These are the elements of official magic ritual formulas, which parents and teachers are urged to inculcate:

> You can do several things to improve American education. First, display the SCANS skills prominently in your home and discuss them, often, with your children. Make sure they understand what you expect. Second, take the list with you to your child's school and find out where and how the school is equipping your child with these skills. (United States *What Work Requires* 6)

Depersonalization, the identification of people as things, governs the SCANS directives: The Foundations Skills are presented without human nouns or pronouns; there are no grammatical subjects, only behaviors. People charged with these behaviors have been abbreviated away, or at best standardized into ciphers—owner, client, worker, supervisor, operator—whose skills are entirely operational. In the beauty shop, writing functions to index the client along with other inventory.

FREIRE'S MAGIC CONSCIOUSNESS

For Adorno and Marcuse, the refusal of operationalism and one-dimensional language requires a philosophical language "estranged" from mass culture. Because established reality has so fully "coordinated the means of expression," this may be impossible (*One* 70–71). Yet, attempting to maintain a language of critique removed from the scope of existence remains crucial; as Adorno says in the conclusion of *Minima Moralia*, "Even its own impossibility it must at last comprehend for the sake of the possible" (247). With his advocacy of a philosophy that pursues strange and presently inoperative visions, Marcuse inveighs against philosophers who focus on the ordinary utterances of everyday life. The work of J. L. Austin and Ludwig Wittgenstein, for instance, has become dangerously operational, reducing or eliminating the transcendent ethical/political potential of philosophy by circumscribing the context for the philosophical imagination. Ordinary language philosophy is descriptive of the factual, "restricted experience" rather than revealing of strange alternatives that take place "behind the curtain" (*One* 145).

For similar reasons, the philosophy of estrangement and refusal cannot welcome social constructionism. Gregory Clark, who invokes Mikhail Bakhtin, Richard Rorty, Kenneth Bruffee, and Chaim Perelman in order to construct a "social perspective on the function of writing," locates the importance of dialogue and dialectic in "pluralistic" consensus that materializes "moderate" and "well-balanced" solutions to problems. Clark counterposes "fair compromise" to "coercion imposed in the name of a unique value"; such compromise requires a community that is "proficient in pluralism," and that agrees to continue conversation about its disagreements (56–58). In Clark's exposition, conflict and difference, which constitute a "collaborative testing process," take on the quality of what Adorno calls "serene demonstration" (*Minima* 247). The oracular voice of absolute refusal, speaking the unimaginable, has no role in a group devoted to practical and generally agreeable solutions. Against arguments for the participatory social construction of truth, we hear Adorno and Marcuse wondering whether people really matter when the maintenance of the group is primary.

With faith that radical critical consciousness *can* arise from the dialogic interaction of the oppressed, Paulo Freire sets aside philosophical despair. Freire's Subject is a generative individual who *makes* culture; the *object* is an individual arrested by culture. To become a Subject, one must develop a "permanently critical attitude" (*Education* 5). This is associated with the "capacity for choice," a participatory role which—*contra* Marcuse—is both transformative and plausible.

For Freire, illiteracy coincides with "magic consciousness," which is resignation to the facts of life and the powers that enforce them. This term is particularly appropriate to Freire's Central American peasant culture, whose preindustrial beliefs are more explicitly magical than those of *Times* astrology column readers. At the same time, the peasants who are prey to magical thinking share certain characteristics that coincide with the closed thinking of their one-dimensional counterparts in the United States (*Education* 102–6; *Pedagogy* 50):

1. The uncritical acceptance of facts, without the critical ability to see them in relationship with other facts, explicated in the natural-historical-social world.
2. The tendency to see other forms of thought as invasive.
3. Perception of oneself as "belonging to" a fixed world rather than "entering into" a transformable world.
4. Perception of transformative structures, such as industrialization, as magical phenomena. The "action" of such a transformative structure is not met by "reflection."
5. "A diffuse, magical belief in the invulnerability and power of the oppressor."

Magic consciousness is reinforced by the deposit of "myths indispensable to the preservation of the status quo" (*Pedagogy* 135).[17] The overarching myth is "the model of itself which the bourgeoisie presents to the people as the possibility for their own ascent" (*Pedagogy* 144). Because magical thinking is not changed merely by schooling that continues to deposit this restrictive cultural model, education itself must be reconsidered. It cannot be a process of extension "from those who consider that they know to those who consider that they do not know" (109). Rather, it must be an open (and necessarily slow) dialogue that begins "at the level at which [the illiterate] *are*," not where the teacher thinks they should be (160).

Freire's literacy program is a striking revolution against magic consciousness, founded as it is in generative language, reflection *and* action, and continual dialogue and critique. Freire's opposition of a mechanistic, servile literacy to a dialogic, critical literacy parallels the opposition of arresting magic to generative magic, so that we may think of Freire's insistence upon a liberatory literacy as his magic remedy for magic consciousness. Literacy is itself the offer of a new magic:

> We wanted to offer the people the means by which they could supersede their magic or naive perception of reality by one that was predominantly critical, so that they could assume positions

> appropriate to the dynamic climate of the transition. (*Education* 44)

Grounded in an "active, *dialogical*, critical and criticism-stimulating method," literacy brings with it "an attitude of creation and re-creation, a self-transformation producing a stance of intervention in one's context" (45, 48). Noting Freire's emphasis on the transformative magic of dialogue, I would stress that a Freirean educator's task is precisely the coercive expansion of the possibilities for action, the constitutive inquiry of generative magic.

Freire would move his students, then, from "semi-intransitive" consciousness, which prefers arresting magical explanations to the apprehension of causality; through "transitive consciousness," which is the ability to enter into dialogue with other people and with the world; to critical transitivity:

> The critically transitive consciousness is characterized by depth in the interpretation of problems; by the substitution of causal principles for magical explanations; by the testing of one's "findings" and by openness to revision; by the attempt to avoid distortion when perceiving problems and to avoid preconceived notions when analyzing them; by refusing to transfer responsibility; by rejecting passive positions; by soundness of argumentation; by the practice of dialogue rather than polemics; by receptivity to the new for reasons beyond mere novelty and by the good sense not to reject the old just because it is old—by accepting what is valid in both old and new. (*Education* 18)

Adorno, Marcuse, and Freire are all interested in the democratization of cultural memory, in full mass awareness of the complexities of causality. While the Frankfurt critics appreciate the power of dialectical thought for achieving this goal, they do not think that a community of truly radical counter-magicals is realizable. Freire is exhorting dialogical thought (within a *communal* dialectic), in which an education of "I wonder" rather than "I do" is not pursued in solitude, but rather in a "culture circle" where dialogue is grounded in "generative words" that catalyze linguistic and experiential elaboration.[18]

In a recent reconsideration of Marcuse that serves to validate Freirean pragmatism, Richard Bernstein appreciates the importance of phantasy, because as Marcuse says, it keeps alive "the tabooed images of freedom" (qtd. in Pippin 19); but he would finally bypass Marcuse's absolute refusal, and calls him mistaken for misjudging the "pragmatic movement as being only one more variant of the positivism that [the Frankfurt thinkers] abhorred and detested" (24). Bernstein advocates a "concept of rationality [which is] not only intrinsically dialogical and communicative but places upon us the *practical* demand to work toward that form of democratic socialism" that Marcuse would wish (23). We must move past "determinate negation" and engage in those "forms of *praxis* that are still open to us" (Pippin 27). With such a critique in mind, and placing Marcuse and Adorno alongside Burke and Freire, we are prompted to ask whether generative magic language must be socially estranged, or might be socially engaged.

CHAPTER 5

Grimoires and Witches

"Advertising, Magic and Behaviorism all say the same thing—invoke often!"

—"transcendental Agnostic" Robert Anton Wilson (Adler 396)

ARRESTING THE NEW AGE

The 1993 Conference on College Composition and Communication, held in San Diego, added a three-hour "California Psychic Fair" to its program. In its advertisement of the April 1 fair, the sort of drollery one would expect from academics describing such an enterprise is strikingly absent:

> This day has been set aside by our predecessors for praising the symbolic foolishness of humanity. A Fool's Journey is represented in the deck of Tarot cards by card "0" of the major Arcana. It represents the taking of chances.
>
> The Metaphysical Awareness Project of San Diego is providing some of the best intuitive counselors, gifted readers often referred to as psychics, to interpret various oracular tools for your personal insight. If you have ever been curious about Tarot cards, astrology, and other forms of intuitive counseling, here's the chance to partake of short individual readings and sit in on many symposiums on the modern role some of these ancient practices play. (80)

The initial nod to foolishness here is quickly displaced by the characterization of magic in favorable, even erudite terms that are allied with both academic education and psychotherapy: "intuitive counselors" offer "symposiums" and interpretive "readings" that develop "personal insight." While this episode of welcome for the semblances of magic at our major national conference on English studies is not an indicator of any official rapprochement of the magical and academic worlds, it is one of many signs that magic has reacquired significant visibility in Western culture, and shares the lexicon of more legitimate institutions and practices.

Magic today "attracts more people than at any time since the end of the Middle Ages" (Galbreath in Kerr 13). The numbers of professional astrologers and psychic counselors in this country now reaches into the hundreds of thousands, and horoscopes reach millions (Eliade, *Occultism* 59): between 1967 and 1987, the percentage of daily newspapers running a horoscope column rose from less than 1 percent to 84 percent, constituting the "only significant upward change" during that period (Bogart 196–97). Witchcraft has also become more popular and visible: recent surveys count as many as eighty thousand witches or "pagans" [polytheists who worship nature and practice magic rituals] in the United States; dozens of major pagan and wiccan festivals take place each year; a correspondence course in witchcraft has enrolled more than forty thousand students since the late 1970s; and there are well over one hundred pagan and wiccan newsletters and journals (Adler 418–37; 475–544). The witchcraft manual that we will examine below, Starhawk's *The Spiral Dance*, sold fifty thousand copies between 1979 and 1985, and was reissued in a revised tenth anniversary edition in 1989. For readers, magic is a popular choice, and the literature of magic is widely available, as T. S. Luhrmann points out:

> More occult stores have been and continue to be opened. And in the last twenty years the detective novel has been replaced by fantasy and science fiction as the light fiction of majority choice. Fantasy fiction can be a powerful inducement to magical practice, because . . . the fiction and the practice share many characters, themes and ideals. In the last five or ten years most readers of Tolkien, C. S. Lewis, or Ursula LeGuin have been able to find a local bookstore with instruction books on how to recreate the sort of magico-religious practice characteristic of this fiction, and there quite likely see an advertisement for a coven or a magical course. These bookstores, and the sections on the occult and mythology in old bookstores, have appeared for the most part within the last ten years [e.g., in the decade of the 1980s]. (339)

Robert Galbreath adds that "The most recent occult bibliography of value annotates 1,856 original and reprinted English-language books published in just five years, 1971–75, a figure that confirms earlier statistics of a publishing boom in the occult" (Kerr 20).

The popularity of astrology, witchcraft, and fantasy fiction coincides with widely available instruction in therapeutic techniques for achieving cosmic harmony, such as yoga and transcendental meditation; ecological movements, programs, and policies with origins in nature-worship; increased acceptance of medical and nutritional treatments based upon Eastern mystical practices, such as acupuncture and Ayurvedic medicine; and the proliferation of sometimes dangerous and often bizarre religions such as the Universal Life Church, the Nudist Christian Church of the Blessed Virgin Jesus, and the Branch Davidians.

Numerous theoretical explanations of this occult revival appeared in the 1970s and 1980s, locating its beginnings in the antiwar movements of the 1960s, and in the correspondent urgency during that period for alternatives to the "establishment." The commercial success of magical practices is attributable to both the tolerance that marked post-Vietnam society (Luhrmann 339), and the continuing perception of ourselves as "surrounded by machines, bureaucracies, technologies and planning systems made by human rationality but unfathomable to us personally" (O'Keefe 458); of ourselves as bound spiritually, physically, and intellectually by the limitations of Western thought (Adler 351–71; O'Keefe 561–69; Luhrmann 337–44). Magic answers the need to recast what we perceive as an oppressive and ineffectually complex environment, into *a different form*. It tells us that we can change consciousness and affect reality as we see it through ritual interaction with the natural and cosmological worlds; here, for instance, is Starhawk's "anger spell":

> Visualize a circle of light around yourself. Cup a BLACK STONE in your hands and raise it to your forehead. Concentrate and project all your anger into the stone. With all your might, hurl it out of the circle into a lake, stream, river, or the ocean. Say:
>
> With this stone
> Anger be gone.
> Water bind it,
> No one find it.
>
> Earth the power. Release the circle. (To be done alongside flowing water.) (*Spiral Dance* 130)

Enacting such a spell is not, as Starhawk warns, "a matter of simply emoting." She echoes philosophers of magic like Ficino and

Agrippa with her recognition that the transformation of consciousness depends upon a sympathetic universe populated by a dynamic complexity of forces and energies, a universe so complex as to make any certain invocation impossible. The efficacy of a spell depends upon the right balance of desires, emotions, unconscious motivations, socioeconomic and political forces, and natural cycles (126–27).

However, it is not the subtlety of magic that accounts for its general appeal. Magic spells and incantations are essentially formulaic, and when the cosmos of contingencies for their effective use is set aside in the wake of their popularization, magic becomes interconnected with—indeed, often indistinguishable from—the very forces of mechanism that it may claim to mitigate. Shirley MacLaine indicates as much in an interview with Oprah Winfrey publicizing MacLaine's new video about "metaphysical well-being," called *Inner Workout*, which she characterizes as "techniques for consciousness" (1). The commercial success of magic—in venues such as MacLaine's video—depends upon its promise of efficient techniques. The protean mind is the magician's ideal, and efficiency is the technocrat's; the adaptation of magic to a technocratic culture leads to its considerable speeding-up, and the value of transforming consciousness becomes measured by the immediacy of results. When MacLaine tells Winfrey how crucial it is "to accelerate our own consciousness," Oprah brags a bit about her own efficient powers, recalling a time when it would take her weeks to recover from distress and develop a positive, harmonic relationship with her world, whereas now "it takes three hours or three minutes" (3).

MacLaine's advice on metaphysical well-being is, as Winfrey says, a counter to the "stress and conflict of everyday life" (1). With this purpose, magic retains its traditional function as a subversive, antisocial force, enacted by an individual who is capable of materializing multiple selves and playing multiple roles, of transforming her anger and anxiety into love and peace. To practice "aligning" oneself with the power to control consciousness," the initiate must (1) take full responsibility for her life; (2) think positive; (3) see herself and her world in mechanistic and systematic terms: the seven chakras, or levels of consciousness, constitute for MacLaine the "technology" that synchronizes us with the "solar mechanism Mother Earth" (3–4); and (4) perfect the combination of attitude and technology through everyday practice. For instance, if one is suffering the frustration of a "terrific argument" with a loved one,

MacLaine advises concentrating on those chakra colors that correspond with love and communication (green and blue): "Try mixing [colors]. After awhile, you get adept at this" (4). MacLaine's characterization of magic power is tied to traditional conceptions of phantasy and astral sympathies, with its emphasis on both visualization and the identification of human qualities with nonhuman analogs. But at the same time that this magic promises alternatives to damaging conventional life-states, it adapts itself to the management of critical attitudes and promotes automatism by identifying self-improvement with quick, patterned behavior.[1]

MacLaine's magic lessons are largely indistinguishable from popular advice that is not explicitly magical, but which promises increased personal power while it promotes behavior that arrests negative and unproductive states of mind:

> You can get rid of negative thoughts—and get on with your life—by following an expert's simple four-step program. . . . Admit that you don't know what's causing your problem. . . . Accept responsibility for your problem, but don't blame yourself for it. . . . Gain a fresh perspective. . . . Think positive. (*National Enquirer*, 31 January 1989; 6)

The proliferation of directives such as this in all the mass media typifies the commercialization of a need for magic that may have begun in the 1960s as a vehicle for personal and political revolution, but has been adapted to domestication. Spells that maintain a well-managed public, inculcated as a cultural lexicon, become the elements of mass literacy and define the maxims that constitute conventional public rhetoric; they are the substance of contemporary arresting magic. To construct a full and current definition of arresting magic as an imposition of the current American *fidei lumine*, as well as the inculcation of one-dimensional thinking, I now turn to the *National Enquirer*. Widely circulated and widely read by the American working class, the *Enquirer* represents the abbreviation of inquiry that constitutes American magic consciousness.

THE *NATIONAL ENQUIRER*

Taken together, the major supermarket tabloids—the *National Enquirer*, *Star*, *Globe*, *National Examiner*, *Sun*, and *Weekly*

World News—sell 14 million copies each week. The *Enquirer* is the most popular, selling about 4.3 million copies weekly and reaching eighteen million readers. It is read in ninety-one countries (on every continent except Antarctica), with a circulation of more than 80,000 copies weekly outside of the United States and Canada. Because the *Enquirer* appeals to and accounts for the leisure reading of a substantial number of the working class, it may be taken as an index to working class literacy.[2] The typical *Enquirer* reader is a woman who is not college-educated, with a household income of $27,000. According to a profile of the 1992 *Enquirer* audience, nearly 75 percent of its adult readers have not attended college, and nearly 34 percent are unemployed. About half are married with children. Women readers outnumber men more than 2 to 1.[3]

The *Enquirer* exemplifies the characteristics of arresting magic that we have touched upon repeatedly to this point:

1. Reductive simplification
2. Emphasis on patterned behavior, or sheer "motion"
3. Authorization in the centers of mass culture
4. Inculcation of the absolute
5. Valorization of normalcy[4]

Reductive Simplification

Most *Enquirer* stories are tethered—often explicitly—to a governing maxim; the repetition of very similar stories from issue to issue results in the same maxims "hammered and rehammered into the recipient's mind" (Marcuse, *One* 88), so that they become "proverbial" examples of the magic ritual formulas that Marcuse has in mind. A handful of "proverbs" recurs from issue to issue:

Self-Improvement is Simple. "Simply Eating Certain Foods Will Make You Smarter" (2 August 1988; 23); "Living A Long, Happy Life Is Easier Than You Think" (12 April 1988; 9); "52 Simple Tips That Will Put Thousands In Your Pocket" (12 January 1989; 6–7); "Lay Off The Beer, Stay Cool—& Other Cures For Infertility" (2 June 1992; 16); "How to Teach Your Kids Good Manners—The Easy Way" (14 July 1992; 22); "How To Ask Your Boss For A Raise—And Get It" (21 July 1992; 35); "Free and Easy Ways to Beat the Recession Blues"(3 November 1992; 3);

"Cleaning Your Ears Can Cure A Chronic Cough" (2 March 1993; 9); "52 Ways You Can Be Richer A Year From Now" ("Buy produce only when it's in season. . . . Do not take long showers. . . . Don't open the oven door to peek in when something's cooking! . . . Sew as much as possible") (23 March 1993; 10). Setting aside complexity and difficulty, while advertising discipline, articles such as these extend the American self-help tradition initiated in the eighteenth century by *Poor Richard's Almanac*; as Steven Starker argues, such homely Yankee advice exerts oracular power, and publications that feature it function as latter-day Delphic teachings (1–11).

Success Techniques Apply to Everyone. The *Enquirer* sets aside individuality along with complexity and difficulty. *Generalized* schematic advice—advertising better living through sameness—aligns success with following universal rules. There are five rules for handling mistakes on the job (22 December 1987; 12); seven rules for saving time in the kitchen (27 September 1988; 15); seven rules for getting a promotion (27 September 1988; 20); ten ingredients in the "recipe for a happy marriage" (23 August 1988; 13); and three steps to falling asleep (23 August 1988; 48). In a world where individual differences are homogenized into generalized behaviors, individual psychology is understood only as an instance of universal categories, so that "The Way You Celebrate Your Birthday Reveals Your Personality" (23 August 1988; 12), and there are just nine personalities to choose from; similarly, the way you take compliments, give gifts, and smile, along with your favorite ice cream flavor and the aromas you prefer, allow for self-typing.

Failure is an Attitude Problem. "Six Ways To Better Your Luck" (20 October 1992; 13) is one of the many schematic typologies that prescribe positive thinking and the acceptance of one's lot in life. To get lucky, you must (1) "Try New Things"; (2) "Never Risk More Than You Can Afford to Lose"; (3) "Let Your Talent Shine Through"; (4) "Let Others Know You're There"; (5) "Encourage 'Back Door' Luck" (a variation on the standard astrological advice we saw in chapter 4: do the disagreeable, because something good may come of it); and (6) "Be Persistent."

Success results from the imposition of mind—equipped with the prescribed rules and principles—over matter. And the proper mindset is a positive attitude, a Reaganesque image of "morning in America" in which sniveling about pains and problems is taboo (a regular *Enquirer* feature is "$10 for Happy Thoughts"). The sky diver whose chutes don't open saves himself by refusing to imagine his imminent death, and instead pictures his children, little Ben, a "fantastic little 4-year old, and "his 18-month-old brother Matt, with that dribbly chin that melts my heart." Determined not to die, he meditates himself into "a ball of fat, a rubber ball. I won't get hurt. I'll just melt into the earth or bounce off it," and bounce he does, surviving a two-mile fall (30 August 1988; 3). This is an extreme instance of the "you can be anything you wanna be" attitude that the *Enquirer* insists upon continually, through the very frequency of its success prescriptions.

Medical Technology Can Fix Anything. The power of attitude and discipline to make life better and better is rivaled by the power of technology, mainly medical technology. New machines, drugs, and surgical procedures can make blood clots disappear, eliminate hemorrhoids, remove fat, grow hair, smooth wrinkles, cure arthritis: "Laser Lung-Cancer Surgery Cuts Pain and Speeds Recovery" (14 July 1992; 43); "Amazing Machine Kills Cancer Anywhere In The Body" (27 October 1992; 19); "Doctors Repair World's Smallest Damaged Heart" (23 February 1993; 20); "New Device Can Predict Heart Attacks Years In Advance" (2 March 1993; 2). The general trust in technology is reflected in "Your Fantastic Future: Amazing Changes You'll See Soon," which include laser-powered spacecraft; refrigerated "mailboxes" for the home delivery of perishable food; telephones that translate foreign languages; robots who can drive trucks; video cameras as small as a postage stamp (16 June 1992; 21) While numerous *Enquirer* articles like these reveal such breakthroughs, the most strident and substantial appeal to those who want to make pain, age, and mortality disappear comes through *Enquirer* advertising, with its decided emphasis on fixing one's body. Typically, nearly half of the ads in each issue are selling skin treatments, body beautifiers, reducing programs, indigestion and pain relievers, or ambulatory aids.

Nobody's Safe. At the same time that discipline, attitude, and technology assure personal and professional success, anyone can become a victim or a freak. There are the Australians who are violently allergic to plastic and chemical additives, the little girls who are dying from exposure to light, the boy who won't grow, the boy who can't stop eating, the women who have been unable to stop having babies, the house possessed by demons, the legless Russian orphans, the pregnant man, the bride shot by her groom at their wedding, the woman with two wombs. And celebrities, the culture heroes of the *Enquirer*, are just as vulnerable: Liz Taylor fights back pain, alcoholism, and suicide; television star Alan Thicke is pursued by a terrifying lovesick fan; Ringo Starr fights drug addiction; Oprah Winfrey fails at weight control; Michael Landon and Audrey Hepburn—each portrayed as the epitome of moral virtue—die of cancer; Robert Reed—the TV father of the hyper-wholesome "Brady Bunch"—dies of AIDS; Burt Reynolds goes broke; Kristy McNichol confesses mental illness; Joan Lunden suffers a messy and expensive divorce. From issue to issue, the diseases, deaths, and divorces of the rich and famous illustrate a world of misfortune and tragedy from which no one is protected.[5]

Survival is in the Hands of Providence. A grizzly bear and a "man-eating crocodile" number among the murderous animals who miraculously leave off their attacks, to sighs of "thank God" from their victims. Renegade machines—airplanes, tanks, cars—level property while inhabitants leave unhurt, each repeating the sentiments of Stephen Bright, whose car was sliced in half by a runaway airplane, "I'll thank God every day for the miracle that saved my life" (18 October 1988; 3); and Phil Moulton who, after surviving the demolition of his car by a speeding freight train, is "convinced God engineered a life-saving miracle just for him" (12 May 1992; 7). Scapes from a monstrous death get Providential credit from issue to issue, reinforcing both the traditional belief that life-saving reversals of fortune are ordained by heavenly forces, and the powerlessness of individuals; Stephen Bright and Phil Moulton join the other *Enquirer* survivors who remind readers how easily life can be lost.

As an agent of good luck, the *Enquirer* joins God, advertising its power as an amulet for the suffering. Reading the *Enquirer* is itself featured as the way to survival and happiness. Once or twice a month, the paper prints testimony from grateful readers, who are paid $150 for the publication of "a letter in 75 words or less" that explains how the *Enquirer* has "made an impact on your life or helped you solve a problem." Petta Bourdreault writes, "Thank God for the NATIONAL ENQUIRER—it saved me from a lifetime of agony!" and explains that her seven years of "living in hell" with the pain of shingles ended with an *Enquirer* story about a new cream that "cleared up her pain completely" (2

August 1988; 17). "Hardened criminal" Harold Purnell read an Enquirer article about another criminal who went straight and graduated college, and was inspired to do the same. He graduated in prison and is now out and looking for a job. His father says, "I want to thank the ENQUIRER for helping give our son back to us. Our prayers have been answered" (16 June 1992; 31).

Altogether, the *Enquirer* names the world as, on the one hand, a threatening realm of inexplicable forces, and on the other, a realm where prescribed behavior and technology and a subscription to the *Enquirer* can overcome human pain and poverty. Its maxims define a Marcusean "circle of . . . conditions" that reduces the possibilities for human action, as they praise efficiently delimited solutions to life's problems, while warning that these are no insurance against disaster. Participating in the contradictory worlds of the *Enquirer* has its domesticating effect: one must meet each day with happy thoughts, discipline, and fear.

Emphasis on Patterned Behavior, or "Sheer Motion"

Any behavior that occurs as an *unwitting reduction of complexities* may be classed as motion rather than action. Kenneth Burke makes the distinction by saying that "insofar as a vote is cast without adequate knowledge of its consequences, one might even question whether it should be classed as an activity at all; one might rather call it passive, or perhaps sheer motion (what the behaviorists would call Response to a Stimulus)" (*Grammar* xx). Insofar as the magician creates "simple" solutions to complex problems, he is reducing the scope of human knowledge, reflection, and action to motion. One of the typical *Enquirer* formulas for overcoming personal problems, "Enquirer's No. 1 Plan To Conquer Shyness," developed by two university professors of psychiatry, reveals the magician of motion's work:

> Accept the fact that you are shy. . . . Realize that you have nothing to be afraid of. . . . Observe how confident people behave. Watch people who do well in social situations. . . . By following the advice in this plan you can greatly reduce your problem within a matter of weeks . . . and become happier, more popular and more successful." (22 November 1988: 2)

The emphasis here on watching and imitating, and the focus on repressing distress to reorder one's symptoms rather than investigate their causes (shyness sufferers are told to smile more, nod often, relax, and avoid whispering), is the typical *Enquirer* attempt to prescribe motion rather than action, patterned behavior rather than critical understanding or reflection.[6]

Authorization in the Centers of Mass Culture

Significantly, the creators of magic formulas are almost always university professors (mainly in social sciences and medicine), the class that inhabits an academic "otherworld" relative to the typical *Enquirer* reader who has not been to college. The magicians of culture—those who either invent formulas for success (the professors) or have themselves been transformed by the magic of determination, discipline, and luck (the celebrities)—are called, respectively, "experts" and "insiders." They are secular oracles speaking to a working class on the margins of the happiness, popularity, and success that formulas for self-improvement promise to recover.

Inculcation of the Absolute

The chant of maxims and prescriptions that recurs through each *Enquirer* identifies knowledge with the invariable, suggests that learning about the world means remembering facts and procedures, and proposes that *any* fact is worth knowing. The bimonthly feature that lists miscellaneous statistics, "What Happened Since You Last Read The Enquirer" (recently retitled "What Happened Since Last Week"), joins the other numerical facts that make headlines in each issue, all restating the importance of simplistic empiricism: "Video rentals soar 1900 percent in five years . . . 8 in 10 grocery shoppers bring along coupons . . . 1 in 4 students is a college grad . . . last week Americans spent almost $2 million on maps and atlases . . . last week Americans bought 24,000 guitars, mandolins, banjos and ukeleles . . . there are over 41,000 pizzerias in the U.S." (3 January 1989). This is the *Enquirer* narrative of American life: if it can't be quantified and memorized, it didn't *happen*; if it can be quantified, it's worth knowing. It's not that some things count more than others; whatever can be counted, counts. This is often apparent in *Enquirer* assessments of an individual's success. Johnny Carson is measured by a statistical inventory:

> Johnny has asked his guests more than 110,000 questions over the past 30 years. Some 83 guest hosts have taken Johnny's seat.

> More than three million people have sat in the audience at "Tonight Show" tapings. . . . Last year he earned $2380 for each minute on the air. (19 May 1992; 20)[7]

Valorization of Normalcy

Paulo Freire distinguishes social integration from social adaptation, associating the latter with "magic consciousness":

> *Integration* with one's context, as distinguished from *adaptation*, is a distinctively human activity. Integration results from the capacity to adapt oneself to reality *plus* the critical capacity to make choices and to transform that reality. To the extent that man loses his ability to make choices and is subjected to the choices of others, to the extent that his decisions are no longer his own because they result from external prescriptions, he is no longer integrated. Rather, he has adapted. He has "adjusted." Unpliant men, with a revolutionary spirit, are often termed "maladjusted." (*Education* 4)

Enquirer magic appeals to the desire for normalcy. Shyness, weakness, anxiety, anger, disaffection, and infidelity are debilitating maladjustments. They make happiness, popularity, and success less likely; they make one more like the *Enquirer* freaks of nature, who represent what it means to be abnormal. Nobody's safe, but normalcy, with its attendant docility, is a hedge against adversity.

Repugnance for the abnormal is generally indicated by the *Enquirer's* anglocentrism and homophobia. Apart from regular pieces dealing with the weight and emotional problems of Oprah Winfrey, who has joined the pantheon of celebrity-freaks, and occasional exposés of scandalous behavior by Whoopi Goldberg or Bryant Gumbel, the *Enquirer* presents a white world. Significantly, one of the few black noncelebrities featured in the *Enquirer*, Harold Purnell (see above), is a convicted felon; and another, Lydia Phelo, is a South African peasant involved in witchcraft: the nonwhite world is not inviting. Neither is the gay world: homosexuals are either dying of AIDS or living as freaks, to be feared in either case, as typical headlines suggest: "Nine Out Of Ten Vote No On Gay Scoutmasters" (6 October 1992; 42); "Should Gays Be Allowed In The Military" (1 December 1992; 20); "Wynonna Judd Fights Back: I'm No Lesbian" (12 January 1993; cover); "Fancy Dressing Transvestite Gets In The Fast Lane

With Three Stolen Caddies" (16 March 1993; 7).

Recall that the *Enquirer* magicians are usually university professors whose work contributes to both the formulaic management of abnormality and the ideology of career success. Their characterization as *Enquirer* "experts" alerts us to the ambiguous position of the academy and academics; the more proximate the academy's mission and one's own work is to the tenets of motion that inform mass culture, the more it is likely to entail arresting magic. The professors attacked by the *Enquirer* are those on the margins of practicality, who get government grants for projects that offer no obvious or immediate benefits for mainstream Americans; a typical attack, "Should You Foot The Bill To Dig Up Ancient Mexico," responds with outrage to a National Science Foundation $73,000 grant for studying "Prehistoric Political Economy in Mesoamerica's Northern Periphery" (24 January 1989: 30). "Bug-Brains Bite Taxpayers for $200,000—To Study Ants" (19 May 1992; 14) once again criticizes the NSF (a frequent target), and makes clear that while advancements in technology and behaviorism are admirable, the work of "hard" or "pure" science is inefficient and impractical waste.

With its emphasis on the importance of normalcy, rather than the paranormal and the lurid (qualities which—although formerly associated with the *Enquirer* [Kerr 6, 196]—are now featured in the more offbeat, low-budget, and *Enquirer*-owned *Weekly World News*), the *Enquirer* asks to be taken seriously (a colleague of mine recently cut his attention to the *Enquirer* in a popular culture course because "it isn't sleazy enough," its pseudojournalism is too subtle, too factual, too difficult to dismiss). While regular *Enquirer* readers may be aware of its negative reputation, the paper's straight-faced appeal to conservative mainstream values, the apparent veracity of its prescriptions and statistics, and its disdain for complexity and confusion, assure it a good measure of credibility. Elizabeth Bird concludes from a series of interviews with readers that they neither fully believe nor disbelieve tabloid content, entertaining it "as if" it were true, in a kind of "what if" way (151). Women readers are especially likely to imagine themselves as, for instance, Elizabeth Taylor, in an act of "resistance to everyday realities and [as] material for play" (160):

> The dominant reading of tabloids places them as an example of . . . "the accommodative culture" of the working class, a cul-

> ture which, although accommodated within the dominant ideology, may be at odds with it. I believe the tabloids are to some extent an alternative way of looking at the world that may be valuable to people who feel alienated from dominant narrative forms and frames of reference. (160)

Bird is careful to qualify this conclusion, and finally very skeptical about cultural studies arguments that tabloids can be read in infinite ways, and that readers can use them as a mode of resistance, exploiting their ambiguity.[8] She recognizes the phenomenon that I have documented with the *Enquirer*, that such tabloids work to control readers, and her conclusion emphasizes this as arresting magic:

> The tabloid charms its readers and beckons them into a world where life is dangerous and exciting. But when the journey is done, it soothes them with assurances that, be it ever so humble, there really is no place like home. (209)

Taking the *Enquirer* seriously, reading it with some measure of belief and hope, does mean demonstrating a literacy limited by the information, ideals, and attitudes that the paper enfranchises; a literacy limited by the dictates of arresting magic; a literate susceptibility to the coercive reduction of the possibilities for action. Such a conclusion need not castigate readers as unwitting victims, so much as those for whom the culture and its educators perhaps do not offer much in the way of alternatives to arresting magic. To the extent that mass media generally advertise a reductive, technocratic ideology of adaptation, they are arresting magi. More important, to the extent that education and educators generally advertise a reductive, technocratic ideology of adaptation, they promote Enquirerey rather than inquiry.[9] The very identification of magic with cultural literacy and the rhetoric it grounds "problematizes" the role of the teacher-magician, calling into question every act of education-as-normalization as the invocation of a tabloid epistemology.

MAGIC NUGGETS AND THE VOGUE OF TABLOID EPISTEMOLOGY

A 1993 television commercial for *TV Guide* says, "People love nuggets . . . little bits and pieces," touting the format that was initiated when tabloid-king Rupert Murdoch bought the magazine in 1988: a grab-bag of very brief articles, each offering "the visual equivalent of the 'sound bite'" (Altschuler 85). Small capsules of celebrity gossip, show business statistics, and TV reviews and previews crowd pages that had been devoted—from the 1960s through the early 1980s—to longer, more serious and critical pieces sometimes written by prominent artists and scholarly essayists (Altschuler 67). The "Fact File" is a typical nugget in recent *Guides*,[10] displaying a few television-related statistics printed on a square inch of space designed to resemble an index card; one Fact File presents the "wish list" of Smithsonian Institution curator Ellen Hughes:

> One of Lucy's housedresses from *I Love Lucy*
> An Ollie puppet from *Kukla, Fran and Ollie*
> Beaver's baseball cap from *Leave It To Beaver*
> Mouseketeer ears from *The Mickey Mouse Club*
> A bow tie from Dave Garroway, first host of *Today*
> Groucho's duck from *You Bet Your Life*
> A *Captain Video* cosmic-ray vibrator
> Bill Cosby's *I Spy* tennis sweater (*TV Guide*, 8–14 August 1992; 5)

In nuggets such as this, as with the *Enquirer* presentation of Johnny Carson as an aggregate of statistics, an inventory of facts and artifacts obviates the existence of people themselves: Dave Garroway becomes a bow tie.[11] Another regular *Guide* nugget, "What I Watch," profiles celebrities by listing their favorite television shows: in effect, each individual becomes the analog to that list, in another exercise that points up the viability, and star-appeal, of itemizing identity.

The publishers of our most popular mass market magazines tie reader-appeal to proffering great numbers of easily digestible pieces, with good reason. With its nuggets format, *TV Guide* has maintained "the largest circulation in publishing history" (about sixteen million copies per issue; Altschuler 3, 80) as it competes with a growing number of similar local and regional television weeklies. The *Enquirer* has also been advertising its longstanding nuggets-format recently, with covers that not only boast "Largest Circulation Of Any Paper In America," but also trumpet the sheer number of items in each issue, with "Over 100 Features Every

Week"; some of these features are as long as 750 words, others less than 50 words, each readable in a few minutes or less, with the longer features frequently organized as an enumeration of brief points.

Putting information in small, concisely worded packages coincides with the abbreviation, acceleration, compartmentalization, and quantification that have come to define widely practiced forms of reading, writing, and thinking, and are also central to arresting magic rhetoric.[12] Arresting magic often corresponds with brief and efficient rhetorical forms: for the magus who wants control, the traditional goal has been a singular invocation with an instant result, a "let there be such-and-such." However, the abbreviation and fragmentation that we are moved to reject as elements of debilitating sorcery in tabloids and the like have become common features of writing and broadcasting that claim—with the seriousness missing in the *Enquirer's* tongue-in-cheek appeal to "inquiring minds"—to promote critical thinking. The oldest American high-brow magazine, *Harper's*, was recently reformulated into a colloquy of snippets and provocative statistics, with its editor explaining the change as an acquiescence to new ways of reading and a renovation of the intellectual landscape; the "new" *Harper's* and Lewis Lapham's apology will occupy us presently. Along with the print media, a proliferation of television talk shows—each typically featuring a panel of discussants interacting with audience members over a controversial and often sensational moral or ethical issue—presents the interaction of brief views as an irresolute public forum that generates multiple perspectives without enforcing consensus. The wide popularity of the nuggets-format, in print and on screen, prompts us to consider it more fully as a qualitative indicator of the magic—normative or transformative—at work.

Starting at the "top," I would call attention to the centrality of nuggets epistemology in postmodern academic scholarship. Ihab Hassan's 1980 *The Right Promethean Fire*, an extended juxtaposition of extracts from philosophy, criticism, science, and Hassan's personal journal, has become a well-known representation of the "acute self-consciousness [of] the formal interrogation of forms" now identified with much postmodern discourse and its bias against extended linear development (xvii; see also Hassan, *Dismemberment*). For intellectuals such as Hassan, the avowed purpose of arraying bits and pieces is not an appeal to easy and efficient reading. Quite the contrary: Hassan presents fragments of thought in order to invite interaction among them, as the enactment of a creative imagination explicitly characterized as magical, as a colloquy of invocations that comprise a multivocation:

> Imagination, I confess, is my arch theme; teleological or not, it makes our future, *is* our fate, though we may come to it soon or late. Conjoined to that theme are other recurrent themes: desire, hope, change; ambitions and afflictions of the humanities; the immanence of language, the indeterminacies of knowledge and action; a new play between wholes and parts, or the One and the Many as philosophers used to say; politics, history, the transhumanization of the earth; the role of mind—self-made and from itself concealed—in the universe; death, first literally, then as metaphor of change, finally as a language the cosmos speaks to us when we calm our fears. Are these fit topics or tropes for a gnostic Prometheus? . . . In any case, a study of the postmodern imagination may be forgiven some defamiliarization, deformation, of traditional forms. (xvi–xvii)

It would seem that thought-nuggets can be placed in the service of entirely different kinds of magic. Some kinds of montages—those in the tabloids, for example—seem to domesticate the imagination, while others activate it. This is certainly the position of *Harper's* editor Lewis Lapham, who finds himself caught between Ihab Hassan and the *Enquirer*, as a card-carrying intellectual who wants to increase the circulation of his magazine. Lapham suggests that when bits-and-pieces are themselves epistemological (prompts for reflection and critique) more than ideological (maxims for the governance of readers) they activate the kind of reading and thinking we have associated here with generative magic and the composing imagination, and counter the arresting effects of mass media that may themselves employ similar rhetorical forms. Lapham's justification for his own postmodern editorial practice begins with the recognition that, by the early 1980s, nuggets are common units of discourse. The sensibility that defines the "spirit of the age" had been formed by new media technologies that produce shorter, more filmic, and more wildly juxtaposed texts. Visual and print media have become variations of MTV (Lapham 6). I would add that the very ubiquity of formalized fragmentation and provocative juxtaposition in postmodern mass media makes its defamiliarizing and disruptive function (which Hassan hoped for in 1980) unlikely. Lapham seems to understand this with his recognition of the spirit of the age, and his view that the new *Harper's* is distinguished not by a disorienting postmodern form, but by a lyrical and elitist sensibility. Writing in 1992, Lapham is explaining and celebrating the 1983 revision of *Harper's* that introduced new definitive features that correspond to the MTV model as they attempt "to convey a sense of the world's ambiguity and surprise" (7). Observing that these changes put him in league with the tabloids, Lapham is at great pains to insist that the venerable *Harper's* is not becoming the *Enquirer*, and that the features he associates with ambiguity and surprise are qualitatively different from similar features one might encounter in mass media that "say what the greatest number of people wish them to say" (7). Such media are portrayed in sophistic and magical terms, as the productions of "flatterers" who create a "preferred reality" (7).

Lapham's apology tries to aggrandize and distinguish writing that appears nonetheless to cater to an acknowledged short attention span and appetite for nuggets, those "shorter texts" that are definitive cultural commonplaces. The *Harper's* sections debuting in 1983 are the Index, the Readings, the Forum and the Annotation. The Readings section exhibits fifteen or twenty excerpts and adaptations of longer works, ranging from about 150 words to about 2,000, generally treating political and social issues or offering part of a novel or poem. The Forum arrays the concise views of as many as a dozen differing experts—sometimes in dialogue with one another, sometimes not—on some trenchant topic, for instance, pornography, defense spending, urban gangs, abortion, Iraq-gate. The Annotation presents five or six paragraphs that each interpret a particular item or statistic on a crowded document; for instance, Michael Moynihan points to a few key places on the U.S. government's large table of figures defining the Gross Domestic Product (December 1992, 46–47). With these features—all assemblages of short pieces—Lapham hopes to provide "narrative and metaphor" which, though couched in the provocative, brief forms that have become common to media generally, serve the purpose of generating rather than arresting thought: they are meant to be "epistemological, not ideological."

Harper's Index is the foremost and most popular of its features (recently published in a book-length version called *What Counts*). The monthly Index lists about 40 different but implicitly related offbeat statistics:

Chances that a viewer of an Amy Fisher TV movie can cite a reason for the war in Bosnia: 1 in 5

Chances that a person who has not seen an Amy Fisher TV movie can cite a reason for the war in Bosnia: 1 in 3 (April 1993; 11)

Number of calories in a chocolate chip cookie baked according to Hillary Clinton's recipe : 68

Number of calories in a chocolate chip cookie baked according to Barbara Bush's recipe : 75

Ratio of the number of times President Bush has had his hair cut this year to the number of time Bill Clinton has: 2:1 (October 1992; 11)

In Lapham's view, the Index is a "common folk tale" of American humanity, which invites judgments even as it suspends them:

> Fitted to almost any topical reference, a statistic or a percentage point counts as a closing argument, a proof of virtue, or a judgment of Heaven . . . although in no way definitive, [the Index] marks the weight of the world's desire. ("Notebook" 8)

Both *Harper's* and the mass media respond to the world's desire for closure, virtue, and judgment, but Lapham charges that the latter do so with statistics that sell abstraction and sensation, preferring "data to ideas, celebrity to non-celebrity, allegory to history" (8). Disclaimers aside, Lapham does follow the lead of tabloidism as well as avant-garde postmodernism, conforming *Harper's* to the fragmentation of mass culture and the quantitative measurement of people and events, while assuring readers that "we" at *Harper's* are better than "they" (mass media) are: we enclose you in narrative and metaphor and don't push you around, while they enclose you in faceless, vague facts; our writers and editors have open minds, while they are ideologues motivated by profit. But thought-control and a profit-motive are not inimical to *Harper's*. Like Rupert Murdoch, Lapham knows that nuggets sell. The reformulation of *Harper's* into bits and pieces is an explicit marketing strategy, which Lapham appreciates as a success when he notes that circulation has increased by 1992 to a break-even figure of 202,000.

And as the magazine becomes more like the tabloids it disdains,[13] the erudite readership with which it would identify is maintained by the ideology of the Index enthymemes that inform its statistics (Lapham recognizes the enthymemic quality of the Index, saying that it comprises "closing arguments"). The enthusiasm for facts in general that we find in the *Enquirer* is replaced by the selection of Index facts that flatter a politically liberal audience who disdains and mocks mass culture. "We" smile at the Amy Fisher watchers who suffer from global illiteracy. We are gloating progressive types who caricature conservative values, ready to conclude from the juxtaposition of cookie-recipe calories and presidential haircut habits that overweight or fastidious people are likely to be Republicans. We are the insiders whose occultism lies in our talent for detecting "hidden" meaning in the calculated juxtapositions written by our peers.

In short, *Harper's* and the "we" it represents suggest that the avowal of a generative intellect—however rhapsodic—may disguise arresting forces. Any appeal for regular "subscribers" must define and conserve the "market" of beliefs, values, abilities, and desires that subscribers represent; such an appeal is then, in effect, the creation of a cult. Maintaining a cultish mentality in readers, while promoting the vision of a critical polis engaged with a pluriverse of volubility, may be the paradox attending any nuggets-format vigorously directed away from the proles and claiming critical thinking as its goal.

The Book of the Subgenius revels viciously in that paradox. Appearing in 1983 (the year of the "new" *Harper's*), this production of the mysterious "Subgenius Foundation" spoofs the American urgency for "instant answers to everything" with a 193-page surrealistic collage that elaborates "the sacred teachings of J. R. 'Bob' Dobbs" and his Church of the Subgenius. The *Book* acknowledges our vulnerability to arresting magic with a comic version of social critique in which nuggets of wisdom are admitted as fool's gold, and ideology is a commodity. Its comedy has gained a following: the *Book* has sold nearly 40,000 copies, and produced two sequels, the 1990 *Three-Fisted Tales of Bob* and the forthcoming *Revelation X*.[14] Membership in the Church has been estimated in the hundreds of thousands (Kinney 86). Officials of the Church tour the country regularly, holding Subgenius "Devivals" where they preach the word of Bob and sell T-shirts, books, video tapes, and Church memberships (at $20 each).

The *Book* juxtaposes distorted, cartoonish throwbacks to 1950s magazine ads and science fiction movies, double columns of small print exhorting Bob's teachings, and a barrage of Church mottos and maxims. Thus, at the same time that it illustrates postmodern de-formation, the Subgenius world is like a bad, campy 1950s movie, complete with horrible but inexplicable threats (invasion by aliens), a heroic paragon of normalcy (Bob), and a vague plot—pun always intended—full of sensationalism but void of clear causality. This is a world of phantasy gone wild, and accordingly the Church teachings are products of a protean sophistry: "We must *transcend style* through *nonstop style metamorphosis*. . . . The Teachings contradict each other and yet remain equally true and false" (*Book* 18–19):

SLOGANS

"Fuck 'Em If They Can't Take A Joke"

"Too Much Is Always Better Than Not Enough"

"Pull the Wool Over Your Own Eyes"

"You'll *Pay* To Know What You *Really* Think" (*Book* 7)

Bob's teachings equip Subgenii with the complete cynicism that allows them to make intellectual "PLAY into a *paying profession* or Life Scam" (67) in order to counteract the cultural agents of thought control, abandon all fixed ideas and values, and "slack off":

> *You see what you want to see.*
>
> *So you have to pay to know what you think. You pay Them.*
>
> They've got you so closed off from what you're REALLY SEEING, and have made your most instinctive hopes and desires seem so "impossible" or "impractical" in the *quote* "real world" *unquote*, that you're still looking where *they're* pointing rather than *just looking around*. You can SEE what CAN lie ahead if you'll just *slow down*.
>
> Don't pay them to know what you really think. *Pay "Bob."* It's *much cheaper.* Besides, you owe "Bob" a living. But then, the entire WORLD owes YOU a living. (15)

The earliest Church literature dates to the late 1970s, but Church head Ivan Stang claims he became involved with "Bob" as early as the 1950s. J. R. "Bob" Dobbs is described as a former bit actor and aluminum siding salesman who gathered a following around his professed clairvoyance. "A shadowy figure in the tradition of L. Ron Hubbard and Howard Hughes" (Kinney 86), the Bob of the *Book* is a mythologized composite of American male types and archetypes. Bob's face, filling the cover of the *Book* and appearing dozens of times throughout, resembles Hugh Hefner, especially given the pipe always clenched between smiling teeth. The Hefneresque Bob is a sexual dynamo who is "ALL MAN to all women" (23). But he is also the stereotypical "family man" of the Robert Young/*Father Knows Best* variety who is devoted to his wife Connie; a prophet who warns of doom; a time and space traveler (we read of "Bob sightings" that place him among ancient cultures and in other galaxies); a cosmic warrior who fights star wars against alien invaders; and "the High Sales Man of the SubGenius" (24). He is the always-ironic, guiltless supermerchant, with the power to make himself into anyone in order to get everything:

> J. R. "Bob" Dobbs: on the surface, an average, good-looking all-American "Joe," though of debated parentage; perpetual smoker of a sacred briar Pipe filled with mysterious and, some claim, hallucinatory admixtures; master omni-salesman of legendary abilities (very probably the historical "Traveling Salesman" of mythology) . . . recognized as Patron Saint of Salesmen the world over . . . prophesied savior of the dogma-following and dues-paying Chosen on *X-Day*, July 5, 1998, when his "customers" *the Xists* arrive from "Planet X"; Honorary Pilot of the pleasure-saucer Escape Vessels of the Sex Goddesses; and captain of the Church softball team. (Stang, *Three-Fisted Tales* 15)

> "Bob" is, was, and ever shall be. "Bob" is you. "Bob" is me. "Bob" is the Kama Sutra, the Id, the light that glows in the heart and mind of EVERY free-thinking SubGenius. And "Bob" is a man. (*Book* 15)

The magical ubiquity of the godhead is a traditional religious and magical trope. As Stang mimics it here, we note the close resemblance to current portrayals of the Goddess that are central to current feminist witchcraft and magic:

> The primary symbol for "That-Which-Cannot-Be Told" is the Goddess. The Goddess has infinite aspects and thousands of names—She is the reality behind many metaphors. She *is* reality, the manifest deity, omnipresent in all of life, in each of us. The Goddess is not separate from the world—She *is* the world, and

> all things in it: moon, sun, earth, star, stone, seed, flowing river, wind, wave, leaf and branch, bud and blossom, fang and claw, woman and man. (Starhawk, *Spiral Dance* 22)

Starhawk strikes the tone of great ethical seriousness that Stang's parody of transformative self-improvement subverts. The Church teaches that our need for magic makes us gullible (Levine), liable to accede to the fervently serious beliefs of either The Conspiracy or Dupes of the Conspiracy, which—taken together—fight out "The Battle For Men's Minds" that occupies 99.9 percent of the population of the earth (*Book* 112). "Bob's" transcendent cult is a parody cult: a cult of laughter against the pretense and paranoia that enfranchise idolatries, including the idolatry of the surrealistic form that the *Book* represents:

> [The Church of the Subgenius] is the ultimate secret order for those who "know better" but who demand in their *LUST for GRINS* a spectacular, special-effects laden belief system—a *'stuporstition.'* . . . The Church provides *sure answers* and *miracles* in the service of *SURREAVOLUTION*. (*Book* 12)

Lewis Lapham romanticizes fragmentation as redemptive critical thinking, with paeans to the wisdom and community potential in the Index nuggets; the Church of the Subgenius sees the selling of intellectual license as sorcery among sorceries, just another ploy to get to our pockets through our need to worship the power of something, rather than the everything-cum-nothing embodied by Bob. In sum, the Church of the Subgenius would arrest all of the serious world. While Marcuse's Great Refusal would counter the commodification of culture with a retreat into phantasy practiced as a serious philosophical critique, the Church would explode the Marcuseans along with everyone else, in a riotous acknowledgment that—as Burke, Adorno, and Marcuse fear—the worship of money-as-god-term is universal, and the only effective counter magic is transcendence through nonstop style metamorphosis, the rhetorical facility that evades all bids for belief, and markets whatever stance will sell.

As former Church of the Subgenius potentate Jay Kinney warns, "Consider it all a joke at your own risk" (89). Noting similarities between the Church's devaluation of all moral authority and the tenets of the John Birch Society and the Libertarian Party, Kinney worries that the Church's widespread cynicism is a license for widespread hatred, epitomized at a San Francisco "Devival" by performing Subgenius Guy Deuel, who "looks uncannily like G. Gordon Liddy" as he fondles an Uzi (86). Mindful that the postmodern suspicion and fragmentation of all master narratives may lead to the dissolution of justice,[15] Kinney fears that the Church's absolute cynicism is tantamount to fascism. Sharing that fear, we note that Bob's world is a white phallocracy, and that the officials and members of the Church, and readers of the *Book*, are mainly young men (Miner interview; *Book* 6). In view of this segregated cabal, we must question our laughter at the magic nuggets of wisdom preached by the Church of the Subgenius: while they mock the arresting magic that has its mainstream expression in the *Enquirer* and its genteel analog in *Harper's*, they enfranchise a class of readers united in the practice of deconstruction that is—in terms of both its sexism and its glorification of contempt—cavalier.

OPRAH AND THE WITCHES

> But critical analysis must dissociate itself from that which it strives to comprehend; the philosophic terms must be other than the ordinary ones in order to elucidate the full meaning of the latter. (Marcuse, *One-Dimensional Man* 195)

> We are of all different colors and different faiths, but, again, we are all human beings and we should love each other just because we're human beings, not because of color. (Audience member, "My Parent is a Racist," *The Oprah Winfrey Show* 15)

As language play becomes an ordinary phenomenon, it enforces rather than disrupts the established universe, and its ostensible innovation becomes merely a familiar mode of entertainment. But the television talk show advertises the "play" of language as both entertaining and transformative, offering episodes of New Age therapy during which the performance of open dialogue would effect the better health of participants and viewers. The majority of typical talk show topics speak to social and psychological issues and problems (the following aired between February 18 and March 16, 1992):

> Agressive behavior of successful women; interracial love and marriage; overweight women; violence in families; practicing safe sex; male sexual problems; homosexuals in the military; battered women in hiding; abusive men; communication

> between men and women; feminine beauty standards; women's roles in the 90s; family therapy; obsessive plastic surgery; black women criticize black men; teenage feminists; overweight children and parents; date rape; marriage—pro and con; tabloids and the news; desperate people denied health care; abusive boyfriends; gay stereotypes; couples considering divorce; obsessive gambling; obsessive dieting; drug-addicted babies; solutions for gang warfare; unemployment.

Transformative therapy—the curing of the many ills that this list features—is the explicit purpose of the most popular television talk show, *The Oprah Winfrey Show*, which is seen by nearly 13 million viewers every weekday.

Oprah Winfrey is a magical figure in two respects. Earning 46 million dollars a year, she is a superstar celebrity goddess, whose otherworldly status is indicated by the elevation of her name to "Oprah" alone. And she is a medicine-woman, a shaman, a self-appointed charismatic healer who believes—as the episode with Shirley MacLaine (discussed above) indicates—in the magic power of a positive attitude, and whose show simulates the communal abreaction associated with medical magic.[16] Winfrey often voices her dedication to personal and social reform, and has said that "my show tackles the root of all the problems in the world—lack of self-esteem" ("Everybody's Talking" 12). As part of her mission to help individuals to like themselves and others better, Winfrey regularly presents programs that address family conflicts—among spouses, siblings, parents and children—in the professed hope that the airing of disagreements in a public forum will lead to understanding and resolution. A successful show—as Winfrey indicates with her championing of positive thinking and self-esteem—is one in which warring factions rededicate themselves to one another, or promise to do so, or one in which there are affirmative expressions of therapeutic self-discovery, as with the audience member's declaration of universal love (quoted above), voiced seconds before the final commercial break.

Intent upon global as well as domestic issues, Winfrey presented twelve programs on racism in 1992; the program we will examine here was the sixth in that series, titled "My Parent Is a Racist." As is typical, this program features a panel of noncelebrities with life experiences related to the topic: Ron, a middle-aged white man, appears with his teenaged daughter Lanette, who once infuriated Ron by dating a Mexican. Gloria, a middle-aged white woman, has called her daughter Daphne a "nigger lover" for having black friends. Carole is a middle-aged white woman who can't accept her daughter Melissa's black boyfriend, Brian. Following the presentation of panel members' stories, joined by comments and questions from the audience, nearly every *Oprah* show brings on an "expert," usually a psychologist, who interprets the situations that have been described and outlines behaviors that can produce healthier relationships. On "My Parent Is A Racist," the expert is Jane Elliott, a lecturer on race relations, whose appearance is striking precisely because it shuts down dialogue: Elliot dismisses the comments of the panel and the audience—including the woman above who voices the importance of loving one another—with uncompromising candor.

I would like to use Jane Elliott's appearance to return to the question that closed chapter 4, and which I have held in suspension while establishing more fully the arresting magics of the New Age; that is, must generative magic language be socially estranged, or might it be socially engaged (that is, propagated in group dialogue)? This is the question I raise again here by placing Marcuse's insistence that critical analysis must exercise extraordinary terminology next to the probably sincere but nonetheless familiar declaration by the *Oprah* audience member, that what the world needs now is love. The *Oprah* show is a variant of the Freirean culture circle, where sociopolitically charged issues are catalysts for a dialogical critical analysis; however, I want to propose that the ostensibly transformative purpose of this program is limited by the lexicon its discussants employ. For this reason, its magic—Oprah's medicine—remains a normative rather than a disruptive power.

Disruption requires an extraordinary lexicon, and the figure who gives us this is not the celebrity goddess, however well-intentioned. The generative magic that makes transformation possible is not worked by the executives of culture, but by those on the margins; or, to place such critique in terms of magic, by those who haunt the "hedges" of culture—the "hags," the witches.[17] Admittedly, Oprah Winfrey represents the possibility that a black woman can ascend to tremendous wealth and fame, but she also perpetuates a myth for preserving the status quo, that "anyone who is industrious can become an entrepreneur" (Freire, *Pedagogy* 135). Her popularity rests on the commodification of sociocultural problems into an entertainment package, not their radicalization.[18] The "witch" who appears on *Oprah*, Jane Elliott, does not see herself as such, but certainly behaves like the declared witches that we will discuss—Starhawk and Mary Daly—who reconstitute language as a magical force for cultural disruption, and know themselves as wicked.

I was part of the studio audience for the May 29, 1992 taping of "My Parent is a Racist." A number of other audience members had come prepared to tell on-camera of their experiences with racism, and much of the pretaping "warmup" is devoted to their rehearsal of those experiences for one of the production staff, who evaluates the stories and comments and keeps a chart noting who might offer good televisable remarks. The behavioristic air of all this, in contradistinction to the open forum that the program tries to mimic, is striking: we are asked to practice yelling "Oprah, Oprah" excitedly, warned to stand up if recognized, and encouraged to respond with Ooohs and Ahhhs to provocative remarks. As Oprah Winfrey enters the sound stage, she receives the welcome of an adored charismatic figure, a spontaneous standing ovation.

For about the first half of the show, the panel participants tell their stories, punctuated at several points by the general egalitarian sentiments of the younger white panelists whose parents have been bigots: Melissa stresses that we must appreciate the goodness of each individual regardless of race or sex; Daphne seconds the irrelevance of what she also perceives as superficial physical differences, with her conclusion that "we're all the same" (6). Enter Jane Elliott. A small, middle-aged, gray-haired white woman, Elliott has enjoyed some visibility as the orchestrator of a "blue-eyed/brown eyed experiment" that she performs for business and education groups. People with brown eyes are segregated from those with blue eyes, and the blue-eyed people are treated with contempt and told that they are inferior in every way, while the brown-eyed people enjoy courtesy and admiration. The blue-eyed group in any of these demonstrations usually consists mainly of white males, who typically respond with terrific anger when, according to Elliott, they experience for a brief time what "women and people of color" endure every minute of every day (7). With her blue-eyed/brown-eyed exercise, Elliott effectively casts a spell on the traditionally well-treated that completely disrupts the pattern of their lives; she transforms the patriarchal oppressors into the impotent oppressed, largely by *telling* them that they are inferior to brown-eyed races. While some of the castigation of the blue eyes is unfounded, conjured in order to demonstrate the mythology of domination that operates in this country, it also entails reminders of the brown-eyed contributions that our racist society has forgotten: brown-eyed people, Elliott declares, are the inventors of literacy, technology, and all major religions. Most of us don't know this because, as Elliott explains angrily, we get our information from a "racist school system" that continues to hang anglocentric world maps on schoolroom walls and until very recently taught children that a peach-colored crayon was to be used for flesh tones (8–13).

Elliott—like Winfrey—wants to work a version of medical magic. Calling racism a "mental illness," she wants a cure. The cure that Elliott insists upon results from the re-spelling (what Mary Daly calls the Be-spelling) of valuative categories and their attendant lexicon. To do so is, as Elliott admits, wicked: her pronouncements provoke anger and even death threats from the "Rotarian" types she curses (8). And those vocally liberal white folks who, like Melissa and Daphne, say "everyone's the same," or "we're all alike on the inside" are cursed as well; Elliott berates them: "We are *not* the same on the inside. . . . The differences are important" (12). Elliott prohibits what she calls "melting pot" sentiments that homogenize individuals into vague ideals, and thus silences the dialogue that prefaced her arrival on the stage. The many who told stories appealing for harmony and "colorblindness" during the warmup, and who were seated on the aisles ready to make their cases on the air, never get to speak, in the face of Elliott's declarations that such sentiments are lies, and because Elliott holds the floor with lengthy castigations. She seems scarcely interested in dialogue with the panel members and the audience, intent upon the urgency of her own message. Even the audience member quoted above who exhorts love is told by Elliott to mind her tongue; the gospel of love has, after all, been around for centuries, but "we have yet to get justice" (15). For Elliott, love becomes yet another vague ideal whose invocation so often evades the social inequities it claims to address. She recognizes that a lexicon of clichéd liberal benevolence continues a malevolent society, and directs her own malevolence against educators who inculcate the sorts of falsehoods that the studio audience reiterates, and against all who are unwilling to curse the myth of color-blindness unequivocally.

As I stated in chapter 1, imagining and arraying alternatives to a presumably healthy body of official knowledge are the traditional practices of the counter-cultural magus, and are always potentially wicked because they violate the *lumen fidei*. In the history of magic, the figure consistently associated with such violation is the witch. The term witch has long been applied to enemies of established culture, usually women, and their persecution—which reached its height between the late fifteenth and early seventeenth centuries in Europe—was carried out based on unverifiable male characterizations of "real" demonic females. Such characterizations of the witch—as a creature who can with her spells steal the intellectual, spiritual, and sexual power of men—get their most infamous and influential exposition in the *Malleus Maleficarum*, or "Witches' Hammer," published in 1486 with the blessing of Pope Innocent VI and used for several centuries as a guidebook for inquisition and persecution. While the professed history of witchcraft is founded less in actuality than in ideology, modern witches are affected by it, and have responded by making the witch a feminist heroine, and revising the "Craft tradition" to emphasize radical politics:

> WITCH is all-woman Everything. It's theater, revolution, magic, terror, joy, garlic flowers, spells. It's an awareness that witches and gypsies were the original guerrillas and resistance fighters against oppression—particularly the oppression of women—down through the ages. Witches have always been women who dared to be: groovy, courageous, aggressive, intelligent, nonconformist, explorative, curious, independent, sexually liberated, revolutionary. (This possibly explains why nine million of them have been burned.) Witches were the first Friendly Heads and Dealers, the first birth-control practitioners and abortionists, the first alchemists (turn dross into gold and you devalue the whole idea of money!) They bowed to no man, being the living remnants of the oldest culture of all—one in which men and women were equal sharers in a truly cooperative society, before the death-dealing sexual, economic, and spiritual repression of the Imperialist Phallic Society took over and began to destroy nature and human society. (Morgan 539)[19]

Starhawk is the most well-known American feminist witch, who locates social justice in both the reformation of language that determines oppressive hegemonies and their institutions, and in the collective practice of political activism and spiritual health.[20]

As we will see, Starhawk never attacks patriarchy as vigorously as Morgan does above; in general, she never writes ferociously about the social conditions she criticizes. But she is a committed activist, who has been arrested repeatedly for illegal protests at nuclear weapons facilities, and like Jane Elliott, she believes that the way in which we name our experience determines the kinds of personal and social powers we invoke and sustain:

> There is a corollary to the principle that knowing something's name [which is for Starhawk a complex magical process of determining both its physical and spiritual characteristics] gives us power-with it. It is this: that the names we choose, the language that we use, also have power-with us, and shape us. Names embody thought-forms. They carry both the idea and the context. When we choose a false name, we place an idea in a false context and its shape changes, becoming, perhaps, something we do not intend. And because our language has itself been shaped by the culture of estrangement, whenever we choose the names that make things sound comfortable, acceptable, respectable, academically sound, scientific, we are almost always placing the thing we name back into the context of estrangement—removing its power and our own, alienating ourselves yet again. The names for the thought-forms of immanence, the names that carry power, often sound simple, childish, or threatening, sometimes they sound funny. They are uncomfortable words—take *Magic*, for example.
>
> Or *Witch*. (*Dreaming* 25)

Different types of power entail different languages. Starhawk distinguishes three powers operating in the world: power-over, power-from-within, and power-with. Power-over speaks the "language of law, of rules, of abstract, generalized formulations enforced on the concrete realities of particular circumstances"; its technology is "mechanistic science," and it motivates adherence through fear. Power-from-within speaks the language of "poetry, metaphor, symbol, ritual, myth, the language of magic"; its technology is magic, "the art of changing consciousness," and it motivates adherence erotically, by calling upon those "deep drives" for human community. Power-with speaks the language of gossip, which is in a positive sense the language of collective friendship and consultative leadership; its technology is dialogue, and it is motivated by the desire for justice, and harmony with the elements of the universe (*Truth* 4–27).

Starhawk's emphasis on community as the site for political and transcendental magic leads her to define the witch less as a wild and shocking figure, more as a welcoming one. In the second edition of *Spiral Dance*, she emphasizes her appreciation of multiculturalism, multisexuality, eroticism, and equality; interconnectedness and diversity both inform the magical sympathetic universe. However, this celebration of diversity seems to soften the kinds of individual differences that Jane Elliott insists upon so wickedly, to dissolve the individual into relativism, and to dilute the power of naming. Starhawk will not, for instance, distinguish male from female qualities, instead universalizing them into a gender-less, value-neutral, vague spirit:

> However, as [traditional qualities of the God rather than the Goddess—aggression, physical power, and ability to pursue personal goals] became mine, I ceased to identify them as male. They became simply qualities, which I as a woman had as much access to as any man. . . . So today I would say that, for a woman, the God is whatever begins to happen when you invoke him, should you care to do so. (*Spiral Dance* 234)

Here, "false naming" would be for Starhawk the estrangement of qualities of the God from the Goddess, and the designation of their respective powers with precision that denies that the God/Goddess may mean different things to different people. A vision of culture as the embodiment of a universal spirit coincides with a lexicon of global terms: "If we are to reclaim our culture, we cannot afford narrow definitions" (208).

While Starhawk acknowledges a world filled with horrors, she features the practice of magic as protest through affirmation. All that is connected, is good (*Spiral* 142): "The universe is a dance of energy, a uni-verse, a single song of ever-changing rhythms and harmonies" (*Spiral* 153). The universe is ambiguous but not antithetical: spirituality and politics are, for instance, complementary: "they are both true" (201). Drawing such harmonic connections requires a conception of language as an infinitely transformable system that gets us beyond denotation and connotation, beyond politics, into a mystical realm of "poetry, not theology": "Magical systems are highly elaborated metaphors, not truths . . . through them we identify ourselves and connect with larger forces" (204). Finally, because spirit takes precedence over words, precise definition is a moot issue: the god is the goddess, everything is everything. Reality is messy, people are different, life is full of inequities, but social and self-transformation are possible through the collective recognition that we are all part of the world-soul:

> The All-That-Is-One is not now and never has been separate from this existing physical world. She is here, now, *is* each of us in the eternal changing present; is no one but you, is nowhere but where you are—and yet is everyone. To worship Her is to assert, even in the face of suffering and often against all reason that life is good, a great gift, a constant opportunity for ecstasy. (*Spiral* 208–9)

Starhawk is an activist witch, but not a radical. Her cheerful tolerance for pluralism and relativism, coupled with her emphasis on the transcendence rather than the explication of differences, allies her with the universal love/we're-all-alike-on-the-inside sentiments that Jane Elliott curses, as obstacles to incisive and uncompromising critical discourse with curative social power.

Mary Daly is a radical witch, but one actively disengaged from the society she scorns. Perhaps our most infamous feminist philosopher, Daly believes that social reform consists in steering an "outercourse" from the ever-present "fatherland," and that doing so involves wild acts of wild language. Starhawk presents magic as a mode of embracing humanity at large; Daly, a self-proclaimed Hag, conjures an exclusive sisterhood that denies admission to all individuals and all language that maintain patriarchal institutions, or even strike a compromise. Daly recognizes, along with Starhawk, that every word has multiple meanings, and appreciates Starhawk's effort to break out of the "thought-forms that are shaped by patriarchal culture" by shifting "the shapes of our consciousness" (*Pure Lust* 392). However, Daly departs from Starhawk by asserting that value-neutral definitions do not exist, and that we must radically redefine or eliminate words with oppressive power; in *Outercourse* Daly recounts her failed struggle in the early 1970s to "save" the word God by attempting to mitigate—as Starhawk has—its patriarchal associations:

> I wanted to keep "God" without "the Father." Unfortunately I did not realize that "the Father" is an irremovable appendage of "God." Certainly, it can be rendered invisible. It can be denied. It can drop to a subliminal level. But this apparently incidental appurtenance immutably hangs on to "God." Goddess knows I tried hard enough to castrate this concept. For example, in a

section [from *Beyond God the Father*] entitled "Castrating 'God'" I wrote:

> The divine patriarch castrates women as long as he is allowed to live on in the human imagination. . . . The problem is one of transforming the collective imagination so that this distortion of the human aspiration to transcendence loses its credibility.

I analyzed all the phallacies associated with this word/concept and proposed ways of getting "beyond the inadequate God." It would take just one slight step beyond this to my full realization that "God" simply is hopelessly, irremediably inadequate. (161)

Daly's *Wickedary*, a "dictionary for witches" reminds us—in its vicious parody of Webster's patriarchal dictionary and the sexist epistemology it enforces—that the root of the word "grammar" is "grimoire," that language is a book of spells, and that a reformed cosmology of powers requires a new lexicon. Devoting a chapter to "Grammar: Our Wicked Witches' Hammer," Daly counters the *Malleus Maleficarum* and the amnesiac state it has enforced, by noting that the established usages of grammar and glamour ignore their interconnection, reducing the former to the "tidy arrangement of words" and the latter to cosmetic virtues touted in the title of a mass-market magazine. Glamour, which originally referred to a magic spell, was once a variant of grammar, and conjoining the two reveals the connection between magic spelling, the elements of rhetoric, and the fundaments of literacy. By "unfixing" grammar, "Websters [Spell-Weavers] become Muses" (24). Such unfixing replaces etymology with Meta-etymology, the disclosure of what is "behind" conventional definitions; words like "hag" and "crone" are transvaluated, capitalized in order to make them "proper" nouns, and re-defined in order to invert their normal defamatory meanings:

> CRONE: Great Hag of History, long-lasting one; Survivor of the perpetual witchcraze of patriarchy, whose status is determined not merely by chronological age, but by Crone-logical considerations; one who has Survived early stages of the Otherworld Journey and who therefore has Dis-covered depths of Courage, Strength, and Wisdom in her Self. *Examples*: a: Harriet Tubman, rescuer of slaves, psychically/physically fearless Foresister; b: Ding Ling, twentieth-century feminist activist and author, Survivor of multiple political purges, one of China's best-known and most prolific female writers (114)

Such definitions are the work of "Word Witches, practitioners of Word-magic whose Be-Spoken words are wands emitting vibrations that Transverse the archetypes of the State of Deadly Deception, overturning and reversing its reversals" (17). The *Wickedary's* spell would recover "lost words" (55) that "make the world Weirder" (43) and produce a state of Anamnesia (60). Language is a transformative agency for change:

> METAPHORS, METAPATRIARCHAL [*metaphor* derived fr. Gk. *metapherein* to transfer, change, fr. *meta-* + *pherein* to bear—*Webster's*]: words that function to Name Metapatriarchal transformations and therefore to elicit such change; the language/vehicles of transcendent Spiraling; words that carry Journeyers into the Wild dimensions of Other-centered consciousness by jarring images, stirring memories, accentuating contradictions, upsetting unconscious traditional assumptions, eliciting Gynaesthetic sensing of connections, brewing Strange Ideas. *N.B.*: Metapatriarchal Metaphors are by no means to be confused with the mere "figures of speech" that are described in textbooks on composition. Rather, they are bearers of complex multiple meanings which reflect the complexity and diversity of life itself. (82)

Daly's celebration of complex multiple meanings entails the magical disestablishment of "archetypal mummy terms" that are "reiterated in the halls of academentia" (242), a radical recognition that magical thinking can coincide with a liberatory rhetoric, and a warning that we choose well the discourse—and the attendant powers—that we invoke.

The claim that changing language can change power structures has its critics. Meaghan Morris argues that "Mary Daly works to transform signs, but not discourse" (35). For Morris, Daly's work addresses acts of the composing imagination but not the material conditions of women's lives, creating an essentialist universe of wicked discourse isolated from contexts of use:

> 'Words' are [for Daly] like the magic formulae of the alchemist: they transform the user, not the material world. And just as spiritual strength is inherent in all women (but more so in some than others), so there is a strength-potential in isolated signs which is sufficient to overcome the histories of their use. The word *race*, for example, can be cheerfully put to 'new' political purposes by reviving the dictionary 'meanings' of rushing onwards, or of two tides meeting in a choppy sea—while the

> function of *race* in certain particular discourses, the history of those discourses, and the histories which those discourses have made and still make possible, remains, in Mary Daly's poetics, entirely beside the point.[21] (42)

Feminist linguist Julia Penelope also warns against a too glib association of transformative language and magical power, given in "the simplistic linguistic advice being urged on us by New Age rhetoricians, namely, that what we say will make some aspects of reality appear and others disappear":

> This is good advice, properly taken, but it is also dangerous, especially to the self-esteem of oppressed people, because it implies that we are responsible for our oppression, that, if we really wanted to, we could end our experience of oppression by describing it out of existence. Obviously, a disabled woman can change the way she describes and thinks about her disability, but neither will alter her physical reality or enable her to do more than what her body can do. Likewise, such claims not only trivialize oppression and the social structures that maintain, it, they also blame the victims by ignoring the fact that differences in power among African-Americans, Native Americans, Latinas, Chicanas and whites, women and men, lesbians and gays and heterosexuals, the differently abled and the able-bodied, the poor and the rich, the powerless and the powerful, are institutionally supported and that those who benefit directly and indirectly from such differences in economic and political power have investments in keeping for themselves the privileges they enjoy. Changing our descriptions won't immediately change reality or eliminate white supremacy or male dominance, but it will change the way we perceive power imbalances and the conceptual structures that make them appear to make sense to us. (214; see also Langbauer in Carr 123–31 on the "bias toward unifying")

Morris and Penelope maintain the suspicion of aristocratic or elitist magic that we initially associated with Yeats's "Magic" at the outset of chapter 4; that is, the essentialist or transcendental or—for the Church of the Subgenius—cynically phallocratic construction of magic social redemption as an act of will exerted by some "chosen" group. Under this suspicion, both Starhawk and Daly can be understood as "arresting" witches. While Starhawk voices respect for diversity, she homogenizes individual and cultural differences, subsuming them to an overarching spirit that exists outside of language and governs all souls. While Daly posits Spelling and Grammar as acts of imagining a new Self who disallows patriarchal abuse, her imaginative realm of complex multiple meanings is unconditionally exclusive of any women, let alone men, whose material conditions complicate an absolute refusal of the patriarchal world (Daly even excommunicates Mother Teresa for her "woman-betraying" Christian beliefs [*Pure Lust* 213–14]). Like De Quincey, who revels in the centrifugal force of his magical imagination, Daly's dictionary is a travel guide out of this world, to a journey "over the moon" (*Outercourse* 337–45). And yet she insists that the magical imagination is itself a form of protest, and its loss an invitation to abuse:

> If women continue to lose our Deep Memories, then the images propagated by the pornographers, the obscene experiments of the reproductive technologists, the mutilation and murder of women's bodies by the sons of Jack the Ripper, and the mutilation and murder of women's minds by omni-present woman-hating propagandists will go unprotested. Unprotested also will be the rape and murder of the planet. (*Outercourse* 130)

As Julia Penelope concedes, changing the perception of the concepts that bind us—which is, in the terms of this study, an act of phantasy—*can* affect our responses to them. Radical phantasy begins with the great and uncompromising refusal of conventional wisdom, a refusal that has always identified the countercultural magician, even when (as Agrippa demonstrates) the world believed in magic. From the vantage point of refusal, by working in Daly's "lunar workshop" to materialize, abominate, and thus commute what Marcuse calls the magic-ritual formulas of culture, the magus-witch generates language that bespeaks the incommensurable. This is dangerous work, both because it affronts institutions and ideas that have actual power over life and death, and because the absolute commitment to disruption can itself become tyrannical. The first of these dangers is unavoidable, and in the magician's view, indispensable. The second requires that the desire for the unknown be tied to the desire for justice (*pace* Lyotard 67), that the oracular voice speak *against* all mesmerizing discourses, that magic-rhetoric teach an intellectual liberty and a wicked literacy founded on the intolerance for commonplaces that do harm.

NOTES

INTRODUCTION

1. Another version of Young's essay is titled "Arts, Crafts, Gifts and Knacks: Some Disharmonies in the New Rhetoric," in Freedman and Pringle (53–60).

2. In his antimagical argument, Winterowd explicitly targets Peter Elbow, whose *Writing With Power* concludes with a chapter titled "Writing and Magic." Winterowd concludes that *Writing With Power* "is like a book on cabinet-making with no illustrations, no suggestions about materials, and no explanations of techniques" (343). Elbow advocates a process-approach to the teaching of writing, but also believes that successful writing can involve access to a mysterious power that may or may not materialize the "right" words. *Writing With Power* appears in 1981, just prior to Emig's and Young's dismissal of magical invention; we can be sure that Young, for one, has Elbow in mind.

3. Jerry Rubin's *Do It!*, the 1970 manifesto for the yippie revolution, is a montage of slogans, anecdotes, and pictures that concludes with a vision of the disrupted society that no longer listens to voices of "reason" and instead thrives on hallucinogenic drugs and Eastern mysticism:

> At community meetings all over the land, Bob Dylan will replace The National Anthem.
>
> There will be no more jails, courts, or police.
>
> The White House will become a crash pad for anybody without a place to stay in Washington.
>
> The world will become one big commune with free food and housing, everything shared.
>
> All watches and clocks will be destroyed.
>
> Barbers will go to rehabilitation camps where they will grow their hair long.
>
> There will be no such crime as "stealing" because everything will be free.
>
> The Pentagon will be replaced by an LSD experimental farm.
>
> There will be no more schools or churches because the entire world will become one church and school.
>
> People will farm in the morning, make music in the afternoon and fuck wherever and whenever they want to.

> The United States of Amerika will become a tiny yippie island in a vast sea of Yippieland love. (256)

The cover of the paperback *Do It!* features Rubin-as-shaman, his face brightly painted as he entrances an unseen throng.

4. Feyerabend calls "Objections to Astrology" an example of "how scientific institutions try to impose their will on the rest of society," and goes on to question the accuracy and authority of the *Humanist* scientists' characterizations of astrology (*Science* 91–96).

5. The value of invention and exploration, and the appreciation of the inherent ambiguity of language, has been widely emphasized during the last thirty years. Each of the composition theorists I have discussed does so in the articles cited here and elsewhere; see, for instance, Winterowd's "Creativity and the Comp Class," and Young's "Paradigms for Teaching Rhetorical Invention." In 1987, Young defines an "emerging rhetoric in which invention is the dominant art" ("Recent Developments" 2). For discussions of related contributions from rhetorical theory and critical theory, see Covino, "Making Differences in the Composition Class: A Philosophy of Invention," and *The Art of Wondering* 121–31. I will elaborate Freire's advocacy of a dialectical and dialogical imagination in chapter 4.

CHAPTER 1

1. *Stolen Lightning: The Social Theory of Magic* is the most exhaustive general theory of magic to date, extending to four hundred thousand words, with pointed attention to over one thousand sources. O'Keefe builds his theory largely through the revision of the classic sociological and anthropological statements, primarily those by Marcel Mauss (especially his *General Theory of Magic*), Emile Durkheim, Max Weber, J. G. Frazer, and Bronislaw Malinowski, with repeated attention to Freud as well. He critiques and synthesizes a broad range of modernist, structuralist, and poststructuralist contributions from sociology, anthropology, philosophy, psychology, critical theory, and intellectual history. The resulting "general sociological theory of magic" is constituted by thirteen postulates:

1. Magic Is a Form of Social Action.
2. Magic Social Action Consists of Symbolic Performances—and Linguistic Symbolism Is Central To Magic.
3. Magical Symbolic Action Is Rigidly Scripted.
4. Magical Scripts Achieve Their Social Effects Largely by Pre-Existing Or Pre-Figured Agreements.
5. Magic Borrows Symbolism from Religion and Uses It to Argue with Religion in a Dialectic that Renews Religion.

6. Logically, and in Some Observable Historical Sequences, Magic Derives from Religion Rather Than Vice Versa.
7. Magic Is a Byproduct of the Projection of Society in Religion.
8. Religion Is the Institution that Creates or Models Magic for Society.
9. Magic Tries to Protect the Self.
10. Magic Helped Develop the Institution of the Individual.
11. Magic—Especially Black Magic—Is an Index of Social Pressures on Selves and Individuals.
12. Magic Persists as an Expression of Certain Aspects of Civilization.
13. Magical Symbolism Travels Easily and Accumulates a History.

2. Kenneth Burke, whose contribution to evaluating rhetoric as magic will be of particular interest in chapter 4, aligns symbolic action with dramatism, which is the interaction of act, agent, scene, agency, and purpose, with a change in one term affecting all the rest. Richards offers a "context theory of meaning" in his *Philosophy of Rhetoric*, and defines rhetoricians as alchemists (9); Jakobson elaborates relationships among addresser, addressee, context, message, contact, and code in "Linguistics and Poetics"; Grassi identifies rhetoric with broadly excursive classical invention throughout *Rhetoric As Philosophy*; Kinneavy triangulates the complexity of rhetorical transactions in *A Theory of Discourse*; Berthoff insists that meaning is a dialectical variable in *The Making of Meaning*; and Eagleton concludes that rhetoric comprises "forms of *activity* inseparable from the wider social relationship between writers and readers, orators and audiences, and [is] largely unintelligible outside the social purposes and conditions in which they [are] embedded" in *Literary Theory* (206).

3. The association of rhetoric with a bewitching spell that "drugs" the soul is common in antiquity (see Gorgias "Encomium"). The counterpositions of magic, rhetoric, medicine, and writing are discussed by Burger, de Romilly, Derrida, and Neel.

4. The analogy between this characterization of government advisors and astrologer Joan Quigley's role in the Reagan administration must be noted.

5. C. K. Ogden and I. A. Richards add that "the function of the verbal symbol is . . . to keep inconsistent attributes forcibly united," and this symbol is used by the metaphysician/magician "according to the presentation of reality desired":

> To classify things is to name them, and for magic the name of a thing or group of things is its soul; to know their names is to have power over their souls. Nothing, whether human or superhuman, is beyond the power of words" (*Meaning* 31)

6. "Voodoo" death occurs when someone is ostracized by a social leader: in primitive societies, a witchdoctor might banish a member of the tribe; in modern societies, a company executive might fire or "retire" an employee. The victim eventually dies as a verification of the "curse," thus illustrating the belief that words can kill (O'Keefe 296–300).

7. Harvey Graff, whose compendious research shows that literacy is "a continuous, widely varying, and nonlinear attribute" in intellectual history (*Labyrinths* 4–5), offers a more neutral definition of literacy than those I am discussing here. For Graff, literacy is reflected by "basic or primary levels of reading and writing" (18; see also *Legacies* 3–4), as illustrated in "a technology or set of techniques for communications and for decoding and reproducing written or printed materials" (19). It is studied less profitably as an ideological construction than as a set of practices whose incidence accommodates coherent longitudinal research: the historian of literacy seeks "systematic and direct indications" that meet "the canons of accuracy, utility, and comparability" (*Labyrinths* 19).

8. The term critical literacy, with roots in Freire's "critical consciousness," is now an established designation in literacy theory, often counterposed to Hirschian cultural literacy, which is usually associated with the banking (Freire's term) of widely established facts.

9. For a reconsideration of psychopathology as illness, see Hillman, especially 56–58. Also Deleuze and Guattari, and Massumi.

CHAPTER 2

1. The Association for Computing Machinery Special Interest Group on Computer Graphics (SIGGRAPH) has grown from inception in 1969 to a membership of 12,000, and sponsors a large annual international conference (with 25,000 participants) "for the interchange of information on the theory, design, implementation, and application of computer graphics and interactive technologies" (*Siggraph* 100). This phenomenon is indicative of the "computerization of society" that Lyotard calls the "postmodern condition" (67); see also Bolter, Landow, and Tuman.

2. Expositors of the phantasm include Gorgias, Plato, Aristotle, Augustine, Pico, Ficino, Agrippa, Bruno, Carruthers, Couliano, Eden, Yates, Kristeller, Nauert, Sorabji, Walker, Watson, and Thorndike. This initial definition draws from all of them.

The Greek *phantasma*, often translated as "image," shares qualities with the *eikon*, often translated as "copy." Eden argues usefully that *phantasmata* are psychological images, and *eikones* are their presentational, or rhetorical, equivalents (90).

3. Gerard Watson proposes (1) that *phantasia* may appear first in Plato's *Republic.*

4. As a writer who deploys shifting forms and meanings, Plato engages himself in such protean magic. See "Plato's Pharmacy" in Derrida's *Disseminations.*

5. Surveying the widespread "presence of magic in Hellenic religion, literature, and history," Thorndike notes that Plato's and Aristotle's views of nature are cognate to those of magic, astrology in particular, despite the authors' protests otherwise (1; 24-32). He also concludes that Cicero, who wrote a substantial attack on divination and also criticized astrology, is "not entirely antagonistic" to the belief that the emanations of stars and planets influence human behavior, and cites in particular the *Dream of Scipio* (1; 273).

6. Watson offers a different reading of Cicero from mine, and misses the rhetoric/phantasy connection, although he does note that the context in which phantasy develops is largely "rhetorical." See 45–6, 60.

7. M. W. Bundy, in his classic history of the imagination (a book to which Gerard Watson is very much indebted), notes that attention to phantasy by both Quintilian and Longinus suggests that it was a familiar term in first century C.E. rhetoric.

Longinus writes, "Weight, grandeur, and energy in writing are very largely produced, dear pupil, by the use of 'images' (*phantasiai*). . . . For the term Imagination (*phantasia*) is applied in general to an idea which enters the mind from any source and engenders speech, but the word has now come to be used predominantly of passages where, inspired by strong emotion, you seem to see what you describe and bring it vividly before the eyes of your audience" (15.1–2; 171).

8. Bundy concludes that classical phantasy "is an ordinary power of reverie, put to practical use in oratory. It is also a capacity which may be readily acquired" (107).

9. Pico is referring to Avicenna's distinction between phantasy and imagination (Caplan in Pico 36n), as recounted and rejected by Aquinas. Aquinas's combination of phantasy and imagination is summarized by Carruthers above.

10. Ernesto Grassi concludes that *De Imaginatione* is a specimen text of philosophical rhetoric, in which "philosophy . . . is no longer a rational, deductive process, but an emotive speech *guided by insight*, which has no rational character and has preeminence" (63, emphasis added).

11. Charles Schmitt reveals that Pico's *De Imaginatione* is an early stage in his eventual turn to radical skepticism in the 1520 *Examen Vanitatis,* a work which has leagued Gianfrancesco with that philosopher of magic, enemy of scholastic reason, and defender of the *fidei lumine* whom we discuss below, Cornelius Agrippa (239–42; see also Nauert 148–52).

12. For a further discussion of Agrippa's influence, see Nauert 322–34.

13. Agrippa lives in the same century with Erasmus, whose elaboration of *copia* identified contemporary rhetoric with skillful amplifications and stylistic variations; with Montaigne, whose *Essays* press skepticism to its pyrrhonistical limits; and with magicians of international fame such as Johannes Reuchlin, Paracelsus, and Giordano Bruno.

14. Quotations from Agrippa's works are based on my comparison of conscientious sixteenth and seventeenth century English translations with the Latin version of Agrippa's *Opera*. Section and page numbers for the English source are given first, followed by the volume number and page number(s) from the two-volume *Opera*. Page references for Book 1 of the English *Occult Philosophy* are taken from L. W. de Laurence's 1913 edition of J. F.'s 1651 translation; page references for Books 2 and 3 are taken from the same translation, as it originally appeared.

Agrippa's reliance on Ficino is especially obvious here. In *Three Books* Ficino says, "the World-soul possesses by divine power precisely as many seminal reasons of things as there are ideas in the Divine Mind. By these seminal reasons she fashions the same number of species in matter. . . . And if in the proper manner you bring to bear on a species, or on some individual in it, many things which are dispersed but which conform to the same Idea, into this material thus suitably adapted you will soon draw a particular gift from the Idea, through the seminal reason of the Soul." (3.1; 243). Kaske and Clark explain that "the seminal reasons which figure so largely in 3.1 were invented by the Stoics and reached Ficino chiefly through Plotinus, who gives them a major role as the lowest agent of the Ideas. In the individual, they can be pictured as performing roughly the same function as does the genetic code according to modern science. Conceived on analogy with the seeds and sperm of organic life, they all reside without extension in the World-soul" (Ficino 428n).

15. Agrippa is referring here to the movement of the stars and spirits through the signs of the zodiac.

16. Allison Coudert summarizes the debate between magic and religion over the belief that letters and words are agencies of transformative spiritual energy (74).

17. In 1509, just prior to completing *The Occult Philosophy*, Agrippa had written *De Nobilitate et Praecellentia Foeminei Sexus*, translated into English as *Female Pre-Eminence*. He finally published this feminist tract in 1532, between the appearances of his *Vanity* and his *Occult Philosophy*. *Female Pre-Eminence* synthesizes Agrippa's occultism, anti-intellectualism, and fideism all at once, arguing for the superiority of women over men from both Biblical and cabalistic evidence.

18. Agrippa's intellectual "itinerance" coincides with geographical and professional restlessness. Through his career, Agrippa travels from job to job—as a lawyer, orator, physician, lecturer, magician—never staying for as long as four years in one city, infuriating and disappointing patrons with his refusal to adopt a consistent, or even identifiable, ideological or philosophical position.

CHAPTER 3

1. The advocacy of an elaborate repertoire of figurative variations finds its central statement in Erasmus's 1512 *De Copia*.

2. The disappearance of phantasy coincides with the reinvigorated oppression of women. As Couliano explains, by the late seventeenth century, "the number one enemy which *all of Christianity* must combat is human phantasy" (203) because phantasy promises the communication with illicit demons. Because women are identified with the sympathetic Nature that is under abolition, and thought prone to consort with phantastic demons, they are subject to the official repression of their feminine—hence demonic—attributes. In terms of fashion, the defeminization begins in Spain where "the bosom is flattened with lead placques, the expressivity of the face is eliminated, the waistline is raised, and the woman is covered from neck to toes; in short, an attempt is made to give her an appearance as masculine as possible" (Couliano 213). By the seventeenth century, throughout Europe, "untidy" women are suspected as witches: the censored imagination is represented by the covered woman, the potential witch whose glamour/grammar must be disciplined and punished. I will deal further with the history and reemergence of witchcraft in chapter 5.

3. Morris Berman understands such statements as the culmination of a developing fear of the mystical "enthusiasm" that was initiated by Descartes and Bacon; a magical epistemology was seen as a radical affront to the Protestant and rationalist establishment of new hierarchies (see also Thomas 641–47). The desire to be part of this establishment leads seventeenth-century intellectuals to renounce both magic and rhetoric. Eventually, even those in the elite class who had once given credence to hermetic, cabalistic, and alchemical philosophies—Isaac Newton, for one—underwent a full "conversion" to science (Berman 115–32).

Ioan Couliano proposes that Newton did not publish his alchemical experiments because he wanted to keep his head on his shoulders (181). Assigning such motives with any certainty is difficult, but it is certain that Newton's interest in alchemy suffused his work, as Betty Jo Dobbs demonstrates in *The Foundations of Newton's Alchemy* and *The Janus Face of Genius*. John Maynard Keynes calls Newton "the last of the magicians":

> Why do I call him a magician? Because he looked on the whole universe and all that is in it *as a riddle*, as a secret which could be read by applying pure thought to certain evidence, certain mystic clues which God had laid about the world to allow a sort of philosopher's treasure hunt to the esoteric brotherhood. . . . He regarded the universe as a cryptogram set by the Almighty. (Keynes 29)

The younger Newton, an enthusiastic student of alchemy, sees the universe as a process of continual transformations, "generating fluids out of solids, and solids out of fluids" (qtd. in Berman 115). This is an alchemical rather than a mechanical universe, quite different from the rigid universe described in a query to the *Opticks* that Newton wrote late in his life: the older Newton describes the universe as "solid, massy, hard, impenetrable, movable particles" that remain immutable so "that nature may be lasting" (qtd. in Berman 115); this Nature mirrors a stable social order (Berman 126).

4. Richard Foster Jones discusses the reduction of figurative language in Cowley's own prose, which reflects "the direct influence which the sentiments and regulations of the Royal Society were exerting upon writers" (98).

5. Michael Spiller summarizes the new science of the Royal Society in terms of its attitude toward language, and its aims to develop a language that is value-neutral:

> For the scientist . . . words are primarily records of things, or of the spatial and temporal movements of things. The moral dimension of words is simply irrelevant, and the unambiguous use of a word is preferable to a rich collection of its varied uses. . . . Such employments of words as metaphors, which are the foundations of mythologies, which in turn hold information about the human behaviour in allegorical or euhemeristic guise, are, as Hobbes calls them, *ignes fatui* of the mind. Hence the observable contempt of the new philosophers for allegory, metaphor, simile, analogy and the other gauds of rhetoric, and their willingness to dismiss poetry as deceit. The capacity of one word to connote and even denote different things is from this point of view unfortunate. (141)

6. I draw from and cite Allison Coudert's survey of the demise of natural language theories in the following quotations and discussion of Boyle and Wilkins.

7. Language reforms initiated by the Royal Society are addressed to men only, and "gentlemen" in particular. As Cowley emphasizes, constructing a universal philosophy is a male pursuit:

PHILOSOPHY the great and only Heir
    Of all that Human Knowledge which has bin
Unforfeited by Mans rebellious sin,

Though full of years he do appear,
(Philosophy, I say, and call it, He,
For whatsoe're the Painters Fancy be,
It a Male Virtu seems to me) (stanza 1)

Those intellectuals admitted into the Society must all be gentlemen, "free, and unconfin'd," according to Sprat, because collaborative inquiry cannot proceed freely among those of different stations: "It is undoubtedly true; that scarce any man's mind, is so capable of *thinking strongly*, in the presence of one, whom he *fears* and *reverences*; as he is, when that restraint is taken off" (68–69).

8. Crowley adds that, "For the first time in the history of rhetoric, the inventional process was focused solely on the individual creative mind of a rhetor working in relative isolation" (32). More so than social isolation, I would stress the rhetor's isolation from the elements of associative itinerance, from participatory consciousness within a live universe of resemblances.

9. Robert Pattison has called Locke "the father of modern Anglo-American literacy," who codified correct writing in his opposition to the "wonderful freedom in spelling and grammar" from the Renaissance. Pattison notes Locke's need for a "correct and authoritative language," so that "the universe could be reduced to manageable and manipulable proportions within the framework of words" (144–45).

Locke's influential antipathy to classical rhetoric is well-established. See, for instance, Golden 167–68; Kennedy, *Classical Rhetoric* 227–28; Bizzell & Herzberg 697–99; Knoblauch and Brannon 55–57; and Crowley, who concludes that "the rhetorical tradition that eventually came to dominate school composition instruction was that fostered by Lockean discursive practice and enshrined in rhetorical theory by the new rhetoricians" (12).

10. As phantasy becomes inimical to determination in the reforms of the Royal Society and their Lockean follow-through, Giambattista Vico is a singular advocate of a generative magic rhetoric, the final heir of the Italian humanistic tradition that blended magic and rhetoric in the fourteenth century. Ernesto Grassi associates Enlightenment rhetoric and philosophy with the debasement of the changeable, and places Vico last in a line of Roman and Italian proponents of the phantastic imagination: Cicero, Quintilian, Ficino, and Pico. In this tradition, the distinction between *res* and *verba*, thing and word, "content" and "style," collapses because—as Vico emphasizes—what is true is what is made ("On the Ancient Wisdom of the Italians"). Human language is not constrained or generated by rules of reason; rather, it is allusive, searching among myths, fables, metaphors, articulating the changeable, creating resemblances. Discourse is not derived from first principles; "first principles" are, rather, tentative consequences of discourse (see above, chapter

1, 27–28). John Schaeffer emphasizes the centrality of phantasy for Vico, as the juncture of memory and common sense (72). For a concise discussion of Vico's place in the history of rhetoric, see Covino, *Art* 57–69.

11. The "Body yellow" in this quotation is gold, which Locke uses repeatedly as an example throughout the *Essay*. As A. D. Woozley points out, the fascination with gold may coincide with the otherwise anti-magical Locke's interest in alchemy: "Locke's repeated and unvaried use of gold as his example, whenever writing in the *Essay* of the defining properties of a material object, may well have been connected with his touching confidence in Boyle's claim to have discovered a formula for the alchemical production of gold, a confidence of which Newton seems finally to have disabused him a few years after the *Essay* appeared." (13)

12. For a discussion of Neoplatonic and mystical influences on Romanticism, see Abrams 141–95.

13.

> To every natural form, rock, fruit or flower,
> Even the loose stones that cover the high-way,
> I gave a moral life: I saw them feel,
> Or linked them to some feeling: the great mass
> Lay bedded in a quickening soul, and all
> That I beheld respired with inward meaning. (3.130–135)

14. This construction of the Romantic tradition has come to pervade the statements against Romantic writing and pedagogy presented above in the Introduction. When W. Ross Winterowd objects to "Romantic solipsism," he is in some measure participating in that deconstruction of the upper-case Romantic Imagination that has become a formidable scholarly project in recent years, so much so that Romantic criticism has come to be regarded as a field of "parties and partisans," with its recent history understood as "the rise of a deconstructive, language-oriented, and rhetorical account of literature and its recent replacement by a more historically and politically oriented model" (Ferguson 100). The first phase of "new" Romanticism is identified with Paul De Man, the second with Jerome McGann. The questions at issue are summarized usefully by Ferguson and Copley. The entrance of De Quincey scholarship into the debate over what McGann calls the Romantic ideology is indicated by John Barrell's *The Infection of Thomas De Quincey: A Psychopathology of Imperialism* and Angela Leighton's "De Quincey and Women."

15. Thus I associate myself neither with those who have seen their critical task as expounding the transcendental Romantic imagination as a secularization of religious impulses (e.g., Abrams), nor with those deconstructionists and new historicists who want to demystify and

recast the traditional view. My approach is congenial to what Don Bialostosky calls a Bahktinian or "rhetorical" reading of the Romantic "tradition," which seeks to explicate the diversity of voices that speaks through the writer; at the same time, I continue to maintain the value of the radical individual imagination—with its multiple voices—over the tolerance of normative consensus, as will become more fully apparent in chapters 4 and 5.

16. J. Hillis Miller seconds this alliance by recognizing that the excursive, "dreaming" quality of De Quincey's visionary essays enacts his theory of rhetoric (45–49). For Robert Ready too, the dream visions illustrate "what De Quincey characterized in 1828 as the action of true rhetoric" (48). Masson's own lectures at the University of Edinburgh define rhetoric broadly; he proposes that "Rhetoric may be as appropriately applied to the production of the poet as to the orator" (Horner 76).

Masson also compares De Quincey's phantasy to Bacon's "feigned history" (*Collected* 13; 6) which is, as Bacon explains in the *Advancement of Learning*, "extremely licensed, and doth truly refer to the imagination . . . [which may] make unlawful matches and divorces of things." Such lawlessness is a necessary (but not—for Bacon or Masson—fully approved) expression of the human spirit, "the world being in proportion inferior to the soul; by reason whereof there is, agreeable to the spirit of man, a more ample greatness, a more exact goodness, and a more absolute variety, than can be found in the nature of things" (*Advancement* 2.4.2; 82).

17. For a full discussion of De Quincey's rhetorical theory, see Covino, "Thomas De Quincey in a Revisionist History of Rhetoric."

18. My page citations refer to Grevel Lindop's edition of the *Suspiria* that originally appeared in *Blackwood's Edinburgh Magazine* 57: 269–85, 489–502, 739–51 and 58: 43–55.

19. "'Dream' for De Quincey is a term of infinite flexibility, used to cover mental states ranging from waking reverie to the dreams experienced in sleep; indeed we might say that he comes to use the word as a synonym for 'imagination' and even at times for literature itself" (Lindop, "Introduction" xiv–xv).

20. De Quincey's association here of the palimpsest with thinking-in-general qualifies earlier implications that opium itself performs a "chemical magic" that creates the palimpsestic imagination.

21. The sort of palimpsest which has today become a child's toy was, for Freud in 1924, a model for how the mind works. The name of the product indicates that it works "like magic":

> Now some time ago there came upon the market, under the name of the 'Mystic Writing-Pad', a small contrivance that promises to perform more than the sheet of paper or the slate. . . . The Mystic Pad is a slab of dark brown resin or wax with a paper edging; over

> the slab is laid a thin transparent sheet, the top end of which is firmly secured to the slab while its bottom end rests on it without being fixed to it. . . . To make use of the Mystic Pad, one writes upon the celluloid portion of the covering-sheet which rests on the wax slab. . . . It is a return to the ancient method of writing on tablets of clay or wax: a pointed stilus scratches the surface, the depressions upon which constitute the 'writing'. . . . [After lifting the covering sheet] it is easy to discover that the permanent trace of what was written is retained upon the wax slab itself and is legible in suitable lights. . . . If we imagine one hand writing upon the surface of the Mystic Writing-Pad while another periodically raises its covering-sheet from the wax slab, we shall have a concrete representation of the way in which I tried to picture the functioning of the perceptual apparatus of our mind. (*Works* 19: 232)

Robert Maniquis concludes that, like Freud, "De Quincey also moves pleasurably with the palimpsest into the place of the hidden and the dead, only to find that everything is reconstitutable in the imagined moment of complete memory" (130).

22. De Quincey resembles the *pharmakeus* whom Derrida locates in "Plato's Pharmacy" in *Disseminations*.

CHAPTER 4

1. Yeats's interest in the occult, in particular his membership in the Order of the Golden Dawn, a magical society that flourished in London in the 1890s, signals his abhorrence of "Science, separated from [metaphysical] Philosophy, [which] is the opium of the suburbs" (Flannery 5; Kinahan 11–12). A survey of the magic materials Yeats used is given by Harper (1–10). *A Vision* (1925) is Yeats's attempt to fully explicate the Mind and Memory he alludes to in "Magic."

2. Yeats was briefly interested in Irish Fascism, and once expressed admiration for the strong leadership of Hitler, Stalin, and Mussolini (Stanfield 20).

3. Jane Blankenship suggests the Romantic foundations of Burke's theory of magic, by noting his indebtedness to Coleridge. John Briggs associates Burke's magic with classical rhetoric's "ideas about inductive, *energeic* actualization," as opposed to "an almost mechanically dialectical scourging and dispersal of desire" (374).

4. In his discussion of Cippola in Thomas Mann's "Mario and the Magician," Burke concludes that this tale of automatizing magic is "explicitly an admonition against Fascism" (*Attitudes* 189n).

5. Burke, Adorno, Marcuse, and Paulo Freire (whom we will also consider in this chapter) are all tied in some way to Marxism. Certainly all four have identified themselves as critics of "orthodox" Marxism and

dictatorial Communist governments, while at the same time, all are incisive and constant critics of the bureaucratized and technologized society encouraged by capitalism.

Armin Paul Frank notes that while Burke joined the post–World War I intellectual ranks of American communist sympathizers, he is best characterized as "an anti-Fascist, Agrarian liberal" who is officially a political independent (25): "the communism which Burke recommends is of an idealistic, tentative kind; and, though there are many references to Marx, the principles of a philosophy of *being* definitely carry Burke beyond any shade of orthodox Marxism" (84).

6. The recent worldwide conversion of the Communist bloc to capitalism attests to a "transcendent unity" constituted by monetary rather than religious systems, a unity that Burke sees already overtaking the world in the *Grammar.*

7. Automatism has been an enterprise of magicians since antiquity (Luck 50–52; Camille 247; Kieckhefer 100–101), and the invention of robotic automata flourished in the thirteenth century. These inventions were castigated as demonic impieties by the churchmen of the day, for whom they were not "spiritual symbols but ugly naked machines—materiality incarnate" (Camille 246).

8. Martin Jay writes that

> The unbridgeable distance between subject and object in [Horkheimer and Adorno's construction of] the Enlightenment world view corresponded to the relative status of rulers and ruled in the modern authoritarian states. . . . All of these changes were reflected in the most basic of cultural creations, language. . . . Man was the sole name-giver, a role commensurate with his domination of nature. Language thus became, to use Marcuse's later term, one-dimensional. Incapable of expressing negation, it could no longer voice the protest of the oppressed. Instead of revealing meanings, speech had become nothing more than a tool of the dominant forces in society. (261–63)

9. For Adorno, the menu of options now available to all general consumers with touch-tone phones would represent standardization endowed with the "halo of free choice or open market" ("Stars" 29n).

10. Some astrologers are attempting to challenge this perception, in specialist journals such as *The Mountain Astrologer* that sometimes feature articles on astrology as a radical activity. See, for instance, Shelley Jordan, "The Repression of the Feminine in Astrology," in the April/May 1992 *Mountain Astrologer* devoted to "Revisioning the Feminine." Jordan argues that traditional modes of astrological interpretation reflect and enforce Indo-European cultural origins and attitudes that are "dualistic, patriarchal, and repressive of the feminine" (14).

11. Jung holds a similar view, which Marcuse appreciates (148).

12. Like De Quincey, Marcuse calls for a revalidation of solitude, which emphases on community life have eroded, and which is the only condition in which "the individual, thrown back on himself alone, can think and question and find" (244).

13. Burke is also interested in arraying contradictions, in the form of multiple meanings; his pentad is a calculus for revealing "the strategic spots at which ambiguities necessarily arise" (*Grammar* xviii).

14. Adorno and Marcuse, although they reject Walter Benjamin's theology, both draw from observations on the decline of language from an originary purity that Jewish mysticism might recover (Jay 262–63). In this passage from "Theses on the Philosophy of History" (*Illuminations* 264), Benjamin connects the suppression of magic with the suppression of memory, makes prayer a parallel to soothsaying, and suggests that subversive mysticism might reveal Adorno's "messianic light":

> The soothsayers who found out from time what it had in store certainly did not experience time as either homogeneous or empty. Anyone who keeps this in mind will perhaps get an idea of how past times were experienced in remembrance—namely, in just the same way. We know that the Jews were prohibited from investigating the future. The Torah and the prayers instruct them in remembrance, however. This stripped the future of its magic, to which all those succumb who turn to the soothsayers for enlightenment. This does not imply, however, that for the Jews the future turned into homogeneous, empty time. For every second of time was the strait gate through which the Messiah might enter.

15. See Lyotard on "performativity" in *The Postmodern Condition* (47–53).

16. The jobs are Childcare Aide, Dental Hygienist, Dietary Manager, Licensed Practical Nurse, Medical Assistant, Medical Technologist, Optician, Personnel Specialist, Graphics Designer, Computer Operator, Programming Technician, Accounting/Financial Analyst, Law Enforcement Officer, Quality Control Inspector, Waiter/Waitress, Food Service Manager, Industry Training Specialist, Hotel Account Executive/Sales Executive, Hairstylist/Cosmetologist, Beauty Shop Owner, Show Operations Supervisor, Excavating Equipment Operator, Farmer, Carpenter, Construction Contractor, Expeditor/Purchasing Agent, Plastic Molding Machine Operator, Blue Collar Worker Supervisor, Shipping and Receiving Clerk, Order Filler, Outside Equipment Technician, Truck Delivery Salesperson/Outside Sales, Telemarketing Representative, Travel Agent, Customer Service Representative, Teacher's Aide, Medical Records Technician, Registered Nurse, Bank Teller, Secretary, Underwriting Assistant, Chef, Front Desk Clerk, Assistant Housekeeper, Electrician, Numeric Drill Operator, Offset Lithographic Press Operator, Inside Equipment Technician, Truck Driver, Retail Sales Person.

17. Denis Goulet calls the language of the established culture, from which Freire's peasants are to be released, "the magic toolbox of those present-day sorcerers, the stewards of the culture of silence" (*Education* viii).

18. I will not rehearse Freire's pedagogical method here. It is described in *Education for Critical Consciousness*, and re-presented in a number of places, notably Ira Shor's *Freire for the Classroom.*

CHAPTER 5

1. Another best-selling example, among hundreds (see Starker 175–92), is Herbert Benson's *The Relaxation Response,* which adapts Eastern mysticism and Western magic to a six-step meditation technique that—in ten or twenty minutes a day—can relieve fatigue, anxiety, stress, and high blood pressure, reduce the desire for drugs, and increase alertness and energy.

The simplification of Eastern mysticism found in such books is just that, a formulary reduction of those millennia-old developments that Georg Feuerstein earnestly calls "spiritual technologies," while he explains that they are not technologies in the modern Western sense. In a compendious guide to the history and practice of yoga that suggests anything but quick results, Feuerstein insists that Eastern spirituality is incompatible with Western mechanism, and thus sets the practices he represents well apart from the specious packaging of consciousness that amounts to "mere imitation" (4–8, 303–4).

2. I must admit the difficulty of defining "working class." The color of one's collar on the job, or whether one holds a job outside the home, are questionable determinants; beliefs and feelings about one's status, and group identity, may be the significant factors (Jackman 38ff.). Identifying class with the power and authority enjoyed by its members, we might, at least, distinguish the working class from the middle class by adopting Daniel O'Keefe's definition of the latter; the middle class are "those who do not run things, but are treated well in return for their loyalty" (O'Keefe 467); consequently, the working class are those treated less well, those Paul Fussell calls "people things are done to" (44). This definition certainly applies to working class women who, according to the U.S. census, "suffer disproportionately from economic marginality, unsatisfying jobs, poor working conditions, inadequate social and municipal services, deteriorating neighborhoods, and alienation from the American mainstream" (Hunter and Harman, 388).

3. Sources for these figures are Randall, Bird, an unauthored article boasting worldwide circulation that appeared in the *Enquirer* on 23 February 1993 (14), and the 1992 "National Enquirer/Star Magazine

Demographic Profile" supplied by the *Enquirer* advertising department. Based upon her interviews with tabloid writers and publishers, Bird concludes that the typical reader envisioned is a middle class white female (113), and that tabloid publishers assume that "tabloid readers are predominantly women who are untouched by feminism, their main concerns being marriage and parenthood" (76). A more detailed demographic profile from 1987 (also supplied by the *Enquirer* advertising department) indicates that the women readers are older than the men (36.7 is the median age for women, 33.6 for men); they are less well educated (80 percent have no college, as compared to 73 percent of men); and they earn less (65 percent of female readers have a household income of less than $30,000, as compared to 60 percent of male readers).

4. For the analysis that follows, I examined *Enquirer* issues from 29 September 1987 through 31 January 1989; 12 May 1992 through 21 July 1992; 13 October 1992 through 30 March 1993.

5. The same advanced technologies that can fix anything also threaten human autonomy and become part of the ominous victimizing forces that affect celebrities and commoners alike, in occasional articles like the one warning, "Robots Will Take Over The Earth!" (3 January 1989; 4).

6. Similarly behavioristic advice, emphasizing traditional gender roles and sexual abstinence, promises that "Anyone Can Find A Marriage Partner Within 2 Years":

> You can find Mr. or Miss Right by following some simple advice from a romance consultant. . . . Make getting married a goal as important as your education or career. . . . Compile a list of qualities you'd like in a mate. . . . Give yourself time to fall in love before you start a sexual relationship. (16 February 1993; 18)

7. Occasional politicized explications of statistics in 1992–93 issues of the *Enquirer* exhort a reactionary audience as they prescribe simple, absolute solutions for governmental and social recklessness:

> Last week the U.S. government used up a staggering 769,000,000 pounds of paper printing new regulations and writing notes. If all that paper were burned instead, it would supply the weekly energy needs of 2,500,000 American homes. (26 January 1993; 44)
>
> Last week party-mad college students in the U.S. spent a mind-boggling $106 million on alcohol! That's a bar tab of more than $10,000 every minute. If college students stopped drinking, they'd save enough money in one week to [fund] 20,000 needy classmates. . . . (9 March 1993; 4)

8. Hoggart's classic study of mid-century British tabloids as determinants of mass literacy expresses similar skepticism (270–82).

9. English professor Daniel McDonald is featured in the *Enquirer* as an advocate of formulaic writing—simple sentences, short para-

graphs, step-by-step organization—who uses the *Enquirer* as a model of successful prose (6 April 1993; 16).

10. I examined *TV Guide* from 29 February to 21 August 1992.

11. Marcuse includes the abridgment of human identification as an element of one-dimensional language; see chapter 4, 109.

12. The nuggets metaphor I am extending here maintains the banking/alimentary concept of knowledge that Freire associates throughout his works with the pedagogy of the oppressed and with the enforcement of magic consciousness. Bankable knowledge is presented in the form of "slogans, communiques, monologues, and instructions," which take on the power of magic ritual formulas that "obviate thought" (*Pedagogy* 57–74).

13. In the same essay we are considering here, Lapham introduces a new *Harper's* feature, the Folio, which debuts in this issue as a novella of about 30,000 words by Don De Lillo. The folio, which will present "essays and stories of substantial length," has been made possible—that is, affordable—by the commercial success of the nuggets-format, or as Lapham rhapsodizes, "the magazine's safe passage through the shoals of perilous transmigration" (9). In the context of the format that has come to define *Harper's*, we are prompted to ask whether the Folio (which in its next two appearances was one-half and two-thirds as long, respectively, as the De Lillo piece) might be one more display of the appetite for brevity, the mini-book. At the same time, the appearance of the Folio does offer some compensation to readers nostalgic for the pre-nuggets *Harper's*.

14. The primary author of all Subgenius books, as well as *High Weirdness By Mail*, a guide to newsletters, books, and other products of numerous fringe groups, is "Reverend" Ivan Stang.

15. See, for instance, Fredric Jameson's "Postmodernism," and his Foreword to Lyotard's *Postmodern Condition*.

16. For discussions of charismatic shamanism and its current manifestations, see Lindholm, especially 156–65, 176–81.

17. From Mary Daly's *Wickedary*, which we will discuss presently:

> HAG [derived fr. ME *hagge, hegge* . . . akin to MD *haghetisse* witch, OHG *hagzissa, hagazussa* harpy, witch; all fr. a prehistoric WGmc compound whose components are akin respectively to OE *haga* hedge and to G dialect [Westphalia] *dus* devil): "*archaic*" a female demon: FURY, HARPY . . . an evil or frightening spirit . . . NIGHTMARE . . . an ugly or evil-looking old woman"—*Webster's*]: *Archaic:* a Witch, Fury, Harpy who haunts the Hedges/Boundaries of patriarchy, frightening fools and summoning Weird Wandering women into the Wild. (137)

18. "Even though the shaman clearly is a charismatic figure, he [sometimes she] is not a radical opponent of the system. Instead,

shamanism serves as the accepted revelation of the holy, and the practitioner is integrated into society" (Lindholm 162).

19. For discussions of the uncertain history of witchcraft and the horrors of persecution, see Adler 41–93; Daly, *Gyn-Ecology* 178–222; Luhrman 42–50; Starhawk, *Spiral Dance* 19–21. Peters discusses the eleventh- and twelfth-century writing on witches as a fanciful rhetorical exercise that nonetheless propagated stereotypes of the witch.

20. In addition to the best-selling *Spiral Dance* (1979, 1989), she has written *Dreaming the Dark: Magic, Sex, and Politics* (1982) and *Truth or Dare: Encounters With Power, Authority, and Mystery* (1987).

21. Jane Hedley sides with Morris against Daly in "Surviving to Speak New Language." See also Audre Lorde, "An Open Letter to Mary Daly."

REFERENCES

Abrams, M. H. *Natural Supernaturalism: Tradition and Revolution in Romantic Literature.* New York: Norton, 1971.

Adler, Margot. *Drawing Down the Moon: Witches, Druids, Goddess-Worshippers, and Other Pagans in America Today.* Rev. ed. Boston: Beacon, 1986.

Adorno, Theodor W. "The Essay As Form." Volume 1 of *Notes To Literature.* Ed. Rolf Tiedemann. Trans. Shierry Weber Nicholson. New York: Columbia UP, 1991. 3–23.

———. *Minima Moralia: Reflections from Damaged Life.* Trans. E. F. N. Jephcott. London: NLB, 1974.

———. "Scientific Experiences of a European Scholar in America." *The Intellectual Migration: Europe and America 1930–1960.* Ed. Donald Fleming and Bernard Bailyn. Cambridge: Harvard UP, 1969.

———. "The Stars Down to Earth: The Los Angeles Times Astrology Column." *Telos* 19 (1974): 13–90.

Agrippa, Henry Cornelius. *Female Pre-Eminence, or the Dignity and Excellency of that Sex, Above the Male.* Trans. Henry Care, 1670. Reprinted in *The Feminist Controversy of the Renaissance.* Delmar, N.Y.: Scholar's Facsimiles, 1980.

———. *Of The Vanitie and Uncertaintie of Artes and Sciences.* Trans. James Sanford, 1569, 1575. Ed. Catherine M. Dunn. Northridge: California State U, 1974.

———. *Opera.* 2 vols. New York: Verlag, 1970.

———. *The Philosophy of Natural Magic.* Ed. L. W. de Laurence. Chicago: de Laurence, 1913.

———. *Three Books of Occult Philosophy.* Trans. J. F. London: Gregory Moule, 1651.

Allen, Michael J. B., ed. and trans. *Marsilio Ficino and the Phaedran Charioteer.* Berkeley: U of California P, 1981.

Altschuler, Glenn C., and David I. Grossvogel. *Changing Channels: America in TV GUIDE.* Urbana: U of Illinois P, 1992.

Aristotle. *De Anima (On the Soul).* Trans. Hugh Lawson-Tancred. New York: Penguin, 1986.

———. *On Rhetoric.* Trans. George Kennedy. New York: Oxford UP, 1991.

———. *Topics.* Trans. E. S. Forster. Cambridge: Harvard UP, 1960.

Augustine. *On Christian Doctrine*. Trans. D. W. Robertson, Jr. Indianapolis: Bobbs-Merrill, 1958.

Austin, J. L. *How To Do Things With Words*. Ed. J. O. Urmson and Marina Sbisa. 2nd ed. Cambridge: Harvard UP, 1975.

Bacon, Francis. *The Advancement of Learning*. Ed. G. W. Kitchin. Totowa, NJ: Rowman, 1973.

Barrell, John. *The Infection of Thomas De Quincey: A Psychopathology of Imperialism*. New York: Yale UP, 1992.

Barrett, Francis. *The Magus, or Celestial Intelligencer; Being a Complete System of Occult Philosophy*. 1801. New York: Citadel, 1989.

Barthes, Roland. *S/Z*. Trans. Richard Miller. New York: Hill and Wang, 1974.

Basseches, Michael. *Dialectical Thinking and Adult Development*. Norwood, NJ: Ablex, 1984.

Benjamin, Walter. *Illuminations: Essays and Reflections*. Trans. Harry Zohn. Ed. Hannah Arendt. New York: Schocken, 1968.

Benson, Herbert. *The Relaxation Response*. With Miriam Z. Klipper. New York: Avon, 1975.

Berman, Morris. *The Reenchantment of the World*. Ithaca: Cornell UP, 1981.

Berthoff, Ann E. *The Making of Meaning: Metaphors, Models, and Maxims for Writing Teachers*. Portsmouth, NH: Boynton/Cook, 1981.

Betz, Hans Dieter. *The Greek Magical Papyri in Translation*. Chicago: U of Chicago P, 1986.

Bialostosky, Don H. *Wordsworth, Dialogics, and the Practice of Criticism*. Cambridge: Cambridge UP, 1992.

Bird, S. Elizabeth. *For Enquiring Minds: A Cultural Study of Supermarket Tabloids*. Knoxville: U of Tennessee P, 1992.

Bizzell, Patricia, and Bruce Herzberg, ed. *The Rhetorical Tradition: Readings from Classical Times to the Present*. Boston: Bedford, 1990.

Blankenship, Jane. "'Magic' and 'Mystery' in the Works of Kenneth Burke." *The Legacy of Kenneth Burke*. Ed. Herbert W. Simons and Trevor Melia. Madison: U of Wisconsin P, 1989. 128–151.

Bleich, David. *Readings and Feelings*. Urbana, IL: NCTE, 1976.

Bogart, Leo. *Press and Public: Who Reads What, When, Where, and Why in American Newspapers*. 2nd ed. Hillsdale, NJ: Erlbaum, 1989.

Bolter, Jay. *Writing Space: The Computer, Hypertext, and the History of Writing*. Hillsdale: Erlbaum, 1991.

Bok, Bart J., et al. "Objections to Astrology: A Statement by 186 Leading Scientists." *The Humanist* 35.5 (1975): 4–6.

Bourdieu, Pierre. *Language And Symbolic Power*. Trans. Gino Raymond and Matthew Anderson. Ed. John B. Thompson. Cambridge: Harvard UP, 1991.

Briggs, John G. *Francis Bacon and the Rhetoric of Nature.* Cambridge: Harvard UP, 1989.

———. "Peter Elbow, Kenneth Burke, and the Idea of Magic." *Journal of Advanced Composition* 11.2 (1991): 363–76.

Brodkey, Linda. "Tropics of Literacy." *Rewriting Literacy: Culture and the Discourse of the Other.* Ed. Candace Mitchell and Kathleen Weiler. New York: Bergin, 1991. 161–68.

Brown, Peter. *Religion and Society in the Age of St. Augustine.* New York: Harper, 1972.

Bruno, Giordano. *On the Composition of Images, Signs, and Ideas.* Trans. Charles Doria. New York: Willis, 1991.

Bundy, M. W. *The Theory of Imagination in Classical and Medieval Thought.* Urbana: U of Illinois P, 1928.

Burger, Ronna. *Plato's PHAEDRUS: A Defense of a Philosophic Art of Writing.* University, AL: U of Alabama P, 1980.

Burke, Kenneth. *Attitudes Toward History.* Los Altos: Hermes, 1959.

———. *Counter-Statement.* 2nd ed. 1953. Berkeley: U of California P, 1968.

———. *A Grammar of Motives.* 1945. Berkeley: U of California P, 1969.

———. *Language As Symbolic Action: Essays on Life, Literature, and Method.* Berkeley: U of California P, 1966.

———. "Logology: Over-All View." *Communication Quarterly* 33 (1985): 31–32.

———. *Permanence and Change.* 3rd ed. 1935. Berkeley: U of California P, 1984.

———. *The Philosophy of Literary Form.* 3rd ed. Berkeley: U of California P, 1973.

———. *A Rhetoric of Motives.* 1950. Berkeley: U of California P, 1969.

Burwick, Frederick. "The Dream-Visions of Jean Paul and Thomas De Quincey." *Comparative Literature* 20.1 (1968): 1–26.

Card, Claudia, ed. *Feminist Ethics.* Lawrence: UP of Kansas, 1991.

Cafarelli, Annette Wheeler. "De Quincey and Wordsworthian Narrative." *Studies in Romanticism* 28 (1989): 121–47.

Camille, Michael. *The Gothic Idol: Ideology and Image-Making in Medieval Art.* Cambridge: Cambridge UP, 1989.

Carr, Glynis, ed. *"Turning the Century": Feminist Theory in the 1990s.* Lewisburg: Bucknell UP, 1992.

Carruthers, Mary J. *The Book of Memory: A Study of Memory in Medieval Culture.* Cambridge: Cambridge UP, 1990.

Cassirer, Ernst. *Language and Myth.* Trans. Susanne Langer. New York: Dover, 1953.

Christensen, Francis. "John Wilkins and the Royal Society's Reform of Prose Style." *John Wilkins and 17th-Century British Linguistics.* Ed. Joseph L. Subbiondo. Amsterdam: John Benjamins, 1992. 133–54.

Cicero. *Academica*. Trans. H. Rackham. Cambridge: Harvard UP, 1933.
———. *On Oratory and Orators (De Oratore)*. Trans. J. S. Watson. Carbondale: Southern Illinois UP, 1970.
Coleridge, Samuel Taylor. *Biographia Literaria*. Vol. 7 of *The Collected Works of Samuel Taylor Coleridge*. Ed. James Engell and W. Jackson Bate. Princeton: Princeton UP, 1983.
Conference on College Composition and Communication, 1993. Program. 1–3 April 1993. Urbana, IL: NCTE, 1993.
Conn, Charis, and Ilena Silverman. *What Counts: The Complete Harper's Index*. New York: Harper's, 1992.
Cope, Jackson I., and Harold Whitmore Jones. "Introduction." *History of the Royal Society*. By Thomas Sprat. Ed. Jackson Cope and Harold Jones. St. Louis: Washington UP, 1958. xii–xxxii.
Copenhaver, Brian. "Astrology and Magic." *The Cambridge History of Renaissance Philosophy*. Ed. Charles B. Schmitt. Cambridge UP, 1988. 264–300.
Copley, Stephen and John Whale. "Introduction." *Beyond Romanticism: New Approaches to Texts and Contexts, 1780–1832*. Ed. Stephen Copley and John Whale. London: Routledge, 1992. 1–10.
Coudert, Allison. "Some Theories of a Natural Language from the Renaissance to the Seventeenth Century." *Magia Naturalis Und Die Entstehung Der Modernen Naturwissenschaften*. Wiesbaden: Verlag, 1978. 56–114.
Couliano, Ioan P. *Eros and Magic in the Renaissance*. Trans. Margaret Cook. Chicago: U of Chicago P, 1987.
Covino, William A. *The Art of Wondering: A Revisionist Return to the History of Rhetoric*. Portsmouth, NH: Boynton, 1988.
———. "Magic, Literacy, and the National Enquirer." *Contending With Words*. Ed. Patricia Harkin and John Schilb. New York: MLA, 1991. 23–37.
___. "Making Differences in the Composition Class: A Philosophy of Invention." *Freshman English News* 10 (1981): 1–13.
———. "Thomas De Quincey in a Revisionist History of Rhetoric." *PRE/TEXT* 4.2 (1983): 121–138.
Crowley, Sharon. *The Methodical Memory: Invention in Current-Traditional Rhetoric*. Carbondale: Southern Illinois UP, 1991.
Daly, Mary. *Gyn/Ecology: The Metaethics of Radical Feminism*. Boston: Beacon, 1978.
———. *Outercourse: The Be-Dazzling Voyage*. San Francisco: Harper, 1992.
———. *Pure Lust: Elemental Feminist Philosophy*. Boston: Beacon, 1984.
———. *Websters' First New Intergalactic Wickedary of the English Language*. With Jane Caputi. Boston: Beacon, 1987.

Deleuze, Gilles and Felix Guattari. *Anti-Oedipus: Capitalism and Schizophrenia*. Trans. Robert Hurley, Mark Seem, and Helen R. Lane. New York: Viking, 1977.

De Luca, V. A. *Thomas De Quincey: The Prose of Vision*. Toronto: U of Toronto P, 1980.

De Man, Paul. *The Rhetoric of Romanticism*. New York: Columbia UP, 1984.

De Quincey, Thomas. *Collected Writings*. Ed. David Masson. 14 vols. Edinburgh: Black, 1890. New York: AMS, 1968.

———. *Selected Essays on Rhetoric*. Ed. Frederick Burwick. Carbondale: Southern Illinois UP, 1967.

———. *Suspiria De Profundis: Being a Sequel to the Confessions of an English Opium Eater. Confessions of an English Opium Eater and Other Writings*. Ed. Grevel Lindop. Oxford: Oxford UP, 1985. 87–181.

de Romilly, Jacqueline. *Magic and Rhetoric in Ancient Greece*. Cambridge: Harvard UP, 1975.

———. *Time in Greek Tragedy*. Ithaca: Cornell UP, 1968.

Derrida, Jacques. *Dissemination*. Trans. Barbara Johnson. Chicago: U of Chicago P, 1981.

Devlin, D. D. *De Quincey, Wordsworth, and the Art of Prose*. London: Macmillan, 1983.

Dobbs, Betty J. *The Foundations of Newton's Alchemy*. Cambridge: Cambridge UP, 1975.

———. *The Janus Face of Genius: The Role of Alchemy in Newton's Thought*. Cambridge: Cambridge UP, 1991.

Duncan, Hugh Dalziel. *Communication and Social Order*. New York: Bedminster, 1962.

Eagleton, Terry. *Literary Theory: An Introduction*. Minneapolis: U of Minnesota P, 1983.

Eamon, William. "Arcana Disclosed: The Advent of Printing, the Books of Secrets Tradition and the Development of Experimental Science in the Sixteenth Century." *History of Science* 22.2 (1984): 111–50.

Eden, Kathy. *Poetic and Legal Fiction in the Aristotelian Tradition*. Princeton: Princeton UP, 1986.

Eliade, Mircea. "The Myth of Alchemy." *Parabola* 3.3 (1978): 6–23.

———. *Occultism, Witchcraft, and Cultural Fashions: Essays in Comparative Religions*. Chicago: U of Chicago P, 1976.

Ellul, Jacques. *The Technological System*. New York: Continuum, 1980.

Emig, Janet. "Literacy and Freedom." *The Web of Meaning: Essays on Writing, Teaching, Learning, and Thinking*. Ed. Dixie Goswami and Maureen Butler. Upper Montclair, NJ: Boynton/Cook, 1983. 171–78.

———. "Non-Magical Thinking: Presenting Writing Developmentally in Schools." *Writing: Process, Development, and Communication*.

Ed. C. Fredricksen and J. Dominic. Hillsdale, NJ: Erlbaum, 1981. 21–30.

Erasmus, Desiderius. *Collected Works of Erasmus. Literary and Educational Writings 2: De Copia, De Ratione Studii.* Ed. Craig R. Thompson. Toronto: U of Toronto P, 1978.

"Everybody's Talking." *For Women First* 30 November 1992: 34.

Ferguson, Frances. "Romantic Studies." *Redrawing the Boundaries.* Ed. Stephen Greenblatt and Giles Gunn. NY: MLA, 1992. 100–29.

Feuerstein, Georg. *Yoga: The Technology of Ecstasy.* Los Angeles: Tarcher, 1989.

Feyerabend, Paul. *Against Method.* Rev. ed. London: Verso, 1988.

———. *Science in a Free Society.* London: NLB, 1978.

Ficino, Marsilio. *Three Books on Life.* Ed. and trans. Carol V. Kaske and John R. Clark. Binghamton, NY: Center for Medieval and Early Renaissance Studies, 1989.

Flannery, Mary Catherine. *Yeats and Magic: The Earlier Works.* Gerrards Cross: Colin Smythe, 1977.

Flint, Valerie I. J. *The Rise of Magic in Medieval Europe.* Princeton: Princeton UP, 1991.

Foucault, Michel. *The Order of Things: An Archeology of the Human Sciences.* New York: Vintage, 1973.

Frank, Armin Paul. *Kenneth Burke.* New York: Twayne, 1969.

Freedman, Aviva, and Ian Pringle, eds. *Reinventing the Rhetorical Tradition.* Conway, Arkansas: L&S, 1980.

Freire, Paulo. *Education for Critical Consciousness.* Trans. Myra Bergman Ramos. New York: Continuum, 1973.

———. *Pedagogy of the Oppressed.* Trans. Myra Bergman Ramos. New York: Continuum, 1970.

Freud, Sigmund. *The Complete Psychological Works of Sigmund Freud.* 24 vols. Trans. James Strachey. London: Hogarth, 1961.

Fussell, Paul. *Class.* New York: Summit, 1983.

Gaur, Albertine. *A History of Writing.* London: British Library, 1984.

Giroux, Henry. "Literacy and the Pedagogy of Political Empowerment." *Literacy: Reading the Word and the World.* By Paulo Freire and Donaldo Macedo. South Hadley, MA: Bergin & Garvey, 1987. 1–27.

———. *Theory and Resistance in Education: A Pedagogy for the Opposition.* South Hadley, MA: Edward Arnold, 1978.

Golden, James L., et al. *The Rhetoric of Western Thought.* 4th ed. Dubuque, IA: Kendall, 1989.

Gorgias. "Encomium of Helen." Trans. Rosamond Kent Sprague. *The Rhetorical Tradition: Readings from Classical Times to the Present.* Ed. Patricia Bizzell and Bruce Herzberg. Boston: St. Martin's, 1990. 40–42.

Graff, Gerald. *Professing Literature: An Institutional History.* Chicago: U of Chicago P, 1987.

Graff, Harvey J. *The Labyrinths of Literacy: Reflections on Literacy Past and Present*. Philadelphia: Falmer, 1987.

———. *The Legacies of Literacy: Continuities and Contradictions in Western Culture and Society*. Bloomington: Indiana UP, 1987.

Grassi, Ernesto. *Rhetoric as Philosophy*. University Park: Penn State UP, 1980.

Grim, Patrick, ed. *Philosophy of Science and the Occult*. New York: SUNY, 1982.

Hairston, Maxine. "The Winds of Change: Thomas Kuhn and the Revolution in the Teaching of Writing." *College Composition and Communication* 33 (1982): 76–88.

Harper, George Mills. *Yeats and the Occult*. Canada: Macmillan, 1975.

Hassan, Ihab. *The Dismemberment of Orpheus: Toward a Postmodern Literature*. Madison: U of Wisconsin P, 1982.

———. *The Right Promethean Fire: Imagination, Science, and Cultural Change*. Urbana: U of Illinois P, 1980.

Hayter, Alethea. *Opium and the Romantic Imagination*. Berkeley: U of California P, 1968.

Hedley, Jane. "Surviving to Speak New Language: Mary Daly and Adrienne Rich." *Hypatia* 7.2 (1992): 40–62.

Hillman, James. *Revisioning Psychology*. New York: Harper, 1975.

Hirsch, E. D., Jr. *Cultural Literacy: What Every American Needs To Know*. Boston: Houghton, 1987.

———, et al. *The Dictionary of Cultural Literacy: What Every American Needs To Know*. Boston: Houghton, 1988.

Hoggart, Richard. *The Uses of Literacy: Changing Patterns in English Mass Culture*. Fair Lawn, NJ: Essential, 1957.

Horkheimer, Max, and Theodore W. Adorno. *Dialectic of Enlightenment*. Trans. John Cumming. New York: Herder, 1972.

Horner, Winifred Bryan. *Nineteenth-Century Scottish Rhetoric*. Carbondale: Southern Illinois UP, 1993.

Hunter, Carman St. John, and David Harman. "Who Are The Adult Illiterates?" *Perspectives On Literacy*. Ed. Eugene R. Kintgen, et. al. Carbondale: Southern Illinois UP, 1988: 378–90.

"Introduction to Adorno." *Telos* 19 (Spring 1974): 2–6.

Jackman, Mary R., and Robert W. Jackman. *Class Awareness in the United States*. Berkeley: U of California P, 1983.

Jakobson, Roman. "Linguistics and Poetics." *Style in Language*. Ed. Thomas Sebeok. Cambridge: MIT, 1960. 350–77.

Jameson, Fredric. Foreword. *The Postmodern Condition: A Report on Knowledge*. By Jean-Francois Lyotard. Trans. Geoff Bennington and Brian Massumi. Minneapolis: U of Minnesota P, 1984. vii–xxi.

———. "Postmodernism: Or, The Cultural Logic of Late Capitalism." *New Left Review* 146 (1984): 53–92.

Jay, Martin. *The Dialectical Imagination: A History of the Frankfurt School and the Institute of Social Research, 1923–1950*. Boston: Little, 1973.

Johannisson, Karin. "Magic, Science, and Institutionalization in the Seventeenth and Eighteenth Centuries." *Hermeticism and the Renaissance: Intellectual History and the Occult in Early Modern Europe*. Ed. Ingrid Merkel and Allen G. Debus. Washington: The Folger Shakespeare Library, 1988. 251–64.

Jones, Richard Foster. *The Seventeenth Century: Studies in the History of English Thought and Literature from Bacon to Pope*. Stanford: Stanford UP, 1951.

Jordan, Shelley. "The Repression of the Feminine in Astrology." *The Mountain Astrologer* April/May 1992: 13–14.

Kaske, Carol V., and John R. Clark. "Introduction." *Three Books on Life*. By Marsilio Ficino. Ed. and trans. Carol V. Kaske and John R. Clark. Binghamton, NY: Center for Medieval and Early Renaissance Studies, 1989. 3–90.

Kellner, Douglas. *Herbert Marcuse and the Crisis of Marxism*. Berkeley: U of California P, 1984.

Kennedy, George. *Classical Rhetoric and its Christian and Secular Tradition from Ancient to Modern Times*. Chapel Hill: U of North Carolina P, 1980.

———. "A Hoot in the Dark: The Evolution of General Rhetoric." *Philosophy and Rhetoric* 25.1 (1992): 1–21.

Kerr, Howard, and Charles L. Crow, ed. *The Occult in America*. Urbana: U of Illinois P, 1986.

Keynes, John Maynard. "Newton, the Man." *The Royal Society Newton Tercenternary Celebrations*. Cambridge: Cambridge UP, 1947.

Kieckhefer, Richard. *Magic in the Middle Ages*. New York: Cambridge UP, 1990.

Kinahan, Frank. *Yeats, Folklore, and Occultism: Contexts of the Early Work and Thought*. Boston: Unwin, 1988.

Kinneavy, James. *A Theory of Discourse*. 1971. New York: Norton, 1980.

Kinney, Jay. "Backstage with 'Bob': Is the Church of the Subgenius the Ultimate Cult?" *Whole Earth Review* 52 (Fall 1986): 86–89.

Knight, Gareth. *Magic and the Western Mind*. St. Paul: Llewellyn, 1991.

Knoblauch, C. H., and Lil Brannon. *Rhetorical Traditions and the Teaching of Writing*. Portsmouth, NH: Boynton/Cook, 1984.

Kozol, Jonathan. *Illiterate America*. Garden City, NY: Anchor, 1985.

Kuhn, Sherman, and John Reddy, eds. *Middle English Dictionary*. Ann Arbor: U of Michigan P, 1963.

Kristeller, Paul Oskar. *The Philosophy of Marsilio Ficino*. Trans. Virginia Conant. Gloucester: Peter Smith, 1964.

Landow, George. *Hypertext: The Convergence of Contemporary Critical Theory and Technology.* Baltimore: Johns Hopkins, 1992.

Langer, Suzanne. *Philosophy in A New Key.* Cambridge: Harvard UP, 1957.

Lapham, Lewis H. "Notebook: New Directions." *Harper's Magazine* 285.1709 (October 1992): 6–9.

Leighton, Angela. "De Quincey and Women." *Beyond Romanticism: New Approaches to Texts and Contexts, 1780–1832.* Ed. Stephen Copley and John Whale. London: Routledge, 1992. 160–77.

Levine, Art. "On the Trail of High Weirdness." *U.S. News and World Report* 14 November 1988: 67.

Lewis, C. S. *English Literature in the Sixteenth Century Excluding Drama.* Oxford: Clarendon, 1954.

Lindholm, Charles. *Charisma.* Cambridge, MA: Blackwell, 1990.

Lindop, Grevel. "Introduction." *Confessions of an English Opium Eater and Other Writings.* Oxford: Oxford UP, 1985. vii–xxv.

———. *The Opium Eater: A Life of Thomas De Quincey.* New York: Taplinger, 1981.

Locke, John. *Essay Concerning Human Understanding.* Ed. Peter H. Nidditch. Oxford: Clarendon, 1979.

Longinus. *On The Sublime.* Trans. W. Hamilton Fyfe. *Aristotle* 23. Cambridge: Harvard UP, 1927. 119–253.

Lorde, Audre. "An Open Letter to Mary Daly." *This Bridge Called My Back: Writings By Radical Women of Color.* Ed. Cherrie Moraga and Gloria Anzaldua. New York: Kitchen Table, 1981.

Luck, George. *Arcana Mundi: Magic and the Occult in the Greek and Roman Worlds.* Baltimore: Johns Hopkins, 1985.

Luhrmann, T. M. *Persuasions of the Witch's Craft.* Cambridge: Harvard UP, 1989.

Lunsford, Andrea, ed. *The Right to Literacy.* New York: MLA, 1991.

Lyotard, Jean-Francois. *The Postmodern Condition: A Report on Knowledge.* Trans. Geoff Bennington and Brian Massumi. Minneapolis: U of Minnesota P, 1984.

MacLaine, Shirley. *Out On A Limb.* New York: Bantam, 1983.

Maffeo, Charles. *The Encyclopedia of Occult Sciences.* 1939. Introd. M. C. Poinsot. Detroit: Gale, 1972.

Maniquis, Robert. "The Dark Interpreter and the Palimpsest of Violence: De Quincey and the Unconscious." *Thomas De Quincey: Bicentenery Studies.* Ed. Robert Lance Snyder. Norman: U of Oklahoma P, 1985.

Marcuse, Herbert. *Eros and Civilization: A Philosophical Inquiry into Freud.* Boston: Beacon, 1966.

———. *Negations: Essays in Critical Theory.* London: Penguin, 1968.

———. *One Dimensional Man.* Boston: Beacon, 1964.

Massumi, Brian. *A User's Guide to Capitalism and Schizophrenia: Deviations from Deleuze and Guattari*. Cambridge: MIT, 1992.

Mauss, Marcel. *A General Theory of Magic*. Trans. Robert Brain. Boston: Routledge, 1972.

McGann, Jerome J. *The Romantic Ideology: A Critical Investigation*. Chicago: U of Chicago P, 1983.

McKnight, Steven A. *The Modern Age and the Recovery of Ancient Wisdom: A Reconsideration of Historical Consciousness, 1450– 1650*. Columbia: U of Missouri P, 1991.

Mebane, John S. *Renaissance Magic and the Return of the Golden Age: The Occult Tradition and Marlowe, Jonson, and Shakespeare*. Lincoln: U of Nebraska P, 1989.

Miller, David. *The New Polytheism*. New York: Harper, 1974.

Miller, J. Hillis. "Thomas De Quincey." *The Disappearance of God: Five Nineteenth Century Writers*. Cambridge: Harvard UP, 1975. 17–80.

Miner, Sydny (editor, Fireside Books). Telephone interview. 2 March 1993.

Morgan, Robin, ed. *Sisterhood Is Powerful*. New York: Random House, 1970.

Morris, Meaghan. *The Pirate's Fiancee: Feminism, Reading, Postmodernism*. London: Verso, 1988

Murphy, James J. Introduction. *Arguments in Rhetoric Against Quintilian*. Trans. Carole Newlands. DeKalb: Northern Illinois UP, 1986. 1–63.

Nauert, Charles G., Jr. *Agrippa and the Crisis of Renaissance Thought*. Illinois Studies in the Social Sciences 55. Urbana: U of Illinois P, 1965.

Neel, Jasper. *Plato, Derrida, and Writing*. Carbondale: Southern Illinois UP, 1988.

Neusner, Jacob, et. at. *Religion, Science, and Magic: In Concert and in Conflict*. New York: Oxford UP, 1989.

North, Stephen. *The Making of Knowledge in Composition: Portrait of An Emerging Fiedl*. Portsmouth, NH: Heinemann, 1987.

Nye, Andrea. *Words of Power: A Feminist Reading of the History of Logic*. New York: Routledge, 1990.

Ogden, C. K., and I. A. Richards. *The Meaning of Meaning: A Study of the Influence of Language Upon Thought and of the Science of Symbolism*. 10th ed. London: Routledge, 1953.

O'Keefe, Daniel Lawrence. *Stolen Lightning: The Social Theory of Magic*. New York: Continuum, 1982.

The Oprah Winfrey Show. "My Parent Is A Racist." Transcript #1502. June 16, 1992. Chicago: Harpo Productions, 1992.

———. "Shirley MacLaine." Transcript #672. April 11, 1989. Chicago: Harpo Productions, 1989.

Oxford English Dictionary. Compact Edition. New York: Oxford UP, 1971.

Pattison, Robert. *On Literacy: The Politics of the Word From Homer to the Age of Rock*. New York: Oxford UP, 1982.

———. *The Triumph of Vulgarity: Rock Music in the Mirror of Romanticism*. New York: Oxford, 1987.

Penelope, Julia. *Speaking Freely: Unlearning the Lies of the Fathers' Tongues*. New York: Pergamon, 1990.

Peters, Edward. *The Magician, The Witch, and the Law*. Philadelphia: U of Pennsylvania P, 1978.

Pico della Mirandola, Gianfrancesco. *On the Imagination*. Trans. Harry Caplan. New Haven: Yale UP, 1930.

Pippin, Robert, et al. *Marcuse: Critical Theory and the Promise of Utopia*. South Hadley, MA: Bergin, 1988.

Plato. *Phaedrus*. Trans. Harold North Fowler. Cambridge: Harvard UP, 1914.

———. *Sophist*. Trans. Harold North Fowler. Cambridge: Harvard UP, 1921.

Popkin, Richard H. Introduction. *Opera*. By Henry Cornelius Agrippa. New York: Verlag, 1970. v–xxii.

Purves, Alan C. *The Scribal Society: An Essay on Literacy and Schooling in the Information Age*. New York: Longman, 1990.

Quintilian. *The Institutio Oratoria of Quintilian*. Trans. H. E. Butler. 4 vols. Cambridge: Harvard UP, 1921.

Randall, Michael H. "Tabloid Turns Housewife Into Zombie: Access to Supermarket Tabloids." *The Fringes of Reason: A Whole Earth Catalog*. Ed. Ted Schultz. New York: Harmony, 1989. 98–100.

Raso, Jack. *Mystical Diets: Paranormal, Spiritual, and Occult Nutrition Practices*. Buffalo, NY: Prometheus, 1992.

Ready, Robert. "De Quincey's Magnificent Apparatus." *Interspace and the Inward Sphere: Essays on Romantic and Victorian Self*. Ed. Norman A. Anderson and Margene E. Weiss. Macomb: Western Illinois U, 1978.

Richards, I. A. *The Philosophy of Rhetoric*. New York: Oxford UP, 1936.

Rosenheim, John H. "SCANS Foundations and Competencies." Handout. Conference on Literacy in Midwest Communities. Chicago, 4 Oct. 1991.

———. "What Works in Workplace Literacy." Conference on Literacy in Midwest Communities. Chicago, 4 Oct. 1991.

Rossi, Paolo. *Francis Bacon: From Magic to Science*. Trans. Sacha Rabinowitch. Chicago: U of Chicago P, 1968.

Roszak, Theodore. *The Cult of Information: The Folklore of Computers and the True Art of Thinking*. New York: Pantheon, 1986.

Rubin, Jerry. *Do It: Scenarios of the Revolution*. New York: Simon & Schuster, 1970.

Russo, Dominick. "Rhetoric in the Italian Renaissance." *Renaissance Eloquence: Studies in the Theory and Practice of Renaissance Rhetoric*. Ed. James J. Murphy. Berkeley: U of California P, 1983. 37–55.

Schaeffer, John D. *Sensus Communis: Vico, Rhetoric, and the Limits of Relativism*. Durham: Duke UP, 1990.

Schmitt, Charles. *Gianfrancesco Pico Della Mirandola and His Critique of Aristotle*. The Hague: Nijhoff, 1967.

Scholem, Gershom, ed. *Zohar, the Book of Splendor: Basic Readings from the Kabbalah*. New York: Schocken, 1963.

Searle, John. *Speech Acts*. Cambridge: Cambridge UP, 1970.

Seligman, Kurt. *The History of Magic and the Occult*. New York: Harmony, 1975.

Sextus Empiricus. *Against the Professors*. Trans. R. G. Bury. Cambridge: Harvard UP, 1949.

Shelley, Percy Bysshe. *A Defense of Poetry*. Vol. 7 of *The Complete Works of Percy Bysshe Shelley*. New York: Gordian, 1965. 109–140.

Shor, Ira. *Critical Teaching and Everyday Life*. Boston: South End P, 1980.

———. *Culture Wars: School and Society in the Conservative Restoration, 1969–1984*. Boston: Routledge, 1986.

———, ed. *Freire for the Classroom*. Portsmouth, NH: Boynton, 1988.

———. *A Pedagogy for Liberation: Dialogues on Transforming Education*. S. Hadley: Bergin, 1987.

Siggraph '92 Final Program. New York: Association for Computing Machinery, 1992.

Sorabji, Richard. *Aristotle on Memory*. Providence: Brown UP, 1972.

Spiller, Michael R. G. *Concerning Natural Experimental Philosophie: Meric Casaubon and the Royal Society*. The Hague: Martinus Nijhoff, 1980.

Sprat, Thomas. *History of the Royal Society*. Ed. Jackson Cope and Harold Jones. St. Louis: Washington UP, 1958.

Stafford, Barbara Maria. *Body Criticism: Imaging the Unseen in Enlightenment Art and Medicine*. Cambridge: MIT, 1991.

Stanfield, Paul Scott. *Yeats and Politics in the 1930s*. London: Macmillan, 1988.

Stang, Ivan. *High Weirdness By Mail*. New York: Fireside, 1988.

———, ed. *Three-Fisted Tales of Bob: Short Stories in the Subgenius Mythos*. New York: Fireside, 1990.

Starhawk. *Dreaming the Dark: Magic, Sex, and Politics*. Boston: Beacon, 1982.

———. *The Spiral Dance: A Rebirth of the Ancient Religion of the Great Goddess*. San Francisco: Harper, 1979.

———. *Truth or Dare: Encounters With Power, Authority, and Mystery*. San Francisco: Harper, 1987.

Starker, Steven. *Oracle at the Supermarket: The American Preoccupation with Self-Help Books*. New Brunswick, NJ: Transaction, 1989.

Street, Brian V. *Literacy in Theory and Practice*. Cambridge: Cambridge UP, 1984.

Subgenius Foundation. *The Book of the Subgenius: The Sacred Teachings of J. R. "Bob" Dobbs*. New York: Fireside, 1987.

Summers, Montague, trans. *The Malleus Maleficarum of Heinrich Kramer and James Sprenger.* New York: Dover, 1971.

Taylor, Anya. *Magic and English Romanticism*. Athens: U of Georgia P, 1979.

Thomas, Keith. *Religion and the Decline of Magic*. New York: Scribner's, 1971.

Thorndike, Lynn. *History of Magic and Experimental Science*. 8 vols. New York: Macmillan & Columbia UP, 1923–58.

Torrey, E. Fuller. *Witchdoctors and Psychiatrists*. New York: Harper, 1986.

Truzzi, Marcello. "Definition and Dimensions of the Occult: Toward a Sociological Perspective." *Journal of Popular Culture* 5 (1971): 635–46.

Tuman, Myron, ed. *Literacy Online: The Promise [and Peril] of Reading and Writing with Computers*. Pittsburgh: U of Pittsburgh P, 1992.

TV Guide Commercial, 6 March 1993, 4:40 PM CST, Channel 34 (The Weather Channel), Jones Intercable, Aurora, Illinois

United States. Dept. of Labor. Secretary's Commission on Achieving Necessary Skills. *Skills and Tasks for Jobs: A SCANS Report for America 2000*. Washington: GPO, 1992.

———. *What Work Requires of Schools: A SCANS Report for America 2000*. Washington: GPO, 1992.

Valesio, Paolo. *Novantiqua*. Bloomington: Indiana UP, 1980.

Vickers, Brian. "Analogy Versus Identity: The Rejection of Occult Symbolism, 1580–1680." *Occult and Scientific Mentalities in the Renaissance*. Ed. Brian Vickers. Cambridge: Cambridge UP, 1984. 95–163.

———. "The Royal Society and English Prose Style: A Reassessment." *Rhetoric and the Pursuit of Truth: Language Change in the Seventeenth and Eighteenth Centuries*. By Brian Vickers and Nancy S. Streuver. Los Angeles: Clark Memorial Library, 1985. 3–76.

Vico, Giambattista. "On the Ancient Wisdom of the Italians." *Vico: Selected Writings*. Ed. and trans. Leon Pompa. Cambridge: Cambridge UP, 1982. 49–78.

Vitanza, Victor. "Critical Sub/Versions of the History of Philosophical Rhetoric." *Rhetoric Review* 6.1 (1987): 41– 66.

Walker, D. P. *Spiritual and Demonic Magic from Ficino to Campanella*. London: Warburg, 1958.

Ward, John O. "Magic and Rhetoric from Antiquity to the Renaissance: Some Ruminations." *Rhetorica* 6.1 (1988): 57–118.

Watson, Gerard. *Phantasia in Classical Thought*. Galway: Galway UP, 1988.

Webster, Charles. *From Paracelsus to Newton: Magic and the Making of Modern Science*. Cambridge: Cambridge UP, 1982.

Williams, Raymond. *Problems in Materialism and Culture*. London: Verso, 1980.

Winterowd, W. Ross. "A Philosophy of Composition." *Rhetoric Review* 9 (1991): 340–48.

Woozley, A. D. Introduction. *An Essay Concerning Human Understanding*. By John Locke. Ed. A. D. Woozley. New Jersey: Meridian, 1974. 9–51.

Wordsworth, William. Preface to the Second Edition of *Lyrical Ballads*. Vol. 2 of *Poetical Works*. Ed. Ernest de Selincourt. Rev. Helen Darbishire. 2nd ed. 5 vols. Oxford: Oxford UP, 1952. 384–404.

———. *The Prelude, or Growth of a Poet's Mind*. Ed. Ernest de Selincourt. Rev. Helen Darbishire. 2nd ed. Oxford: Oxford UP, 1959.

Yates, Frances. *The Art of Memory*. Chicago: U of Chicago P, 1966.

———. *Giordano Bruno and the Hermetic Tradition*. Chicago: U of Chicago P, 1964.

———. *The Occult Philosophy in the Elizabethan Age*. Boston: Routledge, 1979.

Yeats, William Butler. "Magic." *Essays and Introductions*. New York: Macmillan, 1961. 28–52.

———. *A Vision*. New York: Macmillan, 1937.

Young, Richard. "Concepts of Art and the Teaching of Writing." *The Rhetorical Tradition and Modern Writing*. Ed. James J. Murphy. New York: MLA, 1982.

INDEX